Let's Dance

A Celebration of Ontario's Dance Halls and Summer Dance Pavilions

Let's Dance: A Celebration of Ontario's Dance Halls and Summer Dance Pavilions
Peter Young

Published by Natural Heritage/Natural History Inc.
P.O. Box 95, Station O, Toronto, Ontario M4A 2M8
www.naturalheritagebooks.com

National Library of Canada Cataloguing in Publication Data

Young, Peter, 1949-
Let's dance : a celebration of Ontario's dance halls and summer dance pavilions

Includes bibliographical references and index.

ISBN 1-896219-02-0
1. Ballrooms—Ontario—History. 2. Pavilions Ontario—History. 3. Dance-orchestras—Ontario—History. I. Title.

FC3062.Y69 2002   647'.9686'09713   C2002-901424-4   F1057.8.Y69 2002

Front cover images:
    Dorsey Brothers, courtesy of Don McIndoe.
    "Bren Gun Girl," courtesy of National Archives of Canada/PA119765
Back cover images:
    Louis Armstrong– courtesy of Don McIndoe, Ginny Mitchell– courtesy of Joan (Tibbs) Tanner,
    Count Basie's bus– courtesy of Joe Showler, Mart Kenney– courtesy of Peter Young.
Title page image:
    Courtesy of Toronto Harbour Commission PC 2/422
All visuals courtesy of the author unless otherwise indicated.

Cover and text design by Blue Sky Studio
Edited by Jane Gibson
Printed and bound in Canada by Hignell Printing Limited, Winnipeg, Manitoba.

Natural Heritage / Natural History Inc. acknowledges the financial support of the Canada Council for the Arts and the Ontario Arts Council for our publishing program. We also acknowledge the financial support of the Government of Canada through the Book Publishing Industry Development Program (BPIDP) and the Association for the Export of Canadian Books.

Dedication

To the memory of Joan (Livings) Young,
Whose love of singing and dancing was the inspiration.

Foreword

There was a time in Ontario when live music echoed from hundreds of dance halls and pavilions right across the province, filling the air with memorable songs that have stayed with us to this day. In his book *Let's Dance*, Peter Young takes readers on a nostalgic musical journey, visiting many of these popular dance venues. Louis Armstrong's magical night at Dunn's Pavilion, Canada's Big Band King Mart Kenney and his famous Ranch, Rompin' Ronnie Hawkins and the Hawks at Port Dover's unforgettable Summer Garden, lakeside dances at The Crystal Beach Ballroom ... *Let's Dance* recalls the places in which we loved to swing and sway, as well as the legendary entertainers who made us dance.

John Dimon – Publisher, Big Band World

Table of Contents

The Pavilion

Dancing at the Pavilion is always associated with happiness. No matter what the style of music, its infectious rhythm calls people together, to start moving, to dance, to have fun. People meet people; friendships are made; some fall in love. The love-songs the bands play become a very personal thing to lovers. The chord changes, the lyrics, the melody all reach the inner soul and the song becomes "our song." The words may change, but the feeling is always deep, true and enduring.

So another summer at the Pavilion brings exciting groups to provide happy music for you to enjoy, to dance and to make friends.*

* Reprinted from a 1972 Sauble Beach Pavilion events poster

There was a time in Ontario when the May 24th long weekend was the traditional opening date for most of Ontario's dance pavilions. During this annual salute to summer's pending arrival, wooden shutters would be raised, the dance floor lovingly polished until it gleamed in preparation for another season of dancing feet, the refreshment booth stocked up. Posters announcing the season's attractions would be distributed throughout cottage country.

Summer romances, moonlight strolls, the unforgettable music of our youth and hot cars—there was so much fun to cram into July and August when the days were long and warm and the evening breezes gentle. Throughout the province music soared from dance halls and beckoned us. And we responded to the call. Practically every night of the week there was a dance within driving distance of your home or cottage. Whether you swayed to the mellow sounds of the Big Bands or rocked and rolled to some of Ontario's best rock groups, dancing was the highlight of people's summers for well over 50 years at some locations.

At one time in Ontario there were literally hundreds of dance halls and dance pavilions. Practically every town, city and lakeside resort had at least one dance hall operating anywhere from two to six nights a week. But as time marched on, these palaces of musical pleasure began to fall like bowling pins. Some buildings were torn down, some mysteriously burned, while others were converted into marinas, auto body shops and flea markets.

Scant physical evidence remains of most dance halls which played such an integral part in our lives for so many years, but in some cases there are reminders of the places where music once reigned supreme. For instance, the breakwall with carved dancers marks the spot where Fort Erie's famous Crystal Beach Ballroom once stood. A stone monument where the Humber River empties into Lake Ontario commemorates Toronto's Palace Pier. A foundation with a set of stairs leading to a field of weeds on Highway 2 is all that's left of the Golden Slipper where many a person from Kingston and area danced the night away.

As a number of people who love Ontario nostalgia are discovering today, it's an adventure to make a personal visit to sites around the province where some trace of the past may still remain. To see an old foundation or walk through a door where crowds of people once danced, can be a very intense experience. With this book you have the opportunity

Bunny hoppers snake around a dance floor during the 1950s. *World-Wide Photo, courtesy of Jack Lomas*

to embark upon a journey of musical discovery, searching for places where you may remember dancing, or sites where perhaps your parents or even grandparents first met. But this book is not solely a trip down memory lane. Fortunately there are a few dance halls still in operation, such as London's Wonderland, Toronto's Palais Royale, Oshawa's Jubilee Pavilion, The Kee to Bala (formerly Dunn's Pavilion), The Dard at Wasaga Beach and others. All of these sites will be visited.

This writing about buildings has been more than just a chronicling of structures. What did these halls and pavilions mean to people? Why were they special places? What was so magical about a wooden building that was, in many cases, a large barn-like shell? Yes, I wanted to document the halls, but also I wanted to write about people. Researching this book began strictly as a project about Ontario's wooden summer dance pavilions—unheated gathering spots that would open on the long weekend in May, and close down on Labour Day or Thanksgiving weekend. However, it quickly became obvious that there were just too many other dedicated dance halls—or ballrooms—which operated on a year-round basis and should also be included. It is hoped that you will see your favourite hall in the book.

Much of this book has been made possible because of information provided from interviews and letters from hundreds of generous people—former dance pavilion and dance hall owners, managers, staff, musicians, and of course, those who came to dance. Thanks to their recollections,

The Modernaires performed at most of Ontario's major dance halls, such as Wonderland in London and Grandbend's Lakeview Casino during the Big Band era. *Courtesy of Jack Lomas*

This is a story about people of all ages whose lives have been touched by music

personal insights, photographs and printed material which they so willingly shared, I feel that *Let's Dance* is more than simply a slice of Ontario's social history. Rather, it is a story about people of all ages whose lives have been touched by music, romance and soft summer nights.

It was the music that brought out the people, and so I have tried to devote space to a sampling of the talented local musicians who have played throughout Ontario. These people were the troupers, the road warriors who gigged around the province.

Is this a book of nostalgia? Well, due to the nature of the subject—dance pavilions—much of the material is based on the era when these halls were running full tilt, that is predominately the years between the 1930s to the 1960s. Some background is provided about dancing in the 1920s and earlier, and I have brought the book up to date in terms of the halls that are still operating today. Although the emphasis is on the Big Band era, a number of pavilions were able to make the transition from swing music to rock 'n' roll in the early 1960s. Some of these halls enjoyed their most successful period as they began to cater to the Baby Boomers

Edith and Marshall Louch sway across the dance floor to the sound Big Bands.
Courtesy of the late Marshall Louch.

LET'S DANCE

entering their teenage years. Teen Towns sprung up, rock bands threw their equipment in the back of panel vans and a whole new generation of young people flocked to the pavilions. Their good times parallel the same fun that generations of people before them enjoyed at the pavilions. Although the dress code was relaxed, the owners welcomed them with the same hospitality they had been extending to couples who swayed across the floor to Big Bands, dressed in much more formal attire.

So please join me for an adventure as we take to the road to visit many of Ontario's Dance Pavilions, and meet some of the people who devoted a good part of their life providing entertainment for people who loved music.

Many of Ontario's dance pavilions were running full tilt predominately between the years of the 1930s to the 1960s.

x

Chapter One

INTRODUCTION TO THE ERA OF PAVILIONS AND DANCE HALLS

The great Satchmo drew record crowds at Dunn's Pavilion in Bala. *Courtesy of Don McIndoe.*

The Period of Growth

Dancing has included just about every type of movement and gyration known to humankind over the years. Various steps and styles like the Charleston, the Varsity Drag, waltzes, tangos, the Big Apple, fox trot, jitterbug, the Shag, the twist, Wahtutsi, square dancing and line dancing have all drawn dancers onto the floor. Each generation can brag that its particular form of dancing was the best, or the most romantic, or the most creative, or the most intricate. One person, in comparing some of the more graceful dance forms of the Big Band years, shook his head and commented that after Rock music became predominant, "People just stood in one place and wiggled!" Well, every generation has its own special way of moving— or not moving as the case may be—to the music

enjoyed by all.

The opening of the 20th century, with the advent of automobiles and radios, allowed people's lives to expand. By the early 1930s, although the country was still in the grips of the Depression, there were well over a half million radios in Canada bringing live music broadcasts from both American hotel ballrooms and Canadian venues into living rooms across the land. People became aware of a world beyond their own community, a world filled with exciting music they were able to discover and enjoy in their own homes. At one point, Toronto's CFRB radio was running remote broadcasts from the King Edward and Royal York hotels, the Old Mill, the Silver Slipper and the Club Embassy. Radio affected people in two ways: it enlightened them and entertained them in their homes, and enticed them to look

1

The Varsity Entertainers *(left)* were a group of university students who earned their tuition during the summer playing music. Here they are featured at the Coral Gables Casino in the village of Trent River. Left to right: Al Mueller, drums; Les Clegg, trumpet; Bob ___; sax; John Griffin, piano. *Courtesy of Agnes Nazar.*

Dansemere *(above)* is an excellent example of a basic early summer dance pavilion, complete with shutters which would be opened on dance night. This operated in the earlier 1900s within the summer resort community along the St. Clair River in Port Lambton. *Courtesy of Alan Mann.*

"Bren Gun Girl" *(right)* Ronnie Foster jitterbugging with Michael Graig at the Glen Eagle Country Club, Toronto, Ontario. Dated May 10, 1941. *Courtesy of National Archives of Canada/PA-119765.*

The Romanellis *(below)* were one of Toronto's premier music families. Luigi led the King Edward Hotel's house orchestra for many years. This photo shows Don Romanelli's jazz band in the late 1920s on board the *Cayuga*, a Lake Ontario excursion ship. Dancing on board these cruise vessels was a very popular summer activity at this time. *Courtesy of Jack Lomas.*

beyond their own four walls to experience the music live in a pavilion or dance hall.

The classier ball rooms in the King Edward and Royal York hotels as well as Casa Loma in Toronto were home to some of the greatest early names in the music business. Cruises on Lake Ontario to various towns and cities always included an orchestra on board for dancing. Outside the large cities people also wanted to come together for socializing, and gathered in community halls and even one-room schoolhouses for dances. While these sites were perfect for winter events, the summertime begged a different type of setting for dances, especially if a community was fortunate enough to be located near a body of water. One glance at a map of Ontario immediately shows the Great Lakes and hundreds of interior lakes where cities, towns and villages are located. Small dance pavilions and halls started to spring up around the province where people could attend dances up to six nights per week throughout the summer.

Just as rock 'n' roll spawned many small bands emulating the emerging groups from Britain and the United States in the 1960s, the popularity of Big Band swing music made it feasible for many young men to form orchestras in the 1930s and '40s to perform the music of their era. A number of these groups were coined "Collegiate" or "Varsity" bands as they were formed by university students who would play summer gigs.

By the late 1930s and into the War years, dance halls and pavilions were everywhere. Some would open on the second or third floor of a downtown building and survive just a year or two, while others became more established as destinations for good music where people could meet and dance. On Oshawa's lakefront the Jubilee Pavilion and Barnhart's Pavilion operated side-by-side for four decades. Cities such as Toronto, London, Kitchener-Waterloo and Kingston had so many spots to dance that people could go out three or four times a week to a different place each evening. Resort hotels inevitably included a dance floor or ballroom as part of their complex. Even many campgrounds offered some type of facility for dancing.

The significance of a pavilion or dance hall

to an individual is often not based on its size, or the bands who played there. Some people have a special place in their heart for that little-known hall beside a small lake where they had the best summer of their lives, while others may look back to a major ballroom as their favourite hall. It all depends upon the memories a particular place evokes.

Basic wooden pavilions were fairly inexpensive to build. They were just shells with the beams exposed, although owners often camouflaged the primitive interior with paint, flags, crepe paper and other ceiling hangings. The dance floor itself was usually constructed with hardwood such as maple or oak, and was maintained fastidiously. Long benches usually hugged two or three of the four walls of the building, with the stage at one end, and a refreshment booth at the other. In many of the earlier summer pavilions, indoor washrooms were a luxury. Even any type of heating device in the hall was a rarity. Initially some were without hydro and were forced to rely on coal oil lanterns and battery power—singers in this case were forced to perform with a megaphone, like Rudy Vallee. As the years progressed, many of the pavilions and halls created a night club atmosphere and were improved by the addition of tables and chairs, decorations such as arbours and flowers, a fountain perhaps, and coloured lighting.

Shutters were a common feature on most dance pavilions and would be propped open on

Greenhurst Dance Pavilion would open its second floor shutters to let in the cool night breeze.

3

dance night. Some windows had screens, while others simply let in the night bugs. Outdoor terrazzo floors were particularly romantic on warm summer evenings. London's Wonderland Gardens started as an outdoor venue, as did places like Kenwick-On-The-Lake in Bright's Grove, Sunnyside's Seabreeze in Toronto, Hamilton's Wondergrove and others.

From the 1930s into the early '50s, dance halls throughout the province were enjoying the most successful years they would ever experience. Everywhere, pavilions such as Dunn's in Bala, Port Stanley's Stork Club, the Brant Inn in Burlington, Toronto's halls and over to Hull's popular spots, just a drive across the river from sedate Ottawa, were drawing large crowds. All featured the best in local entertainment with lots of internationally known stars thrown in for good measure. To the observer it looked as if the good times for dance halls would continue indefinitely.

Owners and Operators

Constructing a dance pavilion, or purchasing an existing one, was often a labour of love. Yes, it was a business, but in many cases the owners loved music and wanted to share this passion with their customers. Interestingly, many owners were musicians and bandleaders themselves. Jack Marshall took over The Cameo in Fenelon Falls and managed the Edgewater in Bobcaygeon. The Commodores Orchestra in Belleville built and ran their own pavilion for 20 years. Sarnia musician Jack Kennedy established Kenwick Terrace and Kenwick-On-The-Lake, where he performed regularly. Emmett McGrath, who played sax with Ferde Mowry for years, purchased Port Elgin's Cedar Crescent Casino. Wally Scott led his own orchestra in the pavilion that he and Jack Robertson operated in Sauble Beach.

Running a dance operation is a business and a risky one at that. Will the crowd like the band? Will inclement weather affect the attendance? Is there competition nearby that might draw customers away? Is the admission price reasonable? Will the band show up on time? Will there be a fight in the parking lot? Providing entertainment for people is much more demanding than one might realize. The dance business is one of the few types of operations where it is essential to safely welcome hundreds of people into the establishment in less than one hour, give them an evening of entertainment, monitor the crowd's behaviour to ensure that no trouble erupts, provide customers with food and refreshment, oversee staff, deal with the band, comply with all the applicable regulations and bylaws governing such a business, be prepared for unforseen emergencies, and finally see that people leave the premises in an orderly fashion, with the hope that they'll return to the next dance or concert. Whew!

The dance business takes a very special type of person who is able to combine warm hospitality with the shrewd business sense needed to successfully manage a hall. Of course they all wished to make a profit, but the majority of pavilion and hall owners in Ontario truly enjoyed their businesses and the many

Facilities were sometimes primitive in early dance halls. It was not uncommon for patrons to use outdoor conveniences at some locales, such as Crystal Pier's summer dance hall on Crystal Lake, near Kinmount.

Bud Medley began building his own hall in 1946 on property he and his wife Muriel owned in Carnarvon. Their dancing and bowling business opened in 1948.
Courtesy of Bud and Muriel Medley

Owners were no-nonsense people. They respected the young people who came to dance and wanted to provide them with their money's worth of entertainment, but had to be strict in their dealings with patrons, and also with bands who could be demanding and even lazy at times. Helen Lines ruled Greenhurst with a strong hand and a heart of gold; people called her "Ma" with great affection, but were wise enough to obey her hall's rules. Bands also treated Helen with great courtesy and made sure they played their full sets. Or else!

It is not surprising to realize that running a hall was not an automatic ticket to wealth, and was definitely not a "gold mine" as many people believed. When you factor in the variables and risks, the success of a dance pavilion was quite fragile. With the public's taste being so fickle, pavilion owners continually had to experiment, be willing to try new ideas and, in general, keep their fingers on the pulse of the dancing public. The owners who put their customers' tastes ahead of their own—particularly in the area of music—were the ones who could count on good gate receipts.

challenges presented. They looked forward to meeting their customers and giving them a good evening.

They also were entrepreneurs who were independent and driven by a vision. Quite a few of them were builders, if not by trade then certainly by natural talent, with many of them designing and building their own dance pavilions. Some people in Bala thought Gerry Dunn was taking a huge risk when he erected his large Muskoka pavilion, but he proved them all wrong. Bud and Muriel Medley could see the potential in Carnarvon for their dance hall and bowling operation, when others could see only a grassy field. Charles Jones was the driving force behind Wonderland in London, and with his brother Wilf as the visible host, the two made a formidable team.

Booze and Brown Bags

Ontario used to have very restrictive laws controlling the population's leisure time. For example, it has only been in recent years that Sunday shopping was approved. Years before that, sporting events were prohibited on our mandatory day of rest, as were movies. Naturally, dancing was not allowed on Sunday, so promoters of the popular Sunday night sit-down concerts at dance pavilions and halls were forced to serve soft drinks with a plate of cookies to customers, and charge for this food in lieu of admission. In short, we were a grim-faced province when it came to how we could spend our free time.

Charles and Wilf Jones constructed Wonderland Gardens along the Thames River in London Ontario in 1935.
Courtesy of Chuck Jones.

5

When people came to dance, it was only natural that they wanted to loosen up a little and enjoy themselves. Dance pavilion owners knew that they might as well wait for a rooster to lay eggs than try to acquire permits to sell beer or liquor in their dance hall, so many owners did the next best thing—they sold soft drinks and ice to customers. Dancers discreetly camouflaged their jungle juice in a brown paper bag underneath the table, or in a purse. On the other hand, some hall owners had a very strict No Booze policy, and anyone caught drinking was evicted from the premises. Most halls also had one answer for unruly patrons: eviction for the season.

This is not to say that there were not a few dumps, or "buckets of blood" as they were called, where more than one nose was broken in the parking lot. Ronnie Hawkins played in Arkansas before establishing himself in Toronto. "Some of the clubs we played in had chicken wire across the front of the stage to intercept the bottles when someone decided he didn't like something you were doing and threw one in your direction. These were brown-bag clubs ...."[1] Hawkins' drummer, Levon Helm, adds his recollections: "The Delta Supper Club ... was a bottle bar like all the bars in the South. You bring your bottle, and they provide the ice, glasses and food."[2] The practice of brown-bagging was therefore not restricted to Ontario, but it worked as well as it could in this province under the laws of the time.

Jitney Dancing

For a single guy, asking a girl to dance has never been easy. But at least the fellows going to dance halls in the '30s and '40s had one sure-fire way to impress the girls – jitney dance tickets. The finishing touch to a young man's wardrobe in those days was a long strip of 5-cent or 10-cent dance tickets conspicuously parked in his breast pocket, advertising the fact that this gent was ready for action on the dance floor—all he needed was a partner who wanted to swing. Many of the halls and pavilions at this time incorporated a pay-as-you-dance system, where you were charged on a per dance basis, rather than a flat admission rate. The word "jitney" quickly became associated with

this method, since jitney is an old term for a 5-cent bus fare.

In the late '30s and '40s, Bruce Gosnell "worked the ropes" at Wasaga Beach's famous Dardanella which featured a round dance floor surrounded by a railing to facilitate jitney dancing. In a letter he writes: "The Dard was the place to be. Trump Davidson was there for a long time .... If you worked the ropes you got your dances free—four boys worked them.

Herb Rye still has a collection of jitney dance tickets from many Ontario halls. His father, Harold, built Peterborough's famous Rye's Pavilion along the Otonabee River.

There were benches all around the dance floor where mothers and fathers sat watching the dances. Quite a few people sat outside on the sand to listen to the band. As the dance ended, the rope boys met at the centre of the floor and herded the dancers to the exit as the new dancers came onto the floor. As a rope boy you had to leave the dance halfway through the last number so you could be ready to rope the dancers off. You usually arranged with your next dance partner to meet you at the entrance gate so you could get in as much of the dance as possible. Those were fun years for a teenager."

In his autobiography, Canadian bandleader Mart Kenney writes about jitney dancing: "The Waterton Park Pavilion (in Alberta) was a Jitney Dance operation—ten cents a dance and no charge to come into the hall .... Tickets were purchased at the pagoda any time during the evening and in any quantity, and we quickly learned that if we didn't have people on the dance floor we wouldn't be paid."[3]

By the late '40s most halls had abandoned jitney dancing and were charging straight admission,

6

forcing young men to search for new measures to impress the opposite sex.

Big Band/Swing Music

To fully appreciate the general impact that music had on people's lives we have to momentarily leave Ontario, and take a peek at the larger scene that was developing in North America.

From the days of the old gramophones, people were exposed to music on records, ranging from ragtime to opera. The quality was poor compared to today's CDs and surround sound, but it still gave people the opportunity to purchase music and for listening in their homes. Dance music recorded by orchestras is generally acknowledged as having come into its own by the early 1920s. At this time there were a number of all-black orchestras in the U.S. providing a refreshing alternative to the sometimes less-than-exciting music often heard from their white counterparts. It was looser, with more of an opportunity for musicians to solo; these musicians were not necessarily restricted to the written note, preferring instead to *ad lib*. It was the beginning of jazz.

Jazz and Louis Armstrong

Jazz, a uniquely American form of music, began to develop in New Orleans, bringing together elements of African and European cultures. After Scott Joplin's immensely popular ragtime piano music, the first recognizable jazz music was heard in 1900, played by cornetist Buddy Bouldon in New Orleans.

The real father of jazz was Louis Armstrong. He came to personify jazz music and is credited with being the greatest player of his time, a man who understood all music styles, and a musician whose phrasing and clarity of tone have been copied by generations of musicians over the years. Vocalists have also used his instrumental phrasing to interpret

American popular music. Louis Armstrong is the creator of the organized solo on a musical instrument. He was equally proficient as a singer as well as a trumpet player, bringing the same style he used on his instrument to his vocal arrangements. Louis' style of jazz music had planted the seeds for the pending swing era which was to follow.

The more conservative bandleaders of the time could see the trend to more exciting, free-form music and began to hire at least one or two good soloists to spice up their sound. As new clubs became established, such as the Cotton Club and the Savoy of Harlem, [4] more artists had the opportunity to be heard. Duke Ellington arrived in New York in 1923, a great musician, composer, bandleader and innovator. Kansas City spawned a generation of hot new musicians like William (Count) Basie. As radio elevated many of these bandleaders to star status, they became big draws when they would tour on the road and hit the major halls across North America. It is not surprising that they received equally enthusiastic receptions in Ontario when their schedules brought them to the various dance halls in this province.

Some of the Big Band Players

Just who first played Swing music and exactly when it came about is hard to say. The word does aptly describe a period of music that encompasses a number of well-known American bands. Many Canadian orchestras also began playing their own brand of swing music, the better ones able to develop their own unique style with credit usually going to the leader, the arranger (who was also often the leader) and the level of sophistication of the players.

Swing music, as opposed to the straight

7

Swing music arrived at the Palomar Ballroom in Los Angeles on August 21, 1935, when Benny Goodmans's band hit the stage. *Courtesy of Oren Jacoby.*

Glen Miller *(top)* played to a sold-out house at Toronto's Mutual Street Arena on January 23, 1942. He willingly posed for the press, which included music fan Billy Livings.

Victor, Lebert, Guy and Carmen Lombardo's roots were in London, Ontario, but they became famous throughout the world for decades. *Courtesy of the Joseph Brant Museum.*

dance band music that preceded it, contained a strong element of jazz flavouring to the songs and the arrangements. Therefore, much credit does have to go to the early arranger Fletcher Henderson for being one of the first innovators of this new style of music. Henderson's orchestra, formed around 1924, became one of the most important in the development of Big Band jazz.

If one event could be labelled as the beginning of swing music, it would be the night Benny Goodman and the band arrived in Los Angeles to play the Palomar Ballroom on August 21, 1935. The band was completely overwhelmed by the response. That night at the Palomar with the place packed, Benny became an overnight star. Almost two years later, in March 1937 at New York's Paramount, Benny was crowned as America's first pop culture hero as the crowds went absolutely wild over his music.

Another accepted pioneer of swing music was reed man Artie Shaw, who in popularity contests

created by fans, was often pitted against Benny Goodman. After his May 24, 1936, first swing concert at New York's Imperial Theatre, Artie became a hit. His career really began to soar to new heights after signing with RCA which released his first hit record "Begin The Beguine." Shaw also overwhelmed fans at the Palomar Ballroom in Los Angeles, drawing well over 9,000 enthusiastic people. In a later film documentary Shaw said, "It makes me feel good that I created a piece of Americana that will go on and on. You pass on what you know to the future."[5]

If Benny Goodman and Artie Shaw were two of the principle innovators of swing, it was Glenn Miller's danceable music that was so memorable in

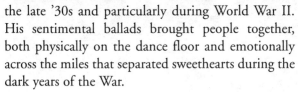

Guy Lombardo *(top left)* **and his Royal Canadians celebrating his 50th Anniversary in show business on June 4, 1977, at the Stork Club in Port Stanley.** *Courtesy of the Guy Lombardo Museum, London, Ontario.*

Count Basie *(left)*. **His tasteful piano playing always complemented his band's orchestrations.** *Courtesy of Don McIndoe.*

Duke Ellington *(above)*, **brought many of his original and familiar songs to the stage at Dunn's.** *Courtesy of Don McIndoe.*

the late '30s and particularly during World War II. His sentimental ballads brought people together, both physically on the dance floor and emotionally across the miles that separated sweethearts during the dark years of the War.

Another anchor of Big Band music, who played a more reserved style than Goodman, Shaw or Miller, was Guy Lombardo. It is important to recognize Lombardo and his family for the more than 50 years they dedicated to making "The sweetest music this side of heaven." Guy's first orchestra included his brothers Carmen and Lebert. Their father made certain that they all practised their instruments without fail for their teacher Professor Pasquele Vanuta.[6] Unlike Shaw or Goodman, Lombardo never tried or pretended to lead a swing or jazz orchestra and there was no room for improvisation. Although it has been over 25 years since Guy Lombardo raised his baton, there is not a New Year's Eve that goes by without people raising a toast, singing a verse of "Auld Lang Syne" and reflecting upon the orchestra which immortalized this tune. Lombardo reached 55 million television viewers every New Year's Eve from 1954 to 1977. His last

9

Murray Anderson presented the biggest names in the business at his Brant Inn in Burlington. Guest artists would often stay in Murray's penthouse suite. Above from left to right – Nellie Lutcher, Evelyn Knight, Larry Adler and Abbe Lane.

Canadian performance was in 1977 at Port Stanley's Stork Club, just a few miles south of his hometown. By touching on just a few of the major artists of the swing music period I hope you are able to either remember (if you grew up with this music), or understand why it played such a significant role in people's desire to dance and socialize. There were so many other bandleaders, musicians and singers who contributed memorable music during this time—Woody Herman, Les Brown, Tommy and Jimmy Dorsey, Cab Calloway, Stan Kenton, Ella Fitzgerald, Billie Holiday, Peggy Lee—their talents and individual styles have been enjoyed by audiences around the world. Many people feel that it was a truly golden era of music and dancing.

Changing Music and Dancing Styles

While Big Bands and their vocalists were still the predominant music force on radio, early television and in dance halls, a completely different music form was quietly developing in the United States. Spiritual music had been part of the American South for a century or more. Various Black artists over the years

interpreted this music and also wrote their own songs, gradually transforming the lyrics into a commentary on the hard life so many of them had experienced. In the 1930s and '40s, acoustic instruments were mainly used to perform the blues. By the 1950s, with the advent of electric guitars and amplifiers, the overall sound of the music changed. Although this music was far from being mainstream, certain producers in the recording industry liked the music and felt it could very well be the leading edge of a brand new style of music. The instrumentation was basic— guitar, drums, keyboard and maybe a sax, and the music did not stray far from simple chord progressions—usually 12-bar, three-chord songs, on which the traditional blues song is based.

Sam Phillips, of Sun Records and Sun Studios, began to have various artists record this new style of music. Jerry Lee Lewis, Roy Orbison, Carl Perkins and even Johnny Cash all started their careers about this time with Sun. As well, artists like Bill Haley and His Comets, Bobby Darin, Pat Boone, Buddy Holly and the Crickets, Richie Valens and many others were all becoming the new teen idols. Black artists such as Chuck Berry, Fats Domino and Little Richard were also being hailed as hot new stars of the 1950s. Yes, rock 'n' roll was here to stay.

But the King of Rock, the man who is really credited with heading this tidal wave of new music that swept the continent and indeed the western world with a surge that had never before been experienced, was Elvis Presley. Writes Levon Helm: "In 1957 the rock and roll craze was at its explosive

Tommy and Jimmy Dorsey *(left)* had personal differences but were complete professionals when they performed together in Bala. *Courtesy of Don McIndoe.*

Sarah Vaughan *(far inset left)* and **Buddy Morrow** *(inset left)* also performed at the Brant Inn. The Brant's Manager Harry Parker, acquired many of the stars' publicity shots with personalized autographs. *Courtesy of the Joseph Brant Museum.*

11

By the early 1960s, hundreds of new young bands began forming throughout Ontario, like the British Modbeats (left) and the Mandala (below). Bringing rock 'n' roll to a whole new generation of kids hungry for the music they were hearing on rock radio stations such as CHUM-AM in Toronto.

peak. In January we all watched Elvis sing 'Don't Be Cruel' on The Ed Sullivan Show … it changed America."[7] Writes Ronnie Hawkins: "… it was Presley who embodied so many of the factors that went into shaping the new, emerging culture of the latter half of the century: its media-friendliness, its talent for instant synthesis, its penchant for larger-than-life personalities."[8] Scott Young writes about his son, Neil's reaction to Elvis: "He was fascinated by Elvis Presley's first TV appearance …. These fans, as consumers, were beginning the long process of forcing the majors in the recording industry to provide something other than Benny Goodman and Artie Shaw and Tommy Dorsey … on which previous generations of music fans had been raised …. The new music was about to sweep the world …."[9]

Luria Catsell, a San Francisco political activist, said in 1965, "Rock 'n' roll is the new form of communication for our generation … music is the most beautiful way to communicate, it's the way we're going to change things. Half the population is teenaged now…. Dancing is the thing."[10] And gone were the long dresses, corsages, ties and jackets. As writer Ralph Gleason notes, "Any kind of dress was permissible … dancing reflected the general attitude of self-expression … the actual demand for dances is going to increase. The whole rock revolution points to dancing …. It is harmless and it is legal. It is, in fact, a delight."[11]

The owners and operators of dance pavilions around Ontario who could anticipate, or at least realize, that change was part of their business were able to make this transition into the era of rock 'n' roll music; as a result, they enjoyed a number of prosperous years catering to a new generation of young people. Other halls began to run country and western dances, as this music gained widespread popularity. Country music has always had a dedicated following, particularly in rural areas. The Ottawa Valley was a bastion of this form of music, with artists like Mac Beattie and His Melodiers as big an attraction here as Bert Niosi and his contemporaries were in urban centres like Toronto.

If the mid-1930s to the early 1950s were the pinnacle of Big Band music, the 1960s and 1970s saw some of the best rock music being performed at halls across the province. Many of these pavilions and halls are about to be visited and experienced through words of the people who were there as dancers, owners and musicians. Each has a unique story to tell. It is hoped there will be as much fun in reading this book as the many contributors had in reliving their memories.

Chapter Two

TORONTO AND SURROUNDING AREA

Eddie Graf at the Palais Royale

The Palace Pier

The Palace Pier condominium tower today sits on the location of one of the most celebrated dance halls in the city of Toronto: the original Palace Pier. Conceived in the late 1920s, The Pier was to be the first section of a half-mile long entertainment complex. The cornerstone for the hall was laid on January 10, 1931, but the grand plans for an Atlantic City-style pier were scrapped as the Depression set in.

      Former Palace Pier floor manager and retired public school principal Ron McLean gives some background on the hall's shaky start: "The building lay vacant until 1941, and then operated under a couple of different names such as the Strathcona Roller Rink and then the Queensway Ballroom." Once The Palace Pier developed its "sea legs," it soon

became a favourite destination for dancers who came to see their favourite Big Bands. All the famous acts played The Palace Pier, including Duke Ellington, the Dorsey Brothers, Harry James and Stan Kenton. Ernie Ince was general manager of The Pier for many years and recalls one bandleader's effect on the audience: "Lionel Hampton would work the crowd into a frenzy. He'd soak three suits in a performance and play louder and faster as the night moved along. The Palace Pier had its heyday between the mid-forties and mid-fifties, when the Big Bands were so popular." He recalls Stan Kenton appearing for the first time and drawing a huge crowd. The Pier was extensively renovated during Ernie's time, around 1951 or '52, and featured one of the largest dance floors around. Three tiers were built with balconies surrounding the dance floor.

13

14

Although just about every well-known Canadian orchestra also performed at The Pier, the musician synonymous with this dance hall from 1944 until 1963 was renowned bandleader Trump Davidson. Over his career Trump became respected as one of the finest self-taught jazz improvisers in the business. CBC radio did live remote broadcasts from the Palace Pier for a number of years, using Trump Davidson's Dixieland combo. According to Ron McLean, "After the dance was over at midnight on Saturday, the rest of his orchestra would pack up and leave, and we would invite anyone in the audience to remain for the live 12:30 a.m. to 1:00 a.m. Dixieland show."

Jimmy "Trump" Davidson *(top)* led the Pier's house band for 18 years. Some of the finest jazz musicians played with Trump. Along with his full orchestra, Trump's six-piece Dixieland band was often featured at the Pier. *Courtesy of Jack Lomas.*

The Palace Pier *(middle)* featured Sunday night concerts since dancing was not allowed on the "Sabbath" in Ontario in the late 1950s. A popular host of these shows was Doug Romaine. *Courtesy Ron McLean.*

Stan Kenton *(bottom)* brought his own style of exciting music – which included loads of volume to the Pier. *Courtesy Gene Smith.*

If there is one word that can describe the resilience of The Palace Pier it is "survival." By the mid-'50s, The Palace Pier had to change direction in order to turn a dollar. As Ernie Ince tells it, "We started booking in country acts like Johnny Cash and Patsy Cline, and it was a very successful move." The Pier also introduced bingo, boxing matches and used the premises for revivals, automobile presentations, school proms, union meetings and political rallies. CHUM-AM radio staged Saturday afternoon dances with live R & B bands with morning man, Al Boliska, MC-ing the show. Ernie continues, "We tried everything to keep the building used during the week because we could still bring in a good crowd of 1,000 on the weekend for dancing." "The only night a dance was ever cancelled at The Palace Pier was the Saturday after Hurricane Hazel."

On the night of January 6, 1963, Ron locked the doors of The Palace Pier for the last time. In the early hours of January 7, fire completely destroyed the dance hall leaving nothing in its wake but grotesquely warped steel girders. In his words, "All that remained of the beautiful white grand piano on stage was mangled wires." Ernie Ince and his young son Patrick raced to the scene but could only stand by helplessly, witnessing the demise of one of Toronto's most famous dance halls. In the cold light of day it was painfully obvious that the building was totally destroyed, and The Palace Pier's life was finished.

On the destruction of The Palace Pier, Ron has some very strong emotions: "It wasn't just the end of a building—it was the end of an era. Those days were done so the property was sold." While many of the people who worked at The Palace Pier have good recollections of this famous dance hall on Lake Ontario, there are likely none who recall the days of the Pier with such affection and vividness as Ernie Ince and Ron McLean. "It was a hall with a million memories," says Ron. "Overnight our jobs were finished. The Pier was another Toronto landmark which disappeared so quickly."

Should anyone wish to experience a slice of the Pier's presence, just walk along the Waterfront Trail and pause at the monument erected in 1994 to honour the past of this wonderful building. It is located just behind The Palace Pier Condominium building. The base of the monument is one of the original concrete pier footings, donated to the City of Etobicoke by the condo residents.

Seabreeze Outdoor Dance Pavilion

The Seabreeze was Sunnyside Amusement Park's outdoor dance pavilion, built in 1932 just east of the bathing pool. Even if it did rain, the Seabreeze was fitted with a slightly sloped floor so the water would run off. With a squeegee mop the dance floor could be cleaned up in a few minutes.

Toronto Star columnist George Gamester related Allan Wattman's recollections of the Seabreeze during the War years: "My friends and I would check the *Star* to see when blackouts were scheduled for the west end. I would then purchase a few 10-cent-a-dance tickets, and make sure I was on the floor with some lovely lady when the blackout occurred. You see, the Seabreeze policy was to allow couples to dance free for the duration of the blackout. I saved a lot of money that way, and met some charming young women." Adèle Bromby writes about the Seabreeze: "The Seabreeze was a delight. It drew us all like a magnet; we loved the lake breeze and the fun we had there. It was the era of the Mills Brothers' 'Paper Doll'—somewhere in my house I have a couple of dance tickets from there." Signs warned patrons before purchasing their dance tickets to behave themselves on the dance floor—jitterbugging and fast dancing were prohibited at the Seabreeze.

Sunnyside Pavilion Restaurant/Club Esquire/Club Top Hat

Constructed in 1917, the new Sunnyside Pavilion Restaurant was very impressive with its Italian architecture and two gardens. Adèle Bromby writes about the outdoor dance floor there: "My husband picked me up at the Sunnyside Pavilion on Labour Day, September 1, 1930. It was a circular or octagonal structure, with the band in the centre. We would stand around the perimeter and watch and flirt and

15

Lining up for tickets at Sunnyside's Seabreeze open air dance pavilion in the early 1940s. The couples all appear to be ready for a night of fun, but as the sign warns, they had to be careful not to jitterbug or fancy dance. Or else!
Courtesy of Toronto Harbour Commission PC 2/422.

The Club Esquire, pictured here in 1937, changed its name to Club Top Hat by 1940 and was one of the most popular clubs in the Sunnyside area of Toronto. *Courtesy of Jack Lomas.*

16

enjoy!" William Beasley took over the business in 1936, renovated the building and opened the Club Esquire. Inside he adorned the walls with large murals of south sea scenes and continued the tradition of providing excellent food, full stage shows and dancing, while the outdoor dance pavilion operated in the warm weather. Three years later William sold the business to Parklyn Holdings and the name was changed to Club Top Hat, the name most people associate with the nightclub which became one of the most popular west end Toronto entertainment spots for the next seventeen years.

Many Toronto bands played the Esquire/Top Hat, including Trump Davidson, Ozzie Williams and

Cy McLean and His Orchestra (above), the first Canadian all-black band, was a regular performer at Toronto's Club Top Hat; they also performed at places such as the Fallingbrook Pavilion and Club Bayview in Whitby. Photo circa 1940s. *Courtesy of Jack Lomas.*

Frank Bogart. Cy McLean, who led the first all-black dance band of note in Canada, played at Club Top Hat for three years starting in 1945. The Club tipped its hat for the last time in 1955 and was demolished in 1956. The final humiliation for the building was being converted into a storage facility for construction equipment used in the building of the Gardiner Expressway.

Silver Slipper

"To dear little Joan, the Sweetheart of the Slipper," read the autograph from Hal McInch, piano player with Frank Otts' Orchestra.

"To our Mistress of Ceremonies," read Otts' personal autograph.

The date was December 21, 1937. "Joan" was Joan Livings, age 11, who performed at the Silver Slipper for six weeks with six other children who were part of the Hollywood Kiddies, a group of talented young people that sang and danced on various stages around the city as well as on radio. They were hired to be part of the floor show at the Silver Slipper on this occasion.

The Silver Slipper was a major player in the lakeshore area dance halls and featured a host of bands let by Frank Otts, Jack Crawford, Ozzie Williams, Billy Bissett (later Billy Bishop), Billy Nelson and many others. The building was refurbished by Babe Karim when he purchased it in the 1940s, and later renamed the Club Kingsway. After this building burned, Babe constructed a new Club Kingsway on the Queensway which later became a renowned bingo palace.

17

Billy Nelson and his orchestra were just one of dozens of bands to play the Silver Slipper, located on Riverside Drive north of Lakeshore Boulevard, east of the Humber River. *Courtesy of Jack Lomas.*

Joan (Livings) Young singing at the Slipper.

The Hollywood Kiddies Revue would often entertain as part of the floor show at the Silver Slipper. Shown in 1937, standing: Joan Livings, Selma Black; kneeling; Lois Garner, __ Worley, Billy Smith, __Worley, Ruth Garner.

Palais Royale

Of all the original dance pavilions and halls in Toronto, the Palais Royale is the only one remaining and still operating as a ballroom and concert hall. Built in 1922 by Walter Deans as a boat-building company and dance hall, the building was later purchased by George Deller and Bill Cuthbert and transformed into the Palais Royale. The land has always been leased from the City of Toronto which has full control of the harbourfront at Sunnyside.

Deller was a great promoter, booking Big Bands in venues all over the city, including the Palais. He built his hall into a major landmark which thrived during the 1930s and '40s with Bert Niosi as the house band. His wife eventually passed ownership along to Joe Broderick, who had been general manager for some years. The Polish National Union of Canada, Branch 1A took over the lease and ran the Palais for many years as both a ballroom and dance hall. In 2000, the Palais' future was in doubt when the lease came up for renewal, but a new group of private investors, Lakeshore Entertainment, now has long-term plans for fully refurbishing and restoring

Sunnyside's popular boardwalk passed right in front of the Palais Royale at one time. As seen on this billboard in the mid-1950s, one of Toronto's finest musicians, Ellis McLintock, brought his orchestra here many times. *Courtesy of Jack Lomas.*

Left: Lake Ontario lapped at the back doors when the business was originally called Dean's Sunnyside Pleasure Boats, circa 1920s. *Courtesy Mike Filey.*

the very historic hall.

Name bands would usually play the Palais every couple of weeks, including Artie Shaw in 1938 who performed four straight nights plugging his new record that he hoped would be a hit—"Begin the Beguine."

"During World War II radio broadcasts from the Palais reached army and air force camps far beyond Ontario, and went to Canadian ships at sea," writes Jean Williams in a letter to the *Toronto Star.* "An announcer would say: 'We are bringing you the music of Bert Niosi from the Palais Royale Ballroom on the shore overlooking beautiful Lake Ontario in downtown Toronto ....'" Toronto resident George Strachan says, "My favourite hall by far was the Palais Royale. I was on guard duty with the RCAF during the War and had to leave the Palais dances at 11 p.m. in order to be at my post on time—it sure was hard

19

This picture *(top left)* captures life on the road for musicians in 1938. Count Basie's bus is unloaded in preparation for a performance at the Palais Royale. *Courtesy of Joe Showler.*

In the 1960s, *(above)* the Palais continued to retain much of its art deco style. The huge memorable colour sketches of bandleaders were mounted on the wall behind the bar to the right of the stage. **James Lewcun photo.** *Courtesy of Joe Showler.*

Mart Kenney and Norma Locke *(left)* at the Palais Royale in 1947. Mart's first performance here took place in September of that year. As part of his 50th Anniversary Tour throughout Ontario he raised his baton here once again on May 10, 1986. *Courtesy of Mart Kenney.*

to leave when the evening was in its prime. We were able to see or dance to the best entertainers and bands."

In his autobiography, Mart Kenney recalls his first booking into the Palais: "In the fall of 1947 the band commenced its first engagement in the Palais Royal Ballroom ... at night, with the lights subdued, the overall effect was pleasantly exciting. The focal point was the bandstand, bathed in coloured light in startling contrast with the rest of the room .... The Palais dance floor was large and superbly maintained .... Business was brisk ... I was in my element with a good dance band making music for plenty of people who really came to dance."[1]

Richard Kosztowniak managed the hall for the Polish Union, and knew the hall even as a youngster. He told me: "We operate on relatively short-term leases from the city." At one time the city wanted to take over the building to store tractors and other gardening equipment in the Palais. On three separate occasions the Polish group fought to save the building from demolition.

Both the exterior and interior of the Palais have changed as additions have been made and taken down, and as the decor has undergone various transformations. "During the War much of the original woodwork trim was removed, many of the French glass panes were painted over and a Florida Art Deco style was incorporated into the Palais," explained Rich. Soft pastel colours of pink and blue highlight the fixtures that were popular in that particular decorating style. Many of the angles were taken out as a more rounded feel was installed, including the semicircular stage which extends into the dance floor. There is even a fireplace in hall.

Well-known Toronto musician and band-

Performers in the 1990's included Eddie Graf (left), and Mart Kenney.

After playing the Club Embassy in Toronto, versatile and talented musician Bert Niosi (seated centre) moved into the Palais in the early 1930s and led the house band for over 30 years. *Courtesy of Jack Lomas.*

leader Frank Evans played at the Palais for many of the Big Band dances. Frank led the house band at Dunn's Pavilion for many years and at the Dardanella in Wasaga Beach for a season. Along with Frank Evans some of the other regular bands to play the premises have included Dino Grandi, Norm Amadio, Vic Lawrence, Gid Rowntree and Eddie Graf. Private groups regularly rent the premises for parties, dances and fund-raisers and ballroom dance school students also make use of the historic site. In recent years, artists such as Colin James have given concerts at the Palais, and on New Year's Eve Blue Rodeo welcomed in 2001.

The true magic of the Palais Royale can really be appreciated on a warm June Saturday night when you step out onto the deck and patio overlooking the lake. Standing out on the verandah and gazing over the still water with the twinkling lights of faraway ferry boats out for an evening cruise, while a great swing band plays the best of the Big Band era can transport you back 50 years or more.

Bert Niosi was often affectionately referred to as "Canada's King of Swing." Roberta Baldwin, Bert's daughter writes with these words: "Dad played at the Palais for over 30 years and made many people happy. He received many letters and phone calls from people giving their gratitude for all the fond memories he provided over the years. Many happily married couples met there."

Born in London, Ontario, in 1909, Bert began his serious musical studies with Professor Vanuta. "He began playing with Guy Lombardo at age 14," writes Roberta. "Unfortunately, when the band started to travel, his mother wouldn't allow him to go, so the

21

The first of three Balmy Beach Canoe Club *(above)* buildings. The upstairs hall featured regular dances, while the lower area was used for boat storage. This hall burned down February 8, 1936. *Courtesy of Jack Lomas.*

"Sea Biscuit" *(left)* was a Palais regular in the 1990s. His moves on the dance floor were hard to match. He is seen with Debra Young in June 1995.

In 1938, the Canadian National Exhibition opened its famous dance tent, located south of the coliseum and just west of the electrical building. Measuring 80 feet by 260 feet, the first year featured Benny Goodman, Buddy Rogers, Guy Lombardo and Tommy Dorsey. Dancing in the CNE Tent continued through the 1940s. *Courtesy of The Pringle and Booth Collection, from the CNE Archives, A14522-4.*

only time he could play was when they performed in London. However, he carried on and became one of Canada's Best." Bert Niosi was regarded as one of the most versatile musicians in the country, proficient on clarinet, flute, saxophone, trumpet and trombone. He was an arranger/conductor as well as player. As Roberta notes, "Playing at the Palais he had the opportunity to play with and for many great stars such as Duke Ellington who tried several times to have him join his band, but he said too many musicians went to the States to make it big. He also played with Jimmy and Tommy Dorsey; they became good friends and used to visit the house whenever they were in town. He wanted to stay in Canada though. In radio he did the *Happy Gang* for many years and *Canadian Hit Parade*. He then went on to television with the *Tommy Hunter Show* and other programs. My father also travelled a lot, entertaining the troops in Cyprus, Gaza Strip, the North Pole and more." When you speak with people who remember the Palais Royale, the name Bert Niosi invariably is never far behind.

CNE Tent

As one of the features of its annual run in Toronto,

the Canadian National Exhibition used to bring in top-notch entertainers to the famous CNE tent just inside the Prince's Gates. Many people, including the Hon. John Arnup, made a special trip just to see a particular star. "The Canadian National Exhibition in the late 1930s and early 1940s had a huge tent covering a dance floor, with tables around its perimeter," he writes. "In late August, 1940, I took 'my girl' to hear and dance to Duke Ellington. At 1 a.m. outside her apartment I proposed to her and was accepted. We were married a year later and have been happily married for 53 years [in 1994]." Practically all of the Big Bands were booked in for a day or two: Artie Shaw, Benny Goodman with Peggy Lee, Glen Gray and the Casa Loma Band, Tommy and Jimmy Dorsey. On September 8, 1939, the Tommy Dorsey band flew to Toronto on the American Airlines American Flagship craft, to appear at the CNE. This was the first time that an entire band had travelled by air, and the band marked the occasion by playing a few tunes right at Malton airport.

Mutual Street Arena

The Mutual Street Arena (also known as Arena Gardens and The Terrace) opened in 1912 between Dundas and Shuter streets. Music fans will remember it best as a concert hall for famous entertainers. When Glenn Miller appeared at there in Toronto on January 23, 1942, all 6,000 seats had been sold in advance and scalpers were receiving an amazing five dollars for a ticket costing a dollar and a half. A family cousin, Billy Livings, brought along his impressive Speedgraphic camera complete with a large flash unit and was immediately escorted to a prime area, just behind the band. At an appropriate moment between songs, Glenn Miller glanced up and Bill asked him for a pose. "Just a minute," Glenn replied, "I'll get my cigarettes."[2] After he lit up, Bill was free to snap a number of shots.

Frank Sinatra's first Toronto appearance was at Mutual Street Arena in 1949. The building was demolished in 1989 to make way for co-op housing. Today, a plaque on the site marks this arena where the Big Band stars played to thousands of cheering fans.

Fallingbrook Pavilion (The Beach)

If you remember the Fallingbrook Pavilion in The Beach then you're sure to recall the famous "One Hundred Stairs" you had to climb down to reach the hall. Today, the pavilion is gone and the stairs have been closed by the City of Toronto under Bylaw 14122, but for over 50 years people made their way to the pavilion at the base of the Scarborough Bluffs. The hall, built by the lake in the early 1900s, featured a concession stand, change rooms, and boat storage. Jazz pianist Cy McLean led a band at Fallingbrook (also dubbed the East-Enders' Paradise) in the early 1940s before moving to the Club Top Hat. More than once the Fallingbrook Pavilion has been irreverently referred to as "The Bucket of Blood," according to Bruce Brocklebank. "I haven't been down those steps in years," he writes. "I attended dances there in my days at Malvern Collegiate ('37-'39)."

Jack Ainslie knew Fallingbrook well: "During my stint in the Navy I took out a girl who lived at the eastern end of the Beach area of Toronto and we frequently danced at Fallingbrook." He recalls the pleasant summer evenings when people would stroll along the beach near the pavilion.

Louaine Parten writes, "Fallingbrook Pavilion, where I attended dances between 1948 and 1950, was considered rather rough. Gangs from the west end caused problems breaking windows and causing fights. One night we were leaving the dance up the narrow flight of steps and the whole stairway sunk a few feet. Boys would often bury bottles of beer in the water to drink during the evening. On the way home from the dance, the boys would sometimes take the pole off the top of the street car and the driver would chase them down the road. I then graduated to more mature dance halls."

Balmy Beach Canoe Club

Toronto's "Balmy" dance style was coined after the popular hall where it was first introduced—The Balmy Beach Canoe Club. Louaine Parten writes about dancing here. "We had our own style of dancing—the Balmy Beach Style. You can still pick out

Doug Kemp and his orchestra *(above)* on stage at the Masonic Temple in the 1950s.

Toronto's venerable Masonic Temple at Yonge and Davenport, seen here in the 1960s, has featured every type of music from Big Band to Hip Hop throughout the years. *Courtesy of Jack Lomas.*

Balmy Beachers at any function today. Dancers would move counterclockwise in a circle. Boys would stand in the middle of the circle, and girls stood against one wall waiting to be asked. We danced to records on Tuesday and Friday, when people came stag, but on Saturdays it was couples only and a live band performed. I met my husband at Balmy Beach in 1948 when I was 18 years old."

The grand old building was similar to many Ontario canoe clubs, with storage on the main level for easy access to the beach, and a large ballroom on the second floor. Couples could dance on the huge verandah which completely surrounded the building, with French doors leading into the hall.

For some years before and after World War II, life member Joe McNulty was in charge of the Balmy Beach Club dances. A witness to the devastating fire in the mid-'30s, he recalls: "The first building burned to the ground on February 8, 1936." Within months a new structure was erected, and dances were back in operation. The Balmy Beach Club dances became known throughout the city of Toronto as one of the most popular places to meet friends, enjoy music and strike up relationships. One of the orchestras to play here was led by local musician Roy Railey, according to Joe's recollections. The second Balmy Beach Club was also lost to fire. Fortunately, the third and present building was built immediately, thanks in large part to the proceeds of

24

the dances which had been held here for so many years, according to Joe. Dances are still occasionally held at the Balmy Beach Canoe Club.

Masonic Temple

Sitting prominently at the northwest corner at the intersection of Yonge Street and Davenport Road is one of Toronto's musical institutions—The Masonic Temple. The temple has been a popular place to dance since the 1940s, serving a number of purposes during its life. Constructed in 1918 by the Free and Accepted Masons, the building's hall was rented to outside parties for a variety of functions. For generations of Torontonians who love music, this hall is synonymous with dancing to the sounds of the

Rhythm and Blues music at Club 888 gave way to rock in the late 1960s as the Masonic Temple was transformed into the Rock Pile, as seen in this 1969 "After Four" ad in the *Toronto Telegram* newspaper.

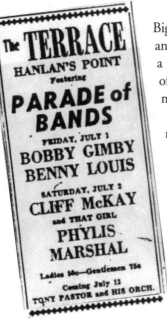

Big Bands, such as Doug Kemp and Paul Whitman who played on a stage adorned with silhouettes of dancers and musical instruments.

In the early 1960s the hall made the transition to other forms of music. A name change was in order—Club 888 was born, offering primarily rhythm and blues bands from Toronto, one of the most popular groups being Dunc & Judy and The Regents. The days of Club 888 waned with the rise in the new heavy rock music from British and American rock bands of the later 1960s. Another name change and new direction in music were planned for the Masonic Temple. Enter The Rock Pile. It is very interesting to look back at just who did visit The Rock Pile in the early years of their career. Led Zeppelin played their first Toronto gig here. And in a one-month period in 1969, fans could see acts like Spirit, Julie Driscoll, Muddy Waters, John Lee Hooker, Lighthouse and Chuck Berry.

Promoters continued to run dances at the Masonic Temple for the next 25 years. In 1995, the hall was sold to the Rosedale Group and renamed The Concert Hall where regular shows featuring name artists in the music business were staged. Then for some time the very future of this historic building was uncertain as the site was considered for a condo development. However, the venerable Masonic Hall has recently been given a facelift and new life appears to have been breathed into this 80+ year-old institution. Currently, the popular late-night Mike Bullard comedy show seen on CTV is taped in the hall.

Toronto Islands

Along with a popular dance hall on Hanlans Point, Centre Island also had a number of dance halls over the years. In 1921, W.J. Reid built a new dance floor at the Park Pavilion, which brought in huge crowds. Storeowner Fred Ginn decided to enlarge his premises and built the Casino, and advertised it as having the best dance floor in the city. Customers from the mainland could dance until the last ferry left; after that the Islanders had the joint to themselves and continued dancing until the wee hours, usually 1 a.m.

The Park Pavilion had a reputation of being slightly rowdy, whereas Ginn's Casino was apparently a little more laid back. A dress code was in effect at Ginn's which specified frocks for the ladies and ties and jackets for the men. By 1955, the ferry's rates had increased, cutting down on the crowds and the Casino was transformed into a bowling alley. It was demolished in 1957.

Ned Hanlan, the world famous sculler, built a large hotel on the section of the Toronto Islands that eventually would bear his name. Within a few years, a major amusement park sprouted up near the hotel, with a ball park, theatre, games, rides and a dance pavilion. By the late 1930s, Hanlans Point Amusement Park had lost much of its attraction as people followed the Toronto Maple Leaf baseball team to their new digs on the mainland. The site is now occupied by the Island Airport. *Courtesy of Jack Lomas.*

Scarborough Bluffs Pavilion

George Gordon remembers the Scarborough Bluffs Pavilion at the foot of Midland Avenue where he went dancing through the 1930s. He writes: "This was a large wooden dance pavilion painted light green, no more than 100 feet back from the edge of the Scarborough Bluffs. The clay cliffs were 310 feet high at that point, and I can recall that on more than one occasion a car would be pushed over the edge on a Saturday night. This pavilion was the home of George Wade and His Cornhuskers, and every Saturday night there was a live radio broadcast for an hour that went from coast to coast. There were all kinds of activities, including dancing, smooching in cars, listening to the music and the broadcast, and crowds of people just milling around. There was also dancing to different bands on other nights at the pavilion. It was a real beehive of activity in the 1920s and '30s. I think it closed up during the War years and was later dismantled because of the erosion of the bluffs."

Bruce Brocklebank maintains that it sat at the eastern end of the Cliffside Golf Course and was still there through the 1940s, but agrees that the erosion completely undermined the foundation of the pavilion.

George Gordon echoes the words of many a Scarborough resident when he writes, "There are probably a good many people around like myself, from Scarborough and the east end of Toronto, who have some fond memories of great music and good times at this old pavilion."

Woodbridge: Elm Park

Bet Armstrong's grandfather, John Christopher Eagleson, owned Elm Park for many years. In fact, one of the reasons the park was called by this name was due to John's passion for planting elm trees. "Every year Grandpa planted many elm trees all over the park," says Bet.

Dances were held primarily on weekends—on both Friday and Saturday nights. Bet recalls as a child she was thrilled to watch one particular group perform. "As part of their show they did a tap-dancing routine which was just great. In fact, Grandpa loved the band so much that after he closed the doors at midnight on Saturday nights, he would have the band continue to perform for the family and friends. With the dance floor empty, the men would have the complete floor to strut their stuff—they were absolutely magnificent."

Bet remembers the glass doors at one end of the pavilion. "As kids we would slide along the floor and end up at these doors, after grandpa had swept and polished the surface." With his strong Irish background, John had used liberal amounts of green to decorate the pavilion.

John later leased Elm Park to other individuals, including the Renouf family who operated it from 1934 until the early 1940s. (The Renouf's son, Reg, later purchased the dance pavilion and marina in Caesarea.)

Cecil Hendricks used to play drums at Elm Park and writes: "My greatest experience was being a member of an orchestra under the name of Kris Morris, a six-piece unit—three saxes, trumpet, piano and drums. We played three summers, three nights a week here during the 1930s. There was no television and dancers filled the pavilion these nights, especially Saturday. We had smart white uniforms with black lapels and a stripe down the pants. The talent in the band was excellent, but of course it was different music then."

Mart Kenney and his Ranch

Dr. Mart Kenney, C.M., LLD., is Canada's longest reigning orchestra leader. Born in Tweed, Ontario, in 1910 and now living in Mission, British Columbia, he has been active in local politics. Kenney still practises his clarinet daily and regularly flies across the country to give concerts.

Mart has toured this country from coast to coast since the 1930s, and there are very few pavilions and dance halls in Ontario where he has not played his horns at least once. In the summer of 1998 Mart made his way up to Bala for a memorable concert at The Kee (Dunn's Pavilion) with Eddie Graf and the

26

Mart Kenney's original Seven Western Gentlemen. Left to right: Glen Griffith, Bert Lister, Mart Kenney, Art Hallman, Jack Hemmings, Ed Emel, Hec McCallum. Bert first suggested the name in 1934; it was immediately adopted by the band. *Courtesy of Mart Kenney.*

Galaxy All Stars Orchestra. He brought back memories of his first gig here in 1942. Mart used to do live radio broadcasts from this same pavilion. Mart Kenney's orchestra was the first band to play at the Brant Inn on a year-round basis and they were a regular attraction at the Palais Royale. Dubbed the leader of Canada's Number One Dance Band, Mart also recorded extensively and was heard regularly on the radio. He led the first Canadian orchestra to broadcast on domestic, American and international radio networks. During World War II, Mart and his band played more than 200 Coca-Cola Victory Parade of Spotlight Bands in Canada radio shows, entertaining over 400,000 troops. In 1992 Mart was named British Columbia's Senior Citizen of the Year. He has been honoured by the Toronto Musicians' Association and was inducted into British Columbia's Entertainment Hall of Fame. Norma Locke, who would become Mart's wife in 1952, joined the band as a regular vocalist on February 4, 1944.

All orchestras have a theme song; Mart's was "The West, A Nest and You, Dear." Mart has always been dedicated to precision tuning and tempo. He writes: "Playing in tune was first, last and always with us. It's part of the magic in music .... One of the things I'd learned was a healthy respect for tempos ... to this day I keep an eye on the crowd to be sure the majority are on the floor ... we have always been a dance band."[3]

By the late 1940s Mart wanted to establish a dance centre of his own and settled on the community of Woodbridge, just northwest of Toronto. He writes: "I bought the land and had plans drawn up for an open-air nightclub with a Western motif."[4] In his bio-discography of Mart Kenney, Ross Brethour writes: "Deciding to bring a little of the west to Toronto and go into the business that he knew the best—music and ballroom—Mart bought the ranch and had the buildings erected."[5] Mart had a private press and celebrity pre-opening on June 23, 1949, and officially opened the Ranch to the public with the Starlit Corral's outdoor terrazzo dance floor on June 24. When the Township of Vaughan permitted the sale of liquor, Mart writes, "For the first time on New Year's Eve, 1966, our clientele didn't have to carry their own supplies."[6]

Anne Kline from Picton tells us her story about Mart Kenney's Ranch. She worked in Saskatchewan and with a number of friends they would listen faithfully to the CBC remote broadcasts from the Ranch and loved them. When she travelled to Toronto she promised to go to the Ranch and get a photograph of her experience to show them. Anne says that she spent "two months wages" on a gown because dressing up was very important to her and others who attended the dances.

The lure to return to his roots in the real West eventually became too great for Mart to ignore. The last dance held by Mart was on May 2, 1969—he and Norma moved West on June 24, 20 years to the day from the Ranch's opening night.

Erin: Stanley Park Pavilion

On the northern outskirts of Erin the entrance to Stanley Park is marked with a cobblestone wall and wooden arch constructed by Charlie Smith in the

Cottagers at Erin's Stanley Park got together in May and raked leaves that had fallen the previous fall. Then they would dance at the Pavilion.

early 1920s. Inside the park you'll see a large, single-storey building with a green metal roof, sitting in a grove of tall white pines. This was the Stanley Park Dance Pavilion, the creation of Harry Austin who erected the building 80 years ago to bring together the cottagers in the park with people in the surrounding area.

Margaret Duggan talked to me about her father's project. "In 1923 the pavilion became a reality, completely designed and built by my dad." The dance floor itself was carefully crafted by Harry with locally harvested and milled lumber from Gillespie's bush and Mundell's sawmill. The dance hall was a hit with the cottagers and continued to attract crowds each year from May through October. Stanley Park was first purchased in 1920 by Margaret's grandfather, Isaac Teeter, who soon sold the property to Harry. The area consisted of a few summer cottages which were rented to people from the Toronto area. Dancers looked forward to many local orchestras, including Willis Tipping from Shelburne, Bud Sutter, and Ben Hokey and his Hawaiian band. Elma Billingsley of Erin writes, "Every May 24th in Erin was opened with a big-name band at the pavilion. I remember George Wade and the Corn Huskers." This old dance pavilion in Erin's Stanley Park is one

of the few such structures from the 1920s still remaining in the province of Ontario.

Innis Lake: Innis Lake III

The large hall, known as Innis Lake III, with its 3200-square-foot dance floor stands proudly on 55 manicured acres surrounding the clear cold waters of Innis Lake, described at one time as having "the best water between Toronto and Owen Sound." When it was built in 1984, the hall became the third dance pavilion to have been located on the property over a period extending back 100 years. The history behind this site is evident the moment you enter the wide foyer of the new hall. The old Mono Road Methodist church pews along the walls were salvaged from Innis Lake II, the predecessor of today's hall. On the walls are pictures of some of the bands from years gone by who have performed here. Hanging prominently above one of the pews are three Mariposa Festival posters from the mid-1960s when Ontario's famous folk music celebration was staged in the park.

Don and Mary Currie, the owners of Innis Lake III, both have strong ties to the property. It was Mary's grandfather who purchased the land in 1902. "Dancing on this property actually goes back as far as 1876, when an open-air dance platform was built for the local folks who would arrive by horse and buggy," Mary explained. "A few years later a proper pavilion was set up and this is where dances were held until 1936." This original building, referred to as Number One, still stands quietly in the trees.

Mary's father, Murving Innis, decided to take the plunge and in 1936 built Innis Lake II, a full-sized dedicated dance pavilion set by the shore of Innis Lake. During its five decades of operation, Murving's hall was the major social stomping ground for hundreds of young men and women in the Caledon area. According to Don, "People always came stag." It was here he first met Mary at this pavilion. Opening night in 1936 featured the mellow sounds of the 10-piece Willis Tipping and his Blue Dragoon orchestra. Big Band music drew hundreds to the pavilion every week. "Innis Lake was the one of the most popular picnic and swim parks in the area before the creation of nearby

Innis Lake II. This venerable dance hall finally succumbed to the long term wear and tear of water damage due to floods. Innis Lake III rose to take its place.

Courtesy of Don and Mary Currie.

MARIPOSA FOLK FESTIVAL 1965

IAN & SYLVIA
PHIL OCHS
GORDON LIGHTFOOT
JOHNNY HAMMOND
THE COUNTRY GENTLEMEN
'SON' HOUSE
ALLEN-WARD TRIO
THE DIRTY SHAMES
JONI ANDERSON
THE YORK COUNTY BOYS
JERRY GRAY
SHARON TROSTIN
LOTVS & RUSS
DAVID REA
ELYSE WEINBERG
THE COMMON FOLK
OWEN McBRIDE
WADE HEMSWORTH
BILL PRICE
AND MANY OTHERS

CHILDRENS CONCERT
CHILDREN ADMITTED FREE

WORKSHOPS
SEMINARS
MARIPOSA CANOE RACE
HOOTENANNYS
CAMPING
SWIMMING
DANCING

TICKETS
SAM THE RECORD MAN
347 YONGE ST.
TORONTO
NEW GATE OF CLEVE
AVENUE RD. & YORKVILLE
TORONTO
MAIL ORDER & INFORMATION
MARIPOSA
FOLK FESTIVAL INC.
20 COLLEGE ST.
TORONTO

PRICES
FRIDAY $3.
SATURDAY (DAY) $1.50

AUGUST 6, 7, 8.
CALEDON EAST
INNIS LAKE
ONTARIO

Conservation areas," says Mary. After 100 years of operation, the family closed the park section to the public in 1980, but the dancing continued.

Thousands of music fans attended the Mariposa Folk Festivals at Innis Lake. It was a perfect site, with its 25-acre natural amphitheatre concert site beside the water. The Festivals featured intimate music workshops, seminars, hootenannies and concerts featuring artists like Pete Seeger, our Gordon Lightfoot, Ian Tyson, the Staple Singers and, as one newspaper wrote, in 1966, "newcomers like Joni Mitchell."

Pavilion #2's fate was sealed after a series of floods weakened the second hall's footings. "We salvaged what we could for the third hall," Don Currie remembered. The couple designed the new hall themselves and were actively involved with the construction every step of the way. The huge stage is two storeys tall, and can accommodate a band on each level while a large balcony surrounds the dance floor. A lot of water has flowed both under the bridge and over the dance floor at Innis, but generations of people have regarded this venue with great affection and hopefully will continue to do so for many more years.

29

Musselman's Lake: Cedar Beach Park Pavilion

A recent view of the pavilion, one dance hall that is still in operation.

In early 1929, Toronto builder George A. Davies was facing a bleak market for his trade. The Great Depression was about to cast its gloom across the land, so George brought his men out to Mussleman's Lake, a few miles northeast of Toronto, where he had originally intended to build a cottage on a lakefront lot. Instead, he erected what would become a landmark on this small body of water—a dance pavilion. George had no portfolio of blueprints from which to work. He knew exactly what he wanted, and with his crew he built his dance hall on the north side of the lake. The grand opening of the Cedar Beach Park Pavilion was in the summer of 1929 and this marked the beginning of a family-owned business—starting with George and his wife Ella—which has now spanned four generations on Musselman's Lake. Vern Davies and his wife Audrey have been the proprietors of the park, with son, George, daughter Janet, and even a grandchild (the fourth generation) involved with the operation.

"During the 1930s and into the 1940s Cedar Beach Park ran dances six nights per week," Vern told me. Some of the well-known bands to grace the stage were Ferde Mowry, Bobby Gimby, Bert Niosi and Jack Crawford. As the dance business began to decline, Vern decided to expand the camping side of his business and established a trailer park. Today Cedar Beach Park is the closest private seasonal trailer park to Toronto, with hundreds of sites. When dancing to Big Bands began to fade, Vern and Audrey chose to go a different route and changed the hall's music policy to country and western. Vern says that this decision was the right one for Cedar Beach Park: "The pavilion developed a loyal crowd who faithfully attended the regular Saturday night dances." Regular country and western dances were held for 25 years.

Gladys Wythe holds Cedar Beach Pavilion very special. "I was from Aurora and went to Musselman's Lake frequently to dance, and I do have such fond and lasting memories of this place," she writes. "The live orchestra at the time—1950-54—was from Oshawa. A couple of girlfriends and myself would rent a cabin for weekends at Mussleman's and had lots of fun with the guys from Oshawa who followed the band." Bruce Brocklebank recalls another pleasant aspect of the pavilion. "I can't remember what bands played there when I danced, but I do remember there were always lots of girls!"

The summer of 2000 saw regular Saturday dances once again being scheduled. Janet Davies and friend Nancy Warton oversaw the renovation of the pavilion and began booking in weekly entertainment.

During the summer of 2001 the Davies family, while retaining ownership of the complex, leased the pavilion to a catering company who will continue to use the premises for private and public functions.

Chapter Three

AROUND THE BAY BY BURLINGTON TO THE SHORES OF LAKE ERIE

Burlington: La Salle Park Pavilion

To mark the occasion of the unveiling of the donor board at La Salle Park Pavilion in Burlington, a grand celebration was held on May 14, 1995, in the park. The $560,000 restoration project of the historic pavilion was ready for the public to enjoy; after years of improvements and renovations, the pavilion would once again be a showcase of unique architecture. The hundreds of people present agreed that after all the dedicated hours of fund-raising and construction, the restored green-and-white pavilion was indeed one of Burlington's historical treasures.

      Older residents recalled the elegant dances which had been held upstairs, while others reminisced about the family reunions and picnics held at the park. People used to take the ferry from Hamilton to attend

Fire destroys historic Burlington pavilion

Above: La Salle Park Pavillion in its glory.

Less than one year after restoration was completed, the historic La Salle Pavilion, originally built in 1917, was destroyed by an early morning fire. *Courtesy of Elaine O'Neill.*

the dances, balls, musical and theatrical performances and banquets held on the second floor. From the upstairs dance floor people could gaze through the casement windows to the romantic view of the bay, and the twinkling lights in the distance. Over the years the La Salle had provided regular employment for local musicians; in 1936 Hamilton musician Jimmy Begg played the upstairs ballroom with Pete Malloy and His Clouds of Joy, while fellow Hamiltonian Dick Wilson was the MC and resident comedian. In June 1945, Eddie Mack and His Band performed. The memories were many.

On May 19, 1995, just five days after the grand reopening, the restored La Salle Park Pavilion was destroyed by fire. Elaine O'Neill, one of the many dedicated workers who co-ordinated the restoration committee of the pavilion, remembers this day: "I followed the smoke and quickly discovered that our pavilion was in flames." Fortunately, the building was insured. The good news today is that a detailed replica of the original pavilion was built and is used practically every day of the week for meetings, special events and larger receptions in the new upstairs ballroom.

Burlington: The Brant Inn

Not far from the Burlington Skyway is the former site of this city's most romantic landmark—the Brant Inn. The Inn's name was coined after Burlington's first pioneer, Chief Joseph Brant, with its history dating back to 1900 when local builder A.B. Coleman erected his new Brant Hotel on the property.

Murray Anderson, the man who would later become the Brant's famous owner and flamboyant impresario began as an employee at the Inn. By 1938 Murray and partner Cliff Kendall were at the helm of one of Ontario's great entertainment venues. Murray set the tone for the Brant, and it could be summed up in one word—class. White linen in the dining room, car jockeys, washroom attendants, a

Murray Anderson of Hamilton *(left)* **began managing the Brant Inn in 1927. With partner Cliff Kendall of Hamilton, they purchased the Brant Inn in 1940 and guided the growth of the club for another 25 years.**
Courtesy of Alex Yackaminie.

strict dress code demanded of all patrons and superb service provided by an outstanding staff all combined to make the Brant Inn a glamorous and romantic destination. As a year round operation, the Brant Inn featured dancing both indoors on the Lido Deck, and outside on the Sky Club, a unique open-air dance floor built over the water. The *Brant News* was introduced as a weekly newsletter to keep people informed about the Brant Inn and related entertainment topics. Murray Anderson made a point of including the Brant Inn on the itineraries of all the famous international acts of the day. Stan Kenton, Ella Fitzgerald, Xavier Cugat, Les Brown, Benny Goodman, Lena Horne, Louis Armstrong, Andy Williams, Count Basie, The Dorsey Brothers ... after one visit the stars wanted to return. Murray became good friends with several of the entertainers who performed at the Brant, and hosted many parties for them in his luxurious Brant Inn penthouse suite.

The Brant Inn, 1955. It hosted the annual Miss Canada Pageant for many years. *Courtesy of Harry Parker*

Murray and Cliff also hired Canadian orchestras as house bands who would perform on a regular, long-term basis. Some of these included Mart Kenney in the 1940s, Gav Morton (1951-61) and Harry Waller (1962-64). Many other top-notch Canadian bandleaders such as Bert Niosi, Frank Bogart, Jimmy Namaro, Ellis McLintock and Stan Patton, played the Brant along with local bands led by Ron "Darkie" Wicken and Morgan Thomas. Disc jockey Paul Hanover's "Meet Me At The Brant" was a weekly highlight, first as a CHML Friday night record program, and later as a cross-Canada CBC live music show.

Murray sold the business in 1964 and the last dance at the Brant Inn took place New Year's Eve, 1968. The contents were then sold and the building was demolished early the next year. Memories of the Brant are all that remain for most people, but there is still some tangible evidence remaining of this great

A.B. Coleman, a local builder, purchased the property in 1892 and erected an impressive hotel in 1900. Across the road he later built his Country Club, which was coined the Brant Inn. This building burned in 1925 but was quickly replaced with the venue most people remember. *Courtesy of Kate Coleman Krenz.*

club on display across the street in the Joseph Brant Museum. In the late 1980s, Burlington Beach resident and Big Band fan Bert Oldershaw organized a series of 'Brant Inn Revival' dances at the Estaminet restaurant, another local landmark. "I scheduled monthly dances on the night of a full moon," Bert told me. Couples could then enjoy an evening beside the lake while the dreamy scene of a moonlit sky reflecting off the water poured through the floor-to-ceiling windows. "It was about as close as you could get to re-creating the Brant's famous Sky Club," Bert reminisced, adding, "The Brant Inn is still close to the hearts of people from all over the province; it touched everyone who came to dance."

Burlington Beach: The Pier Ballroom

Far below the Burlington Skyway lies a strip of beach where many Hamilton and Burlington residents would flock in the summer to escape the city heat.

Guy Lombardo and His Orchestra on stage at the Brant Inn. *Courtesy of Joseph Brant Museum.*

33

Cottages were built along this narrow landform, and as far back as the late 1800s, various attractions were built at the Burlington Canal. It was on this site many years later that the Pier Ballroom was constructed. Louise and Fred Hicks, who owned Hamilton's popular Alexandra and Wondergrove dance venues, operated The Pier in partnership with George Stroud for over five years, starting in 1926. Stroud also owned the Savoy and Palace Theatres in Hamilton. A local newspaper of the time writes that the men would be spending thousands of dollars in improvements and new attractions at the park. "The new company, of course, will also control the $20,000 dance hall, work on which is to be started in the near future. The contract for the building has already been awarded."

Gerry (Hatton) Sterling remembers The Pier. "I was very fortunate to be the vocalist with Jack Ryan's band at The Pier on Burlington Beach," she writes. "I have great memories of watching so many young people having fun dancing, with the breezes blowing right through the pavilion. There were many romances begun there, and couples would saunter outside and sneak under the pavilion, sit on the sand and 'smooch.' The music was fantastic during the War years and many songs immediately make me relive those great nights. On Sunday afternoons we often rehearsed new music, and people strolling the beach would come into the pavilion to listen. I am sure many Hamiltonians will remember The Pier— and smile."

Some of the bands appearing during the summer of 1934 included Jimmie Lunceford, McKinney's Cotton Pickers, and Ozzie Nelson with singer Harriet Hilliard (Ozzie and Harriet!). The Pier peaked as the nearby Brant Inn was coming into its own as one of the premier dance halls in the province. But in the late 1930s and early '40s many more popular big band acts such as Duke Ellington, Tony Pastor and Glen Gray all hit The Pier's stage down by the old canal. The amusement park itself continued operating with rides until 1978, when the City of Hamilton decided not to renew the lease.

Bandleader Ron "Darkie" Wicken. Ron played drums in numerous dance bands for more than 50 years, including a stint with Mart Kenney. *Courtesy Don Buscombe.*

Hamilton: The Alexandra and Wondergrove

If you danced in Hamilton anytime between the 1920s and the mid-1960s, then you likely visited the famous Alexandra downtown, and the romantic outdoor dance floor called Wondergrove at Parkdale and Main. Both locales—owned and operated by the Hicks family—are long gone, the "Alex" succumbing to the wrecker's ball, while Wondergrove closed down

"Darkie" led his own band for thirteen years at Hamilton's Alexandra Ballroom, until the final hours of the hall's existence, May 1, 1964. *Courtesy of Jack Lomas.*

when the lease for the land expired with the city.

Built in 1909, the "Alex" will be remembered best for its dances during the Big Band era. "Our biggest crowd was 2,000 when Charlie Spivak played," family members told me. Local bands led by men like Jack Faregan, Len Allan, Nick Stoutt and Morgan Thomas were popular, but it was Ronald "Darkie" Wicken who would be most associated with this hall. In 1947, Ron was hired at the Alex for a two-week gig and stayed on for another 13 years. His signature "Creole Love Call" song was a favourite with dancers. On January 14, 1960, Ron Wicken played for the last regular dance at the Alexandra. The *Hamilton Spectator* reported that Ron was "as much a part of the Alex as the floor, or the flashing lights, or the music itself. He's Mr. Alexandra or, for hundreds of Hamilton couples, The Beautiful Cupid, who made Beautiful Dreamer replace the bow and arrow."

In 1960, it was decided by the owners to try booking rock 'n' roll acts at the Alexandra. Little Eva, Ronnie Hawkins, Gene Pitney, Duane Eddy, Bobby Vee and Bobby Curtola all played to standing-room-only crowds of over 1,000, but attendance began to fall off and it was simply not feasible to keep the old hall going. As a special nostalgia night held to toast the wonderful years the Alexandra gave to Hamilton, Ron Wicken's Big Band was booked in for a farewell dance on May 1, 1964. Dancers swayed to familiar tunes like "Harlem Nocturne," "Sweet and Lovely" and, naturally, "Creole Love Call," the final music to ever be played in Hamilton's great dance hall. Within hours of the orchestra packing up their gear, the wrecking crew moved in to tear down the building.

It was also the Hicks family in 1935 who conceived and built Wondergrove, billed as Hamilton's scenic outdoor dance floor at Parkdale Avenue and Main Street. In preparation for Wondergrove, a number of willow trees were planted. A large terrazzo floor was poured and a stage, refreshment stand and massive outdoor fireplace were constructed, all styled after the Spanish building Fred Hicks noticed in an old issue of

Wondergrove was a romantic outdoor dance pavilion, set amid willow trees and the thousands of flowers the family planted every spring. Fred Hicks designed the facility and built much of it himself. *Courtesy of Bob Marshall.*

35

An outdoor fireplace may seem strange in a summer venue, but it was one of the highlights of Wondergrove. Johnny Downs and his band posed in front of the set for a photo in 1943. *Courtesy of Johnny and Dorothy Downs.*

the *Saturday Evening Post*. The owners wanted to create an overall ambience of a cosy retreat. Boys with wicker baskets would collect empty pop bottles while people danced. The beauty of Wondergrove was enhanced with chairs and pathways, fragrant with the scent of thousands of petunias and other flowers that the family planted every May 24th weekend. As a special treat for their customers, the family booked in Bert Niosi and his orchestra for the opening night in 1935. Local bands were then hired for the season, which began in early June and wound up on Labour Day. Some of the regulars were Morgan Thomas, Len Allen, Ron Wicken and Johnny Downs from London. Wondergrove operated until 1958.

Welland: Page-Hersey Hall

Tom Zareski of Welland has made music in this part of Ontario for over 45 years. He still plays the drums in the Lincoln/Welland Regiment 17-piece dance band—"a recent off-shoot of the Reg't's Military Band which celebrated its 105th anniversary in 1994," he writes. "The L/W Band is one of three big bands now active in Niagara. We are told by the dancers that they prefer us because we are 'so much easier to dance to.' Consequently, in the last three years, the L/W band has averaged 20 gigs per year compared to six gigs for each of the other bands."

Tom played with the Andy Spinosa Orchestra, a "pretty good band," and had a one-year run at Welland's Page-Hersey Hall, ending in the spring of 1950. The group also had several successful summers at the Lakeside Park Pavilion in Port Dalhousie. He adds, "At both halls, the Spinosa Orchestra was followed by a very good band called The Bruce Anthony Orchestra." Tom also sang with Bruce Anthony at Lakeside Park and Page-Hersey.

The Page-Hersey Hall has a rather unusual background. It is located on Dain Avenue within the confines of Stelco, Page-Hersey Works, where steel tubing is manufactured. Constructed in 1938 as a recreational facility for employees of (then) Hersey-Page Tubes Ltd., it was eventually acquired by Stelco. At that time it was accessible to the public before it was totally fenced-in, as all industrial properties are protected today.

Weekly dances were held throughout the 1940s and early 1950s featuring the area's best big bands—people came from all over the Niagara region to dance. As these weekly affairs waned in attendance, community shows were staged in a concert format. These, too, ended in the mid-1970s.

Tom writes that the Page-Hersey Hall, "in its 'public' heyday, was the largest and grandest ballroom between Buffalo and Hamilton. Its construction in 1938 was financed by a private endowment, and like many such projects—though a monument to its donor and the architect—was ill-planned especially to the location. In my view it never realized its potential as either a public facility, or a facility for company employees."

Port Dalhousie: St. Catharines: Lakeside Park

The dance pavilion in Port Dalhousie's Lakeside Park operated as part of an extensive entertainment complex that at one time drew thousands of people who traveled by rail and steamship every summer from cities such as Niagara Falls, Toronto and Rochester.

Lakeside Park originally started with change houses and a concession booth, with a small open-sided merry-go-round and ball diamond which was added in 1902. A small midway began to develop, offering games, rides and food. With its safe sandy beach, Port Dalhousie became a favourite destination for summertime visitors.

By 1935, Lakeside Park was in full swing and dancing was a major part of summer life here, running six nights per week as well as two afternoons. In the early days you paid ten cents to get in and five cents per couple to dance. During the off-season, CNR Parks Manager J.R. Empringham and his assistant, Sid Brookson, travelled around southern Ontario listening to various bands, and would then hire the one they liked best for the following season.

Dorothy Turcotte writes about the orchestras who played in the pavilion in her book, *Port Dalhousie, Shoes, Ships and Sealing Wax*: "Some of the bands that dancers enjoyed were led by Winn and Ray Phillips from Thorold; Hal Davis from Guelph; Clarence Colton of St. Catharines; Abbie Andrews of St. Catharines; Jack Crawford from Niagara Falls; Jack Evans, Toronto; and Bruce Anthony, St. Catharines. The bands were usually paid $225 a week, plus accommodation in the orchestra cottage. Young people loved to come and dance by the lake, with the moon shimmering across the water in the background. Local girls enjoyed being asked to dance by boys from out of town, while the local lads seethed with jealousy. Sometimes lively rivalries broke out."[1]

Welland musician Tom Zareski played Lakeside Park for many seasons with the Andy Spinosa Orchestra. He writes: "We had several successful summers there in the 1950s; I also sang with Bruce Anthony's Orchestra at Lakeside Park."

On December 20, 1974, the dance pavilion burned to the ground. "This caused a lot of sadness, for many residents of the penin-sula remembered romantic evenings by the lake, dancing to a live band. The pavilion was to have been turned into a theatre."

Fort Erie: Erie Beach Amusement Park

The area at Snake Hill Grove, just above old Fort Erie, was originally a picnic ground when a resort was established in 1885. New owners in 1901 set up rides and renamed the place Fort Erie Grove. Frank V.E. Bardol bought the park in 1910, renamed it Erie Beach Amusement Park, and immediately enlarged the facility to include a full park/recreation resort with more rides, promenades, zoo and an athletic field. The next year, finishing touches were put on the new Casino which featured the most modern dance hall of its days, bowling alleys and, what was at the time, the world's largest outdoor swimming pool. The 130-acre centre once attracted 50,000 people in a single day.

The Park closed its doors for the last time on Labour Day, 1930. Forty-five years later, tall trees grew in the shallow end of the pool. Graffiti covered

The dance pavilion at Erie Beach Amusement Park operated from 1911 until 1930. The park suddenly closed due to the poor economy of the Depression. Also, the Peace Bridge had opened on August 7, 1927, drawing people away from the park to more exotic places like Buffalo. And those who did travel by boat from Buffalo preferred the longer ride to Crystal Beach. The building stood vacant for 45 years, frequented only by graffiti-writing vandals. It was demolished in 1975. *Courtesy of Cathy Herbert.*

37

Two large passenger boats - the *Americana* in 1908, and the *Canadiana* in 1910 - plied the waters daily every summer, ferrying happy holidayers to the park. The *Canadiana* was the most famous of the two boats, and the favourite means of transportation to the park for U.S. visitors. This ship of elegance with its grand staircases was the last passenger vessel built in Buffalo and could hold 3,000 people. Costing $250,000, it featured slot machines and the largest dance floor of any steamer on the Great Lakes. The dance floor on the second level was completely protected from the elements by glass windows. Evening cruises where couples could sway on the moonlit deck were especially romantic occasions. On the last trip of the season during Labour Day weekend the band would occasionally play *Auld Lang Syne*. The *Canadiana's* last year of operation was 1956. *Courtesy of Cathy Herbert.*

Dozens of teams of horse-drawn wagon were used to move hundreds of tons of sand during the construction of the Crystal Ballroom. *Courtesy of Cathy Herbert.*

walls of buildings once offering ice cream cones and soft drinks. Broken glass, rusted steel rods and decades of garbage littered the insides of the three-story dance hall whose walls many years ago were adorned with palm trees and dragon murals.

After a web of bankruptcy and foreclosure which spun over the next five years, a mysterious "covenant on title" eventually emerged, legally forbidding the use of Erie Beach as a recreation site ever again. Rumour had it that the Erie Beach's arch-rival, Crystal Beach, had a hand in the park's demise, to assure ongoing years of competition-free operation.

Crystal Beach Amusement Park Ballroom

On November 3, 1924, the Schultz Brothers of Brantford, along with B & CB Corp., signed the contract to construct the hall at a cost of $80,790—target completion date was May 1, 1925. *Courtesy of Cathy Herbert.*

When the grand Crystal Ballroom at the Crystal Beach Amusement Park officially opened in 1925, 14-year-old Inez Elliott was the first person to have the honour of setting foot with her partner onto the massive dance floor. This marked the beginning of the hall's remarkable 65-year history in the

Thousands came to Crystal Beach Amusement Park for the excitement of the rides and the evening summer dances. The first stage was an octagonal shape, located in the centre of the dance floor. Later renovations to accommodate larger orchestras moved the stage to the south end, opening the space for a capacity of 1500 couples.
Courtesy of Cathy Herbert

park, located on Lake Erie in the Niagara Region.

Crystal Beach symbolized the close relationship between Canada and the United States, and the park soon became affectionately known as Buffalo's Coney Island. As Port Colborne resident and historian Ruby Conway told me, "It's been the water that has brought us together." During the summer months people from Buffalo would hop aboard both the Canadian and American steamers which would ply the short distance across the lake to Crystal Beach. In 1921, the third and largest pier was constructed for the throngs of people disembarking for a day's fun at the amusement park.

As the popularity of the park grew (it was originally established in 1888 as a religious assembly), it was only a natural progression that plans were made to construct a dance hall. Ridgeway historian, Cathy Herbert, obtained the original blueprints and written proposal for the

39

Today, the 3rd pier is condemned. The only reminder of the once popular Crystal Beach Amusement Park is the breakwall with its silhouettes of dancers embedded in the cement. Photo circa 1995.

hall that was to be constructed: target completion date May 1, 1925, cost $80,790. Dozens of horse-drawn wagons were led by workers to level the ground. Before the actual structure could be built, a protective cement seawall had to be constructed. Designers decided to make the wall an extension of the spirit of dancing and included a series of figures in minuet dance poses embedded into the cement. The size of the planned ballroom was to be so massive that architects decided to abandon the use of traditional wooden frame supports in favour of large steel beams, resulting in the largest unobstructed dance floor in North America. The 20,000 square feet available for dancing could hold 1500 couples. The building had many other features as well, including sliding doors, numerous windows which could be opened to allow the heat to escape, and balconies where tired couples could enjoy the evening air. Uniformed ushers escorted couples on and off the dance floor.

Mary Wintle has fond memories of the ballroom. She writes, "As teenagers we looked forward to Saturday nights when we would get all fixed up to go dancing, and hopefully meet some nice boy. The dance floor was so shiny, and up above glittered the huge ball."

During its heyday the ballroom attracted some of the largest crowds of any dance hall. On the

night Stan Kenton drew 7,000, the money was coming in so fast that all cashier Audrey Stockwell could do was sweep the bills onto the floor where it piled up to her knees. The temperamental and sometimes unpredictable Artie Shaw was late for a Labour Day engagement and, while Artie was upstairs later trying to get paid, the dissatisfied crowd decided to riot, tearing mikes off the stands and throwing them at instruments.

Welland musician Tom Zareski not only performed in many of the Niagara region halls, he also met his wife at the Crystal Ballroom. He writes: "In August 1952, while standing 'ringside' at the Crystal Ballroom, totally enthralled by the Stan Kenton band, a very cute young lady of 17 asked if she could hitch a ride into Welland after the dance. Thirteen months later the cute young lady became my wife, and in ensuing years, the mother of our five children."

By the 1980s, Crystal Beach Park itself was becoming a tired amusement centre, despite efforts to make it competitive with other new attractions. Still, attempts were made to revive the site. In 1984, Ed Hall came out of retirement as part-owner of the park and returned the mirrored globe he had retrieved from the hall after an earlier fire. The 13-piece band Buffalo Swing had the honour of being the first band to play in the renovated pavilion on July 6, 1984. As attempts to revive the glory of the Big Band days continued, Lionel Hampton returned for a special show in 1985. "This hall was one of the greatest ballrooms I ever played in," he said. "It's like returning home."[2]

Unfortunately, the glory days of Crystal Beach were finished. On Labour Day, 1989, the park was closed for good and all fixtures were auctioned off. Minutes before the wrecker's ball struck the Crystal Ballroom in June 1991, Cathy Herbert and her father had a symbolic "last dance" on the floor. Meanwhile, the minuet dancers in the cement breakwall remain in their permanent poses, a solid reminder of the magical times people experienced in the Crystal Ballroom at Crystal Beach Amusement Park. Today, a gated community of upscale beachfront homes occupies the site—most purchasers are Americans.

Morgan's Point

When Port Colborne historian and newspaper columnist Ruby Conway was interviewed by a high school history student, one of the questions asked was, "What did you do for fun during the 1930s?" Ruby didn't have to take time to think about that one: "We went to Morgan's Point!" she immediately replied.

Ruby writes: "The girls were not wallflowers. We used to watch for the good dancers and then ask them to dance. It was a long way out to Morgan's Point. After working until 11 p.m. as we did in

Laverne and Donelda (Martinson) Gretsinger met at Morgan's Point near Long Beach on Lake Erie, and eventually purchased a cottage there. The wooden shuttered octagonal-shaped dance hall at Morgan's Point was built by Lloyd "Vic" Neff in the 1920s and was an immediate hit for the local teens, often drawing as many as 600 who came to dance the night away, including Port Colborne historian Ruby Conway. *Courtesy of Donelda Gretsinger.*

Stedman's on Saturday nights, we would hitch a ride with one of the girls, who was going steady with a guy who drove his own car."

The relative innocence of the times is revealed in her letter: "We didn't smoke or drink, and knew nothing about drugs; we just loved to dance. This was the '30s."

Peterborough musician and bandleader Bobby Kinsman spent some time in the Niagara area, playing the local halls. Ruby specifically recalls Bobby's band with musician Del Crary performing at Morgan's Point. Win Phillips, leader of a St. Catharines-based band, played regularly at the Point. Midway through the evening he would leave the bandstand and stroll through the starry-eyed dancers, playing soulfully on his clarinet, while the lights dimmed and people danced cheek-to-cheek.

Ruby says that many couples who are married today met one another at Morgan's Point, where "romances blossomed with the beautiful music." Some years later she met the man she would marry at the dance hall. "He was new in town and wore a white jacket and dark trousers. I asked him to dance and he said 'no,' which upset me and spoiled the evening. The next Saturday he asked me to dance saying, 'I do the asking.' Years later we won many contests, among them the Charleston and Jitterbug."

In the early 1950s, kids could still dance regularly for 25 cents at Morgan's Point and get a hamburger for 37 cents at the restaurant nearby. Both places were owned at this time by Mr. and Mrs. Andy Liptak of Welland.

Harold and Elsie Taylor managed Morgan's Point Trailer Park for 23 years, located just across the street from the pavilion. "The music was all over the area," writes Elsie. "While the dance hall stood, we enjoyed it. On weekends cars were lined up and down the streets. The people from the park and local residents would go up to watch the dancing and hear the music. There was a fellow they called 'Long Beach Joe.' He jitterbugged with all the girls and he really twirled them around—then he would go back to Long Beach to dance."

By 1979 the building had deteriorated to the point where it had become an eyesore and a hangout.

41

Advertisement for Long Beach Pavilion.

It also had not been used for 15 years. At that point the owner, Ron Law, decided to tear down the old pavilion and make room for new house construction on the site. "People don't want the hall anymore," Ron was quoted as saying.

Fifty years of history came to an end in less than two hours as a backhoe from Port Colborne Rock Driller and Blasters Ltd. proceeded to pull down the sagging walls of the pavilion.

"It's the end of an era—that's progress," Ron Law said, as he viewed the work of the backhoe.

Sadly, as Ruby Conway says, "The bulldozer has no respect for memories."

Long Beach Pavilion

Ruby remembers the pavilion at Long Beach as a "larger building which brought in bigger-name performers than we'd have at Morgan's Point—it was where the Americans would go to dance."

Ruby Conway has witnessed first-hand the close ties that have developed between people from Canada and the United States. "The Americans have been a boon to our economy here—they hired local people and were often big spenders." Today, many Americans who have cottages in the area can trace back their families' roots back to six generations of relatives vacationing in Canada. "The lakeshore was founded by the Americans who built their cottages and in many respects, took over." In recognition of the international friendship and neighbourhood that continues to grow between the two nations—more specifically the two cities of Fort Erie and Buffalo—the annual Fort Erie Friendship Festival was founded in 1987 to mark both the Canada Day and Independence Day celebrations.

H.G.R. Williams, the father of Welland resident Patricia Turner, operated the Long Beach

The original Summer Garden in Port Dover, established by Ben Ivey in 1921. *Courtesy of Don Buscombe.*

restaurant and dance hall for a few years, starting in 1939. His daughter writes: "The original dance hall was in the Long Beach park that at one time during the 1920s had an amusement park as well as a large wooden building that housed bathing change rooms below, with a roller rink above. The amusements went to Crystal Beach but when my father built our cottage in 1932, the roller rink and dance hall were still operating.

"The dance hall was a wooden building with open shutters on three sides. A deck with bench-like seats was also built around the three open sides. When my father managed the business, the owner, Gregory Deck of Deco Restaurants in Buffalo, relocated the hall and built a new one further down the road. Dad also ran this pavilion for a couple of years, but after the War the dance hall era seemed to come to a standstill at Long Beach. Ivan Bradden of Welland and Bruce Anthony from St. Catharines were two of the orchestras. Dances were 10 cents or three for 25 cents, and every so often there would be a five-cent special."

Port Dover: Summer Garden

Near the beach on the main drag in Port Dover a bright yellow sign reads "Summer Garden Picnic Area." Today, hundreds of hungry vacationers chow down on ice cream cones and hot dogs here, once the site of three celebrated dance pavilions, all called Summer Garden.

People who remember Port Dover's third and best known Summer Garden likely recall two remarkable aspects about this hall: the unique octagon-shaped building and the legendary man in the white suit and red rose, flamboyant impresario and owner of the business, Don Ivey. Although Don is most associated with Port Dover's beachfront pavilion, it was his father Ben who originally conceived and built all three Summer Gardens, starting in 1921.

Ben's first pavilion was constructed out over the water at the foot of Walker Street. "Our mother, Edith, gave the hall its name—Summer Garden," Gordon Ivey (Don's brother) told me in 1995. It was

erected on a series of wooden supports which had been sunk many feet into the sand below the water. When the big storm of 1929 hit Port Dover, the Summer Garden's wooden building was battered with broken ice and logs until half of the dance hall was demolished completely.

Poster of Lionel Thornton appearing in Port Dover.
Courtesy of Don Buscombe.

But Ben was not to be daunted by the disaster. This "courageous and venturesome man," as Helen Lorriman (Don's sister) described, had Summer Garden #2 open for business in May 1929, wisely locating the building up on the beach. It was built in 19 days thanks to the help of 50 volunteers. Unfortunately, three short years later this large white building burned to the ground. Port Dover resident Leolea McCloy told me that she and other townspeople stood on the hill and wept openly as the pavilion succumbed to the flames. Tears turned to cheers when Summer Garden #3 was erected and opened its doors May 24, 1932, featuring the popular Stan Williams and his orchestra. For the record, Leolea said that Summer Garden #1 opened with the band of Charles Cody, a 12-piece singing syncopated group from Detroit, and Summer Garden #2 featured Emerson Gill on opening night. In the earlier days, these halls were commonly referred to as "ballrooms," and not pavilions, according to Leolea who danced in all three Summer Gardens.

In 1936, the management of the Summer Garden was passed to Don, who really enjoyed the limelight. "Don was a great operational man," said Gordon. "With his white suit and ever-present red rose, he became quite a figure in the town." James

Bentley, who met his wife at the Summer Garden, writes: "Don Ivey managed the ballroom with Ivey League class—wear a tie and jacket, act like a gentleman and the evening was yours."

During the War, the Summer Garden was a natural destination for the servicemen stationed at nearby flying schools. Dancers travelled great distances to visit Port Dover, many coming by the electric rail which made stops in all the towns. Margo Kerber would go to Port Dover during the 1940s for a day at the beach and an evening of dancing. She writes: "We'd take the trolley in Galt for a weekend in Port Dover and the Friday and Saturday night dances. You couldn't wait to get back the next weekend. One of my friends is happily married to the boy she met then in Dover." Here is a poem Margo wrote "years ago when the Dover summer ended for another year":

Don Ivey was affectionately known as "Pop" by most people—the man in the white suit with his ever-present red rose in the lapel. *Courtesy of Don Buscombe.*

Ronnie Hawkins *(below)* and The Hawks considered the Summer Garden their second home on Sunday nights in the early 1960s.

The third and final Summer Garden, built in 1932 and destroyed by fire in 1978. *Courtesy of Don Buscombe*

Summer Romance

Fingers that found mine and locked,
How gentle yet firmly sweet your hand,
While stars leaned low enough to drown their shimmer
In waves softly lapping white sand.

Firm brown cheek pushing tenderly, wind-blown hair
from my face,
While arms turned my body gently into a warm and
heavenly embrace.

This was an old love, a summer romance,
With dreamy phrases, sugared up just so ...
That faded like the leaves of Autumn
Remarking simply, "Angel, you've been nice to know."

Don Ivey's first love was ballroom music, the music that he grew up with and which he brought to his Summer Garden throughout this period. But, he also realized that the younger crowd made his business successful, and he developed a good rapport with the kids. "That's how he became known as 'Pop,' " said Fred Knechtal, Don's friend and business associate. "Don was a memorable person, the kind of man you don't forget and had a gift for the spoken word. He loved his work, and with Don, 'The Show was the Thing.' " With his keen eye for entertainers, Pop Ivey started a Sunday night tradition featuring Ronnie Hawkins & The Hawks, beginning in the late 1950s. After leaving Hawkins, Levon (Helm) and the Hawks—who would later become The Band—continued their gigs in Port Dover, according to Levon in his biography. "On Sunday nights we played Pop Ivey's ballroom for $250. Someone taped our show one night, and the tape still exists .... Richard Manual ends the show with a beautiful version of 'Georgia On My Mind' .... Everybody loved Richard's voice, especially on that song."[3]

Don began the annual Dance of the Roses. People who attended this highlight of the summer dance season remember the thousands of rose blossoms adorning the walls of the Summer Garden. "It was the biggest dress-up affair in Port Dover and was Don's baby," says Fred Knechtal. Over the years the

third dance hall began to show signs of old age. The final show, featuring Roy Hensher, took place on New Year's Eve 1978. "It was the first time I actually saw the ballroom as a customer—it was a grand night," says Gordon Ivey. Eight days later the old hall lay in smouldering ruins after an arsonist torched Summer Garden #3.

From the Big Bands led by Lionel Hampton, Ray McKinley, Count Basie, Louis Armstrong and Gene Krupa, to the rock greats like the Guess Who and Lighthouse, the music was the magnet of the Summer Garden. As James Bentley writes, "Five million people attended the three Summer Gardens, and now it's time to say thanks Don, to you and your father Ben." When Don passed away a few years later, Fred Knechtal had these words: "Music was his life, dancing was his love and ladies were his esteem and he put them all together in a rose."

Poster for Hillcrest Hall. *Courtesy of Betty Coates.*

45

In 1992, the three Summer Gardens inspired the local Lighthouse Festival Theatre to create and produce a hit musical about the pavilion, portraying Summer Garden through the years from ragtime to rock. In late June 1995, an eclectic group of three individuals marked a solemn moment on the site of the Summer Garden—they approximated where Don Ivey's office had been, and left a tribute to Woody Herman where, according to their sources, the musician decided to form his famous Herd.

Perhaps the most suitable words to complete this section on Port Dover are found in part of the poem Don Ivey composed on January 9, 1979, the day after his beloved ballroom burned to the ground:

Summer Garden Farewell

The night is chill, the ballroom deserted
The sound of dancing feet is gone
The sound of music has faded away
There is no sound of voices, they have disappeared
There is no laughter
Farewell, dear old lady Summer Garden.
There are tears I cannot hide, so I smile and say as the flames die
Smoke gets in my eyes ...

Hillcrest Hall/Hillcrest Dance Club

The sign out front of the large store says "Hillcrest No. Two," reminding many people of the years when

The Roosevelt Dance Hall sits in the hamlet of Glen Meyer near Lake Erie. The last dance was held here in 1968.

the busy Hillcrest Hall held weekly dances here. Today it's a furniture store run by Betty Coates. Betty provided some background on the dance hall. "It was built by the late Peter Hegmans in the 1950s and ran until 1965, the last year it was used as a dance hall," says Betty. This hall brought in some of the best country and western music around, and included a little square dancing as well. Some of the bands performing at Hillcrest were Johnny Davidson and the Canadian Hoedowners, the Norfolk Mountaineers and Bill Long. In the front area of her store, Betty has devoted a corner to the dance hall days at Hillcrest. "Customers have brought in pictures which I've put up on the walls," she says. "I've also kept one of the speakers up on the showroom wall, for nostalgia sake."

Simcoe: The Roosevelt Dance Hall

At a quiet country intersection not far from the town of Simcoe, there's an old building partially clad in grey insulbrick with weeds and other wildflowers creeping up the wall. The sign above the front door displays the Roosevelt Dance Hall in thin, rusted metal letters. In the curved front windows, two faded and flaking "Coca-Cola" signs indicate that "Dance" and "Lunch" might be available inside. But expecting to see a band or buy a hot dog in this silent building today would only be wishful thinking. The Roosevelt Dance Hall has been dark since 1968.

Attached to the back of The Roosevelt is a modest house, a contrast to the almost eerie presence of its Siamese dance hall partner. The homeowners, musician Darrin Schott and his wife Allison, told me about this hall's colourful past. The family who originally owned this property grew tobacco and operated a Red Star service station/gas bar in the 1940s. "The family converted the garage into The Roosevelt Dance Hall in 1954 and ran Saturday night dances for 14 years," explains Darrin. As the story goes, the business was suddenly closed down in 1968 after the mother-in-law suffered a third nervous breakdown due to the large crowds and noise of the weekly dances.

The Roosevelt was strictly country and western,

Early days at the London & Port Stanley Dance Pavilion circa late 1920s.
Courtesy of Dolph Coates

Port Stanley: The Stork Club

Visitors to Port Stanley today may be surprised to discover that this quiet tourist/fishing village was once home to one of the largest and most famous dance halls in North America. Later called the Port Stanley Ballroom, and ultimately The Stork Club, the $85,000 London and Port Stanley Pavilion opened its doors to the public on July 29, 1926. More than 6,500 enthusiastic people laid down the 15-cent admission charge and crowded into the pavilion to witness the official opening remarks by dignitaries, and then paid five cents a dance to sway to the Vincent Lopez Orchestra, straight from the Ritz Carlton Hotel in New York City. The 24,000 square-foot gargantuan hall left people awe-struck. A huge balcony surrounded the 13,000 square-foot dance floor, practically free of posts and obstructions.

Opening day was just the beginning of an unforgettable saga of music, romance and the inevitable peaks and valleys that dance halls of this size were to experience in the years ahead. During the busiest periods of summers gone by, Port Stanley's tiny population would swell to over 10,000 on the weekend as people from London and St. Thomas converged by car, electric train and boats to visit the amusement park and pavilion.

With a ballroom the size of Port Stanley's, there was plenty of work for local residents on dance night. Barbara Richards writes: "When I was a teenager in Port Stanley, I sold tickets at 50 cents each so people could get into The Stork Club. They used to come down on the London & Port Stanley (L&PS) Railway and walk across the road to the pavilion." V.P. Smith experienced all phases of the pavilion's life and writes: "As a small lad I watched the Pavilion being built, then I worked there later as a ticket taker for the dances. I learned to dance at the

drawing up to 400 people who would travel from miles around to enjoy bands like George Short. It was rowdy and loud and people had a great time as they celebrated the end of another week of hard farm work. A large indentation in the entrance wall is an indication of the level of excitement that frequently permeated the hall. "A ketchup bottle made that mark," points out Darrin. "The owners left the bottle embedded in the wall for two years."

It was as if time stood still when the young couple in 1994 discovered the dance hall in the same condition as it was when the last patron left the building in 1968. Says Darrin: "There were still streamers on the wall; even the ashtray that the two elderly ticket takers used had old butts in it." On the interior walls of the ticket booth are hundreds of pencilled figures calculating the attendance at various dances. People stop by to optimistically ask if it will ever open again. Probably not, but if The Roosevelt should ever open its doors to the public again, Darrin—and many other people as well—feel that the crowds would be back for the regular Saturday night country and western dances. And as for any potential nervous breakdowns? Just send the mother-in-law out to Bingo on dance night.

47

Dancers arrived at the ballroom in Port Stanley by car as well as by train, which brought them right to the front door. Circa 1930s.

Pavilion and spent a few New Year's Eves there." Alf Murray writes: "I used to work at The Stork Club on the weekends for a dollar a night. Almost all the major U.S. bands played here."

The capacity of the hall made it feasible for management to bring in the best Big Bands in North America. Its sheer size impressed even the most celebrated entertainers as they played to spirited audiences of two thousand and more; the acts who performed here included practically everyone in the music business. Benny Goodman and his band even took time to play a game of baseball with Morgan Thomas and His Orchestra. People associate Guy Lombardo with The Stork Club because of his fre-

quent appearances in later years. The orchestra's first performance here was in 1941; Guy's final job took place here in 1977, just months before he died.

It was also the local orchestras playing their very danceable music night after night, whom many people remember. Alf Tibbs, Frank Crowley, Jack Pudney, Richard Avonde, Benny Palmer, Lionel Thornton and Johnny Downs were just a few of the local London-area men to lead orchestras for lengthy engagements at the club. Performing his special brand of "Sophisticated Swing," Johnny's house band at The Stork Club likely held the record for playing more years at the pavilion than any other orchestra.

Owned and operated originally by the

Multi-coloured houses built in the 1990s now occupy the space once home to The Stork Club.

London & Port Stanley Railway, the Public Utilities then assumed responsibility for the pavilion, leasing it to various individuals. It was sold to private interests in the late 1960s, but a series of problems actually forced the closure of the building in 1973. Then businessman Joe McManus Sr. rode in on his white horse to rescue the tired grand hall, promising to bring back the glory days of The Stork Club. In late 1973, people's spirits soared as workmen arrived to refurbish the club, both inside and out. On the

evening of Friday, June 24, 1974, Harry James and His Orchestra mounted the stage and played to 1,500 ecstatic fans who came out to experience the new Stork Club, relive old memories and look optimistically to the future of the pavilion.

Gerry Costello managed The Stork Club from 1975-77. "Joe hired me to turn the place around," says Gerry. "He handed me the keys and told me to make it work." During Gerry's tenure the dance hall did begin to show an "operational profit."

49

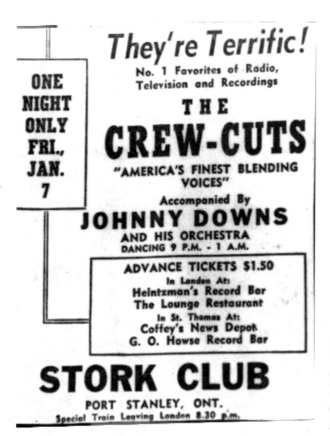

They're Terrific!
No. 1 Favorites of Radio,
Television and Recordings

THE
CREW-CUTS
"AMERICA'S FINEST BLENDING
VOICES"

ONE
NIGHT
ONLY
FRI.,
JAN.
7

Accompanied By
JOHNNY DOWNS
AND HIS ORCHESTRA
DANCING 9 P.M. - 1 A.M.

ADVANCE TICKETS $1.50
In London At:
Heintzman's Record Bar
The Lounge Restaurant
In St. Thomas At:
Coffey's News Depot
G. O. Howse Record Bar

STORK CLUB
PORT STANLEY, ONT.
Special Train Leaving London 8.30 p.m.

Rides on the beach were introduced once again, barbershoppers strolled the boardwalk and various contests were staged all in hopes of bringing back the people to the beach. Some of the old elegance was reintroduced as staff at the hall wore white gloves, the Memory Lane corner was enlarged, and wedding receptions were encouraged in sectioned-off areas which enabled people to celebrate their special occasion.

The Stork Club enjoyed moderate success during the next few years, varying the entertainment to feature pop groups like the Shirelles, The Drifters and Chubby Checker, but there was never an attempt made to turn the pavilion into a rock 'n' roll hall. The last dance staged at The Stork Club was on New Year's Eve 1978, featuring the band Daybreak. On January 13, 1979, a fire set in a garbage bin near the southeast corner of the building destroyed about 20% of the club. By 1979, the days of large crowds dancing to Big Bands were over; Joe McManus Jr. felt that it simply was not worth restoring and auctioned whatever could be salvaged, including the dance floor. Parts of it were later used to create souvenir plaques and cutting boards.

Not long after the fire, with the cool wind off Lake Erie blowing through the charred hole which the fire had created, Johnny Downs and some friends played a few numbers on stage as a symbolic farewell to The Stork Club. The hall later was the inspiration for a musical, entitled "Bandstand," produced by Smile Theatre Company.

Norma Aitkin's writes about The Stork Club: "We especially have fond memories of The Stork Club, because it was there on a beautiful summer Saturday evening, July 17, 1944, that my husband proposed and I got my ring. We celebrated our 50th anniversary on August 3, 1995. This particular evening there was a name band playing—Tony Pastor. Of all the dance halls in the general London area, The Stork Club retains our fondest memories because it was always a 'big event' to go there for an evening—especially when you have a brand new sparkling diamond ring catching the coloured lights flashing from the revolving globe on the ceiling, dancing to wonderful music with all the doors on the lakeside open and the moon glinting off the water!" A small development of houses clad in colourful siding today rests on the Lake Erie beach site of The Stork Club.

Chapter Four

ACROSS SOUTHWESTERN ONTARIO FROM WOODSTOCK TO AMHERSTBURG

**Johnny Downs
and the Rondeau Park Pavilion**
Courtesy of Johnny and Dorothy Downs.

Woodstock: Southside Park Pavilion and the Green Grotto

Woodstock had two very well-known dance halls. Isabel Archer writes about the dances she attended at both of these popular pavilions: "My first recollection of the pavilion at Southside Park was when I was 14 or 15, when my sister came home from university and my father allowed our brother to drive us from Norwich to the dance. It was a great time for my sister and me. Back then it was jitney dancing, costing 25 cents admission and then ten cents a dance. There were four places to enter the dance floor and a young fellow stood at each one to take tickets for each dance. In September 1941, we moved to Woodstock and my father worked in a Massey Harris war plant. There was an army camp at the east end of town where the fairgrounds are now, so there were lots of boys to dance with. By now it was straight admission to the dance. My girlfriends and I would walk all the way to the park, dance all evening and walk home. We liked to go stag. It was more fun to dance with lots of partners, rather than just one date. When I say I danced all evening, I mean I danced all evening. Although it was war time, it was a good time for me with lots of boys to dance with, and always good crowds. There was rarely a fight or any trouble. I hardly ever sat out a dance and thoroughly enjoyed going to Southside regularly every Wednesday, Friday and Saturday nights for modern dancing and, on occasion, old-time on Thursdays. There was a booth outside the pavilion by the creek where refreshments could be purchased, but I never did. I would dash out to the fountain between the dance hall and the booth

The Benny Palmer Band, photo taken at the London Free Press Radio Station in June 1940. Benny Palmer is seated at the piano. Standing left to right: Ed Pudney, Harry Vandersluys, Russ Lansing, Johnny Lombardi, Carl Palmer, Ed Cowie, Lionel Thornton, Rocky Volpe and Lloyd Lansing. *Courtesy of Harry Vandersluys.*

and then dash back in to be sure I did not miss the next dance. It was all live bands and we had such good times. Lionel Thornton was one of the band-leaders—he was very good.

"In the winter we went dancing at the Green Grotto, on the second floor above the bowling alley across from the Capitol Show. The same bands played there, three times per week and, oh, what good times, good memories and good dancing. There too was only a row of benches around the edge, and people danced—no sitting and drinking. I didn't meet my husband at a dance, I met him at work. For a long time he did not dance, but I went anyway. As

the song goes, 'I could have danced all night!'"

Stratford: The Casino and Tony Cryan and his Band

Thousands of devotees of live theatre trek through the Stratford Festival complex every year, enjoying the best in professional productions. Many of these patrons would likely be surprised to know that long before Shakespearean plays began receiving ovations on this site, dance fans were applauding their favourite bands at the Casino, Stratford's celebrated dance pavilion.

To learn more about the Casino and the people behind it, we'll turn to 82-year-old Don Markle, who helped operate the hall.

"Stratford was my hometown before I moved to Woodstock in 1941 to run my own business," he writes. "Gus Morello operated the Casino in Stratford and was a good friend of mine. His connection with the dance hall business started with a hall outside of Woodstock called the Little Casino. He closed this down when he acquired the Stratford Casino. I worked for Gus for many years at the Casino, which was great because I loved dancing. I became his right-hand man. We also had an excellent staff to work with. Jitney dancing was common in the 1930s and '40s. We had several orchestras that played the Stratford Casino—Tony Cryan and his Band, Herbie Fink and his Band, Tibbs and Tim Eaton from London, Benny Palmer and his band from St. Thomas. One of our favourites was Lionel Thornton from London. Mart Kenney and his band was there for special occasions.

"Gus joined forces with Murray Anderson at the Brant Inn in Burlington and the operators of the Port Stanley Pavilion. These three dance halls brought in well-known bands from the U.S.A. They would come across at Fort Erie or Windsor and play three-night stands at Stratford, Burlington and Port Stanley. We had Glen Gray, Russ Columbo, Blue Baron, Little Jack Little. Of course, I can't forget to mention Guy Lombardo.

"We had a good following of people from the surrounding area which helped to make it a popular dance hall for many years. Since that time, it has been taken over by the Stratford Festival and has become a playhouse. Before becoming a dance hall, the Casino was a curling rink. This building had an excellent dance floor. Later, it housed the Badminton Club in the winter. The location of the Casino could

Shortly after this photo was taken outside the Stratford Casino, May 1934, Len Shaw and His Band became Tony Cryan and His Band. Shown here *(left to right):* Len Shaw, Tony Cryan, Eric Illingworth, Murray Corman, Jack Smythe, Edward Eglinton, Alvin Robb, Stephen Hart, Bailey Bird, Gordon Beadle, and George Scott.
Courtesy of Duff Johnston.

not have been better—it was on the River Drive in a parkland setting with lots of parking. By the way, I met my wife at a dance at the Casino. We have enjoyed dancing at all the places I have mentioned."

At the peak of dancing's popularity, there were at least eight hot spots where people could go in Stratford. The Casino, the Winter Garden, Blue Room, Country Club, Canadian National Railway Assembly Hall, Masonic Hall, Queen's Park Pavilion and the Collegiate Auditorium all ran dances.

One of Stratford's most popular hometown orchestras was Tony Cryan and his Band, whose base was the Casino where they would play to a crowd of 1,200 on a Saturday night.

Gordon Beadle was drummer for the band and clearly recalls the memorable times the group had as they travelled around this part of the province playing hundreds of gigs. Gordon joined the Stratford Musicians' Association, Local 418, A. F. of M., in 1922. He became Secretary-Treasurer of the Local for 25 years and writes that he "attended conventions in every state of the Union, making acquaintances with Executive officers of the various Locals. This was a wonderful experience."

53

During the life of the band, 38 members came and went, but the original ten were: John David "Tony" Cryan, Eric "Tim" Illingworth, Murray A.C. "Hap" Corman, Jack Smythe, Edward J. "Ted" Eglinton, Alvin Robb, Stephen Hart, Bailey Bird, George D. Scott and Gordon Beadle.

In a 1992 interview with the *Beacon Herald* newspaper, Gordon said, "Our music was always danceable and we played for profit both for ourselves and the proprietors, who in turn always wanted the band for return engagements. Operators would hand you their date book and ask you to take as many engagements as you had available. We carried door keys for many local halls and always had a rehearsal hall at our disposal, free for the asking."

The group had a running repertoire of over 150 songs, and travelled to their gigs by Cadillac, cabin trailer and a Fargo one-ton panel truck, always polished and painted with the silhouette of a couple dancing and the logo, "Music Styled For You—Tony Cryan and his Band."

St. Thomas: Pinafore Park – West Pavilion

One of the few examples of a grand old wooden dance pavilion still standing and in apparent good shape can be found in Pinafore Park in St. Thomas. The large green painted structure with red trim is labelled the West Pavilion and, although weekly dances are no longer held, music once floated from the second-storey windows across the treed parkland. T. Murray Lynch writes these words about dancing in St. Thomas: "Pinafore Park's dance pavilion was across from the entrance to the ball park. Len Langley and Benny Palmer were two of the local bands I danced to there."

Harry Vandersluys has enjoyed music his whole life in the London area. "I played with the Benny Palmer band back in 1939 until 1942," he writes. "I later played with Lionel Thornton's Casa Royal Band for 17 years. We performed in all the dance halls in and around London, including the Stork Club. There would be 6,000 people there on Sunday nights for concerts, especially with the armed forces from nearby bases. I have a letter sent to me from Satchmo Armstrong in 1941, as we became friends from being the stand-by band for him when he played here at the Stork Club, and the old London Arena." In Louis Armstrong's letter to Harry, he writes:

"You're a fine fellow, and a fine Musician also .... I enjoyed your music very much .... Don't fail to mention this to the rest of the boys in youall's [sic] Orchestra. Also, tell Benny and the boys that Myself as well as my boys were very pleased to have met them ... and do hope that we all meet some day and have one grand and glorious time .... I'll say goodnight my friend and it's really been swell meeting you and the boys .... So 'Take Them Slow' (as we say here in the U.S.A.), which means take good care of your health, etc. Am Musically yours, Louis Armstrong."[1]

Lakeside: Circle K Dance Hall

In 1974, Connie Kittmer and her late husband,

The way to Lakeside Summer Resort and Danceland.

Burns, built the Circle K Dance hall on their farm, northeast of London—the crowds have been dancing there ever since. Connie is now assisted by her son Terry and daughter-in-law Nancy. As the name implies, the music provided is country and are all welcome at Circle K. Along with dances, Connie also stages craft shows and old time fiddling jamborees in the hall.

Lakeside Summer Resort and Danceland

At Lakeside Summer Resort the facade of Danceland is new, but the original hall behind the renovated building still remains; this old pavilion is remembered by many for the dances which can be traced back many years. Daniel Wilson writes about his strong personal ties to Lakeside and the pavilion:

"The Lakeside Pavilion goes back to 1900. The pavilion was known for miles around. My parents met at Lakeside Pavilion and eventually married. Stanley Skipper of St. Marys formed his dance band and played regularly at the hall. My father, Jack Wilson, joined as drummer. The band continued until 1977 and were regulars at the Lakeside Pavilion and surrounding areas of St. Marys, Thedford and region. My father recorded many dances on reel-to-reel tapes. These fond memories bring back pleasant thoughts for me as a little guy around nine or ten, going with my father and watching him set up his drums and rehearse before the evening dances."

Cecil Pearson also remembers Lakeside very well. He writes, "This resort is under new management; the pavilion has been extensively upgraded and has a new dance floor. The beach area has been enlarged and the small lake is still ideal for small boats and swimming. The seasonal camping has also been expanded. I still enjoy attending dances there with friends!"

Over a hundred years after its inception, the park continues to attract summer campers and dancers.

Thamesford: Riverview Pavilion

Located at the intersection of Highways #2 and #19,

just east of London, is the quiet town of Thamesford. The dance pavilion here is chronicled by Ellen Wallace:

"In 1929 the Riverview Pavilion was erected by Bill Holt, on the east river flats near the corner of Dundas Street and the Ingersoll Road. The building was about 60 by 30 feet with a two foot stage on the south side projection for the band or orchestra to play for the dances. The outside was painted a dark green with a sidewalk surrounding three sides. Some of the walls had large openings which could be raised for 'open air' dancing in the summertime. The ticket booth was separate and to the northwest of the main building. Little outdoor 'washrooms' were to the southwest. The driveway

Johnny Downs was not only one of London's most popular band leaders, he also owned a record company and, along with his wife Dorothy, operated a popular restaurant in town, The Latin Quarter.
Courtesy of Johnny and Dorothy Downs.

55

to reach the pavilion came down the road bank from the north, 60 feet east of the bridge, on a steep hill with a 15-foot drop. It is reported Model A cars would spin tires and throw gravel and stones as they tried to climb onto the road. Jim Patience remembers taking tickets at the door which had been purchased at the outer ticket building—he was only about 12 years old at the time. A five-cent ticket was needed for each dance. People often brought a gallon of wine with them. Bootleggers, at that time, were plentiful and one dollar could purchase a gallon of 'pure white' which, it was reported, 'kicked like a mule.' Mac McKinnon, who had the lunch booth across the corner, was always open for Saturday night dances. He had a jukebox and some slot machines, causing much traffic back and forth across the road. Guy Lombardo played in this pavilion with his band and Russ Patton often played as well. The Thamesford Pavilion was torn down in 1935. The hardwood dance floor was used in the new Holt home being built at 153 Allen Street."

An old dance poster advertised the dance floor to be the "finest in the province" and the music as "snappy."

London: Wonderland Gardens

The city of London is synonymous with Big Band music. One of the most successful bandleaders of all time—Guy Lombardo—hailed from this town, and since 1985 London has hosted the annual Royal Canadian Big Band Festival on the July 1st weekend. When your thoughts turn to London, great music and Lombardo, one of the most unique and popular dance pavilions in southwestern Ontario also comes to mind—Wonderland Gardens.

Built in 1935, this historic site is located on

The finished outdoor stage and dance floor at Wonderland. *Courtesy of Chuck Jones.*

The Mickey McDougall Orchestra opened Wonderland on Friday, May 24, 1935. Back row, left to right: Tiny Smith, piano; Billy McLintock, vocals; Harold Corrie, drums; George Upshall, bass. Front row, left to right, Harry Carpenter and Bobby Leitch on trumpet; Cliff Locke on trombone; Mickey McDougall, Jimmy Moore, Bill Kelly & Roy Sommerville all on sax. *Courtesy of Chuck Jones.*

GRAND OPENING

1935

FRIDAY, MAY 24

CANADA'S MOST BEAUTIFUL OPEN AIR

DANCE PAVILION "WONDERLAND

SUMMER GARDENS"

TWO MILES WEST ON SPRINGBANK DRIVE AND TURN TO YOUR RIGHT — ALSO SPRINGBANK CARS AND BUSES TO THE PARK

Free Admission---Free Parking

DANCING 5c

ONE OF CANADA'S FINEST DANCE BANDS DIRECT FROM THE SILVER SLIPPER, TORONTO, and CFRB RADIO ARTISTS FOR LAST SIX MONTHS

MICKEY McDOUGALL

AND HIS 10-PIECE ORCHESTRA

"WE ARE INDEED PROUD TO PRESENT THIS ORCHESTRA."

the banks of the Thames River, nestled in the natural beauty of the trees and gardens that have made this venue so remarkable. Wonderland continues to operate under the careful eye of Chuck Jones, son of the founder of the business. Charles Jones had a deep love for Big Band music and felt that the city would benefit from a well-run dance pavilion providing music throughout the summer. He set his sights on a large parcel of land beside the Thames and obtained a lease on the property from the Public Utilities Commission. Springbank Park, owned by the city as well, was just down the road from the Wonderland site and already had its own pavilion. Since the electrical railroad transportation was set up and running,

57

Charles knew that it could also service Wonderland. The cost of developing Wonderland was $18,000.

From opening night on Friday, May 24, 1935, with the popular Mickey

Alf Tibbs *(left)* was one of London's most respected musicians and bandleaders. *Courtesy of Joan (Tibbs) Tanner.*

The photograph *(below)*, taken in 1925, shows an early Tibbs band at the Masonic Temple on Queen's Avenue in London. Left to right: ___ McDonald, Lock Elliot, Stan Daw, Rus Steeck and Alf Tibbs. *Courtesy of Joan (Tibbs) Tanner.*

McDougall Orchestra on stage, Wonderland was a success, operating six nights a week. Couples loved moving on the 6,000-square-foot outdoor Italian marble floor. A Spanish fountain was installed in the centre of the floor and below the fountain was a gold-fish pond. At either end stood an ornate pedestal urn and a miniature clump of evergreen shrubs. The orchestra performed on a stage set in a Spanish-style bungalow. The site of Wonderland was most conducive to romance. Charles loved nature, designing the pavilion so that most of the trees were left intact and, even today, Wonderland is still dotted with fountains, bird houses and nature paths.

In 1941, after seventeen out of twenty Saturdays had been rained out at Wonderland the previous year, Charles erected a large covered building where bands could play and people could dance. The new facility opened on May 20th with Jimmy

Namaro playing in the open portion and Bubs Jamieson in the closed portion. This same building was completely enclosed and insulated in 1959, which has allowed Wonderland to run events year-round to this day.

Although Charles was the driving force behind Wonderland, many Londoners also remember Charles' brother, Wilf. According to Chuck, "Our Uncle Wilf was the visible partner—an up-front man and a real showman who introduced the entertainers and made regular appearances on stage to speak to the crowd." Wilf was usually attired in a tuxedo, which set the tone for dress at the dance hall—ties and jackets for the men and dresses for the ladies. During the 1940s, most of the well-known Big Bands played at Wonderland—Lombardo, the Dorsey Brothers, Woody Herman and many others. Two of the best known London bands to work Wonderland on a regular basis were Lionel Thornton and Johnny Downs, who played to consistent crowds of 500 to 600.

As his sons Don and Chuck began to grow up, Charles Jones gave them a free hand in running the business. With Don's promotional skills and experience, he was able to give the kids just what they wanted—rock bands like Alice Cooper, Deep Purple and Emmerson, Lake and Palmer. The late Frank Zappa came up to perform at Wonderland and was so enthralled with the location that he insisted a boat be set up so he could water ski.

Wonderland now houses the comfortable and popular Riverside Restaurant—once the original snack bar—with dozens of old Wonderland photographs covering the walls. Wonderland is also an integral player in the annual London Big Band celebration. It seems fitting that the two of the most significant musical and social gathering spots London has given to the public today sit side-by-side: the Guy Lombardo Music Centre and Wonderland Gardens.

Here are a few wonderful Wonderland memories from people:

From Nick Corrie: "My father played drums starting in 1920. I remember as a youngster going with him on band jobs both during and after the War. He was playing with the Mickey McDougall

Ginny Mitchell was the vocalist with Alf Tibb's band.
Courtesy of Joan (Tibbs) Tanner.

Orchestra in May 1935, when they opened Wonderland Gardens";

From Mr. J. Frarey: "I was among those present when Wonderland first opened. It was regarded as a considerable financial gamble as it competed with the popular Springbank Park dance hall, which had additional attractions such as the Ferris wheel and arcade";

From Tom Hammond: "Wonderland was one of the most beautiful indoor and outdoor dance floors in Canada with its gardens and swimming pool";

From Norma Aitkin: "I often went to Wonderland Gardens and would dance 'stag' with a group of girls. There would be lots of tables of single girls and plenty of tables of single young men, usually in one of the services. We would just drink pop and wait for someone to come and ask us to dance. The evening was spent like this and the girls usually went home in a group as we came, but sometimes you would meet someone you hit it off with and

59

might accept his invitation to escort you home";

From Dorothy Ratcliffe: "Wonderland was the place to go—it really was wonderful. I went for the first time about 1938 when they had jitney dancing. Wonderland had a great marble outdoor floor under the stars—it was very romantic. There were lights here and there in the surrounding bush. It was my favourite place to dance."

London: Springbank Park Pavilion

While Wonderland Gardens is warmly associated with nearby Springbank Park, it's interesting to know that the first dance pavilion in this area was built in the park itself. In fact, for a few years after Wonderland opened, both dance pavilions competed for customers, but there was always plenty of business for the two halls.

The best details of Springbank Park and its pavilion are supplied by E. Beatrice Pickles who shares her recollections with us in the following letter:

"The Springbank Dance Pavilion was situated in a small amusement park. The London Street Railway brought picnickers, including school children for some years. In my high school days it was great to come down for an evening's dancing or a picnic. The pavilion was a large two-storey building in Springbank Park with a snack bar downstairs and a ballroom above. My mother and her sisters danced there around the turn of the century. The building was very tall with great supports and a large hardwood floor. It was roofed with shutters that would be opened during dances.

The amusement park had a ferris wheel, a large wooden roller coaster, bumper cars and many game booths such as a fish pond, etc., as well as the large dance hall.

When the Second World War started, I was living about half a mile from the Springbank Dance hall. My husband, a teacher, drove extra buses for Brown's Bus Line, Byron's off-and-on transit system as the need arose. Each night in the summer all Brown's buses loaded up at the Belvedere Hotel at Dundas and Talbot streets in London from 7 to 9 p.m. or so, dropped off the men at the dance hall

stop, and returned later to take them back to London. Gas was rationed so the buses were jammed with passengers.

By 1945 at the end of the War, the dance hall was somewhat the worse for wear. Leonard Smithson purchased the pavilion and late in 1945 and early '46 refurbished the building. The grand opening was early in the summer of 1946, a benefit for the Women's Service League of Victoria Hospital. We had a very active Teen Town in Byron, and they allowed us to hold our end-of-season dance the night before the official grand opening. I recall the kids in their woolly socks sliding up and down the floor, pushing polishers in the afternoon—as usual, preparations were behind schedule. At night, however, young ladies with corsages and gentlemen danced the night away. There was even a floor show with some air force vets who were demobilized and back at university. At the end of summer our Teen Town had another dance, so we both opened and closed the Springbank Dance Hall in 1946.

In late February, 1947, my husband and I were awakened by a fiery glow in the sky. All my husband could think of was the school, but he only had to go as far as the dance hall. The tinder dry building was engulfed in flames, fire balls were shooting up and out across the road. He was the first one there so he alerted the neighbours. The pavilion burned to the ground."

Here are a few more reminiscences about Springbank from other people:

From Elda Barr: "My husband John and I met at the Springbank Park pavilion on June 2, 1945, at a dance. He had come to London from Nova Scotia, just after the War ended. One of the popular bands there was The Melody Makers. Len Masse and Ward Allan were two players I remember";

From Liley Yeates: "When I was 15 to 20 years old my girlfriends and I would get dressed up for our Saturday night ride on the trolley car to Springbank Park at Byron. On the right side there was a beautiful picnic park, and on the other side was the amusement park with the large pavilion where we danced. It was ten cents a dance and we didn't sit many out";

From Dorothy Dobbie: "To quote Charles Dickens, 'It was the best of times, it was the worst of times.' World War II was raging with sadness, even so, the movies and the Big Band Era brought much happiness and made one forget for awhile, the young boys and girls we knew who were fighting and dying to preserve our world. I was 17 when the War started, and London filled with soldiers, airmen and sailors. Many a young heart was broken as the young lovers had to part. Springbank Pavilion was a favourite of many, and my girlfriend and I began going to dances. When I was younger I would practise dancing with a broom and soon became very good";

From Tom Hammond: "One of the pluses of being my age now is that I was a young man and part of this dance era. Because of finances many people went stag, and the joy of asking a good-looking girl for the next dance is a fond memory. But some girls knew the best dancers and waited only for them to ask. I met my wife at Springbank Park."

Other London Venues

The 401 Plaza was built in 1955 by musician Bruce Cowin and his family. Norma Aitkin, who often danced at The 401, noted in a letter, "In more recent years we danced many a Saturday evening all year round at The 401. A large orchestra always played there, called the Modernaires, featuring the Glenn Miller sound, led by Ron Shadbolt." This 16-piece outfit led by Ron, brought back the sophistication and style of the Big Band Era, dressed in their blue tuxedos as they played the music of Benny Goodman, Tommy Dorsey, Harry James and Artie Shaw. The late Dr. Morris P. Wearing wrote to me about The 401. "Shortly after The 401 opened, Ron Shadbolt bought London bandleader Johnny Brenan's book and formed the Modernaires. They remained the house band at The 401 for over 20 years."[2]

The old London Arena, built in 1923 at the southeast corner of Bathurst and Ridout streets, was one of this city's classic dance and concert sites. Dr. Wearing wrote about this event: "Glenn Miller

played the Arena on January 24, 1942, before a sold-out audience of 6,000. Scalpers were selling $1.50 tickets for $5.00. On the afternoon of the 24th, Miller did his weekly radio broadcast—Sunset Serenade—to the Armed Forces. Members of the RCAF Station London were guests of honour at the broadcast which was carried over both the CBC and the Mutual Radio Network, with Elwood Glover as the announcer." As the Big Band era passed, the music turned to country and western and rock. By 1976 the Arena was declared unsafe by the Department of Labour and was torn down.

Delaware: Town Hall

In a 1955 *London Free Press* newspaper article, Gertrude Johnstone wrote about this little hall in tiny Delaware, west of London.

"During World War I we were teenagers and members of the Youth and Beauty Club, still attending school and looking forward to the Friday night dances in the town hall. It had been built in 1842 in the centre of the village. Meanwhile in London, Papa Lombardo was training his children's band thoroughly. The Lombardo boys rehearsed hour after hour in their father's tailor shop. The time came to try their wings and in the summer of 1917 Guy Lombardo's first band was formed, with Guy, barely 16, on violin; Carmen, two years younger was on flute; Leber, quite a small boy played the drums and Fred Kreitzer played piano.

Courtesy of Brass Factory Bulletin.

61

The Bob Jacks Orchestra in Wallaceburg, 1945. The leader, Bob Jacks, is at the piano. Standing, left to right: Doug Wickens, bass; Gord Welch, Alf Crist and Jack Stacey, trumpet; Fergus Ewing, trombone; Peter Mitchell, drums; Tom Platt *(front)*, sax; Bill Christian, trombone; Dave Forsyth, Don Boyce and John Dugit, sax. *Courtesy of Alan Mann.*

We were looking for an inexpensive orchestra. Papa Lombardo was looking for a clientele for his boys. So the Lombardos played for $10 for an evening, including transportation. Guy Lombardo and his newly formed band gave us their best. In spite of their amateurishness, their music was sweet and rhythmic, although sometimes too loud, and they played with enthusiasm and showmanship. Carmen sang, and sometimes their sister Elaine sang. Papa Lombardo was very stern. He watched the boys, critical and unsmiling and permitted no sloppy playing or mannerisms. Sometimes Guy joined us for a dance or two. Sometimes tired little Leber almost fell asleep at his drums, but his father was always sitting near to give him a poke. We little realized the bright future that lay ahead for this group. After standing for 107 years, the Delaware town hall was torn down brick by brick in 1949."

Wallaceburg: Primrose Gardens

When you think about dancing in Wallaceburg, two memories invariably come to mind: Primrose Gardens and the Bob Jacks Orchestra. In October 1995, the Brass Factory Big Band paid a special tribute in Wallaceburg to the Bob Jacks Orchestra during a weekend that saw many surviving members of this local group reunite for one gig. Instrumental in arranging the reunion was Wallaceburg historian Alan Mann. Excerpts from Alan's weekly column for the *Wallaceburg News* give us a look at Primrose Gardens (published in 1985):

"The mid-1980s have brought about a multitude of changes to the face of Wallaceburg. Amid the reports concerning the core area alterations, indications point to the possible razing of one of the town's "all-time" favourite locations, Primrose Gardens. Located in the Quality Point on the busy Water and Margaret corner, this building is, perhaps a bit tired having enjoyed its heyday, but has served the local populace well. It has been host to a multitude of activities since its construction in 1918 and can be considered as one of Wallaceburg's most versatile sites.

"Henry Joiner of Tupperville moved to town and decided to erect yet another entertainment auditorium. It was built as a dance hall when it opened just after the Great War. However, due to circumstances, the hall took on a role far divorced from its original purpose. In 1921 and 1922 the site became a temporary school. In 1928, James Cooper, founder of Cooper Leaf and Tobacco Company, leased Primrose Gardens for the processing of tobacco products, mainly cigars.

"When the Cooper interests vacated the building, Ivan Wickens, well-known Wallaceburg sportsman and businessman, began a long and pleasant association with Primrose. One of his first moves after leasing the site was to open Primrose as a roller skating arena. Doug Wickens recalls that in 1936, his father Ivan began the popular weekly dances. The Tom and Isan Campbell group became popular and played for 52 straight weekend engagements. From 1939 until 1941, well-known Sarnia bandleader, Jack Kennedy and his orchestra, started a tradition of Big Band music that proved extremely popular for Wallaceburg over the next few decades.

"The famed Bob Jacks Orchestra began in 1941 what can be termed the 'golden era' of Primrose Gardens. Three times a week, Wednesday, Friday and Saturday, Primrose was the place to go as a large segment of Wallaceburg dancers and music listeners flocked to the site. What a treat it was to hear the band playing 'Sentimental Journey' or 'String of Pearls!' Doug Wickens, who spent a good portion of his life at Primrose, recalled recently that one New Year's Eve saw a record 936 paid admissions to a Bob Jacks dance.

"By the 1950s Big Band music was on a downturn and the days of the Bob Jacks Orchestra were numbered, drawing to a close in 1952. That same year a new approach was employed by Primrose—a record hop. The 'Primrose Hop' was a first in Kent County as other centres soon joined the trend. Teen Town became a popular term as youngsters still shook the old Primrose floor, but this time to recorded music. From 1955 until 1971, under the

ownership of Doug Wickens, Primrose became a banquet centre, meeting hall and a site for a multitude of uses.

"In 1972, Gord Childs purchased Primrose Gardens, gave it new life and turned it into a banquet and bingo centre. Now into its near 70th year, time has taken its toll. Its sister Primrose II perpetuates the name far from the familiar Gardens. If and when the famed corner takes on a new role, it will be difficult to think of a name other than Primrose Gardens, a site that definitely belongs in the Historical Hall of Fame." [3]

Primrose Gardens and the Bob Jacks Orchestra were recalled by many people in *The Brass Factory Bulletin*, leading up to the 1995 band reunion:

"Margaret (Lashmore) Johns from Earlysville, Virginia has two 78 rpm records with Bob backing singing groups on the piano. The recordings were made January 10, 1948, at Primrose by Fleming Studios of Chatham. Jack Stacey remembers the virtually full houses on Wednesday, Friday and Saturday nights during the War years, along with the migration to Felger's (Fiesta) Grill and later to Lloyd's for cokes and hamburgers after the dance. Bob Lawson who was at Primrose from the very beginning, fondly recalls, 'When four or five of us got together we were all in High School and just wanted to have some fun. Bob and I became good friends. He was one of the best musicians I ever heard.' Gord Welch wrote: "Bob Jacks was to me a very special person who gave me a chance, as he did with so many young people, to play in his band. He was a musical institution as a bandleader and a fine musician." [4]

Chatham: The Pyranon Ballroom and Rondeau Pavilion

At the Colborne Street building supply store in Chatham, customers might be surprised if they knew that not too many years ago this same structure housed the city's premier dance hall—The Pyranon Ballroom.

Maurice Smyth is the person most synonymous with the dance business in Chatham, having

The second Rondeau Park Pavilion, located inside the park, ran dances from 1939 until the late 1960s. The building burned in 1973. *Courtesy of Johnny and Dorothy Downs.*

constructed two of the best known pavilions in this area of southwestern Ontario, The Pyranon in Chatham and the third pavilion at nearby Rondeau Park on Lake Erie. "On opening night in October 1945, the plumbers were running out the back door as the crowds were coming in the front," Maurice recalled. Al Edwards and his band from Windsor opened the Pyranon. Maurice operated the business for many years in Chatham, overlapping with his other dance hall near Rondeau Provincial Park, appropriately called the Rondeau Pavilion, which opened in 1952.

The Pyranon was not only a dance hall, but also provided a venue for wrestling, banquets, proms, fashion shows, political gatherings, bingos and all kinds of community group activities. When record hops were tops, as many as 1,600 young people would turn out on a Friday night to dance to Elvis Presley and Pat Boone records. Both of Maurice's halls drew huge crowds: "People came from all over—Detroit, Ohio, Sarnia—many of the kids came in groups by bus." He booked in all the Big Bands at

the Pyranon, such as Sammy Kaye, Victor Lombardo, Vaughn Monroe, Cab Calloway, Duke Ellington, The Glen Miller Orchestra, Les Brown and Gene Krupa.

The interior of the hall was based on the Latin Quarter in New York City, with a very large stage. "It was very classy in style with three levels and large boxes forming a 3-D effect, drapes that could be pulled up, and a grand piano covered in mauve. The metal lighting was indirect, giving a very professional look to the entertainers on stage." CFCO, the local radio station, did live remote broadcasts for an hour every Saturday night, beaming their signal up as far north as the Bruce Peninsula, and down into the United States. Maurice's philosophy for a successful dance at both of his places throughout the years was simply this: "We put on a party, made sure it ended well and tried to ensure that everyone got home safely." It's a philosophy that lots of people from Chatham and beyond still remember.

One of the local orchestras to perform at the Pyranon regularly was the Wilf Lancaster Orchestra. Cheryl Sanregret is the daughter of the late bandleader, and shares some background on the musical contribution this popular musician made in the Chatham area:

"Dad began playing the drums in bands in and around Chatham about the mid to late '30s. He played at Erie Beach, and in Chatham the band played at a couple of outdoor dance pavilions during the summer and at the Pyranon Ballroom as well. In 1966, Dad began putting his dream of a band reunion together with several of the old members. The First Annual Reunion of the Big Band Sound of

An old postcard circa 1913 depicting the Bob-Lo Pavilion on Bois Blanc Island, set in the Detroit River near Amhertsburg. If not the largest dance hall, Bob-Lo must rank in the top three or four. The impressive building resembles a place of worship, or the Great Hall of a major university more than it does a dance hall.

Wilf Lancaster was held in October, 1966. The curtain rose to the playing of 'With A Song In My Heart' (his theme song chosen in 1938). The hall was absolutely packed. I was indeed privileged to be a part of that night, as my dad had included a part for organ in the arrangements. Due to poor health, he was forced to give up playing. On Friday, October 13, 1970, the curtain came down on the band. As we were playing the theme song for the very last time, I looked over at my dad and saw one big tear trickling down each cheek. It was all I could do to keep playing. On that night the baton was handed over to Fred Foster and Bill Pritchard. Dad passed away in June 1973, but I know he would be so very happy to know that his band continues to play to this day under the name of The Lancaster Band."

In 1952, Maurice Smyth built his own pavilion just outside the Rondeau Provincial Park's gates, the third and last dance hall at Rondeau. "On some dance nights there would be over 1,700 people lined up at the Rondeau Pavilion .... We had bands like Bob Seeger, The American Breed and Alice Cooper all play at Rondeau." Maurice decorated the walls in his hall with palm trees, lit up by coloured fluorescent lighting. The timing was perfect for those early rock 'n' roll years. Many of the new groups who would later become very famous played his hall. Pat Bélanger remembers in a letter that "Seeger was a relative unknown at that time, and would sit between sets with the patrons." Maurice added more activities over the years as dancing declined, such as movies, roller skating and bingos. He also tried other forms of

65

Interior of Bob-Lo Dance Pavilion, 1914. *Courtesy of PA 30076.3.*

dance music including country and western.

Maurice picks up the sad ending of his hall after he had sold it: "After a Halloween dance on October 31, 1980, a fire started in a garbage can, likely due to a cigarette." With the demise of this pavilion, dancing at Rondeau Park was finished. Throughout eight decades of music at Rondeau's three pavilions, music was an essential part of life as people waltzed to orchestras, swayed to the Big Bands and then danced to rock. The romantic walks along the beach with the strains of music floating through the summer night are now just pleasant thoughts for the lucky people who remember dancing at Rondeau Park.

Amherstburg: Bob-Lo Island

An old postcard depicting the pavilion on Bob-Lo Island describes it as "Canada's Largest Dance Hall."

The 50,000-square-foot structure with its towering glassed entrance was designed and built by architect Albert Kahn, who was commissioned by Henry Ford to erect the hall on the former Bois Blanc Island.

Burns Bedard gives us a few more details. He writes, "It was a very popular dance pavilion in Bob-Lo Island Amusement Park, which was located across the water from Amherstburg, Ontario, at the mouth of the Detroit River, entering into Lake Erie. My wife and I both worked on the Island during our summer vacations. Matti Holli and his orchestra from Windsor provided the music, and any evening we had some free time from our work we would rush over to the hall to dance. People would journey down the river on the Bob-Lo Island boats from Detroit to enjoy summer activities on the Island—swimming, dining and dancing." The huge cement edifice is still magnificent today and has been eyed by a developer as an ideal location for a casino.

Chapter Five

PAVILIONS ON BEACHES FROM OWEN SOUND
TO THE SHORES OF LAKE HURON

Built on the site of the King's Royal Hotel torn down in 1916, the Balmy Beach Pavilion was erected in the mid-1930s and was one of the largest dance halls of its kind with a floor area close to 15,000 square feet. Lumber from the dismantled dance hall (1962) was sold at general auction. *Courtesy of Gayle McLauchlan.*

Owen Sound: Balmy Beach Dance Pavilion

Set in the beautiful surroundings of McLauchlan Park for more than 30 years, the Balmy Beach Pavilion was the centre of social activity for people in the Owen Sound district. Ken Bowes writes: "I played trumpet with the Lloyd Kibbler Band during the 1950s. During the summers we played at Balmy Beach, Sauble Beach Pavilion and the Port Elgin Casino on Lake Huron. The Balmy Beach Dance Pavilion had the recognition of the best dance floor in Ontario during the late 1940s and '50s." Vicki Storm grew up in Owen Sound. "I have wonderful memories of the dance pavilions and Big Bands around Owen Sound," she writes. "The greatest dance pavilion of all time was Balmy Beach Pavilion where Lloyd Kibbler's orchestra played. What wonderful times!" The building was

demolished in June 1962 and the land subdivided for home building lots.

Oliphant: McKenzie's Pavilion

William "Mac" McKenzie gives us some details about his family's pavilion built in 1921: "When my father William came back home from the First War, he suggested to Grandfather Murdock and his brother Tom that a dance operation might be a good idea." During the '30s and '40s McKenzie's Pavilion attracted dancers from up and down the Lake Huron and Georgian Bay shores of the Bruce and from the city of Owen Sound. Mac remembers working in the dance hall. "Our job—brother Don and myself, dressed in white short pants and blue blazers made by my mother—was to take the tickets as couples entered the floor and to make certain that all left after the second dance." Mac notes that eventually the pavilion was used only for the annual Civic Holiday Regatta dance. Upstairs you can still see the original

The old upright piano stills sits on the stage in the Oliphant pavilion's second floor. It, however, poses a major challenge for the piano tuner.

stage, with a small railing in front of it. Mac remembers the piano which maintains a lonely vigil here: "It belonged to the pavilion where it spent the frigid winters in solitary splendour on the bandstand. In late June the piano tuner would arrive—the first sign that the season began again. Often when I drift off to sleep on a warm summer night in Oliphant, I can still hear the strains of 'Amapola,' 'Yours,' 'The White Cliffs of Dover,' 'Begin the Beguine' and 'Stardust.'"

Sauble Beach: Danceiro

Stewart Wilson operated Danceiro between 1967 and ran it until 1972. Many name rock bands often played here, including the

Stampeders who had a number of hit songs. Stewart then decided to hire local bands which played a more versatile style of music. Stewart's son Steve later took over the building and operated it as an auto body shop. Today Woody's Flea Market opens on the site during the summer months.

Sauble Beach Pavilion

Sauble Beach boasts one of the cleanest, purest sandy beaches this side of Florida. The original pavilion here, built in 1933, was called the Octagon after its unique shape. In 1945, two couples visited the beach and a chance meeting with the owner would forever change their lives. Wally Scott and his wife, Esther, along with Esther's brother, Jack Robertson, and his wife, Marg, met Bob Walker who asked them if they would be interested in purchasing his pavilion. Esther remembers, "Wally and Jack thought about it and a price was later agreed upon for the business."

Wally also led his own band, and it was this orchestra that opened the hall July 1, 1946, under its new name: Sauble Beach Pavilion. Later they added a

Wally Scott and his orchestra, in 1946, in front of the Sauble Beach Pavilion owned jointly by himself and partner Jack Robertson. Wally would sometimes promote his Sauble venue when his band performed down the road at Port Elgin's Cedar Crescent Casino, but it was all in good fun. *Courtesy of Esther Scott*

68

terrazzo floor to the east so couples could dance under the bright stars on warm summer evenings. According to Esther, "The [old] Octagon was rather primitive inside," so Wally and Jack decided in 1950 to flatten the now rather old structure and build their new pavilion on the same site, leaving the open-air portion as it was.

The owners were never ones to stand still and, as the beach grew in popularity, the men opened up the Sauble Gift and Bowl, the Driftwood restaurant, Starlight Roller Rink and the Dahmer Lumber company. But even as their beach empire expanded, the heart and soul of Sauble was the Pavilion. Esther recalls, "We always received good crowds." The new building with its enlarged interior and outdoor floor could hold up to 2,500 dancers. Being located on the beach beside the lake gave the pavilion a very romantic atmosphere for those summer evening strolls. Along with regular dances, beach people came to the Pavilion for weekly bingos, family movies and

Wednesday night country dances with Don Robertson's Ranch Boys. During the Big Band era, one of the popular orchestras to play the pavilion on a regular basis was led by Warren Ovens from Kitchener.

Both Wally and Jack were very aware of the changing music tastes of their customers. Esther remembers that after they heard the The Beatles' music in the early '60s, the men said, "Let's start booking rock!" By the later 1960s, rock dances were held three nights per week, as well as on Sunday midnights during the long weekends. As the price of bands rose, and the drinking age was lowered, Jack and Wally decided it was time to think about getting out of the pavilion business. Crowds fell off and the pavilion could not survive on bingo and movies. Given the economic reality, as Esther notes, "The decision to tear the place down was made in the fall of 1978 and that was that!"

Geri Kirkpatrick of Owen Sound has some

Warren Ovens (standing) on trumpet and his orchestra on stage at the Sauble Beach Pavilion in the mid-1950s.
Courtesy of Warren Ovens.

Aerial postcard shot of the Sauble Beach Pavilion, circa early 1960s.

69

great memories of the Sauble Beach Pavilion, and writes: "We usually spent most of the summer at the family cottage at Sauble in the still-innocent 1950s. There was a group of about eight of us doing things together. Imagine our reaction when we heard that a Canadian Navy ship and an American destroyer had both made port in Owen Sound. One of the sailors, Jerry, had been an Arthur Murray instructor in Chicago. We ended up doing almost every dance together. Sometimes, we were the only couple on the floor, being cheered for our 'expertise.' During intermission, we had to go out to the edge of the water, so that I could soothe my feet from so much dancing. I will never forget that wonderful, perfect evening at the Sauble Beach Pavilion. Sometimes when I hear the song 'Come Dancing,' I feel a little sad that the Sauble Beach Pavilion is no longer there, and I relive that great memory of it. It still warms my heart."

The local history book, *Green Meadows and Golden Sands: A History of Amabel Township*, states, "The Pavilion was the focal point of the activities at the Beach for many years, and we doubt if Sauble Beach will ever be the same again as it was when everyone got together and had a whale of a time."[1]

Southampton: The Breakers Lodge

The Annex at Southampton's Breakers Lodge was once a popular dance pavilion before it was converted into guest rooms. Russell Knowles built the dance pavilion during the 1920s, bringing in well-known orchestras such as Guy Lombardo and His Royal Canadians, Ferde Mowry's group and many others. After 103 years in business, the owners, in 1991, decided to tear down the town's historic hotel. The cost of bringing the building up to current safety standards was far too large a sum for a business operating three months of the year.

Port Elgin: Cedar Crescent Casino

Port Elgin's Cedar Crescent Casino was one of the crown jewels along the extensive Lake Huron coastline. Owners Emmett and Pat McGrath considered

the greatest honour bestowed upon them was the recognition by the Stratford Musicians' Union for operating a first-class dance hall.

Emmett played sax for years with the famed Ferde Mowry orchestra, the house band at Toronto's Embassy Club. In fact, it was the Embassy's owner who encouraged the McGraths to make the move into the entertainment business and in 1944 the couple purchased the Casino. The long (24 years) warm relationship the McGraths had with the people of Port Elgin, the tourists and the bands made Cedar Crescent Casino a place regarded with great affection by everybody connected with the hall. The Port Elgin couple developed the Casino into a paradise of wholesome and enjoyable entertainment for all ages. Emmett and Pat were devoted to the pavilion and pampered it throughout the years, realizing that it was also one of the town's major attractions on the sandy beach.

Built in 1924 by William Brigden and O.E. Boehmer, Cedar Crescent Casino officially opened on June 28th of that year. Dances ran six nights per week, attracting hundreds of eager residents and summer vacationers. From 1950 to 1964 Lloyd Kibbler's Big Band from Owen Sound was the Casino's house band. As music and dance styles changed, so did the McGrath's music policy: "We had to move with the times," Pat told me. When the Twist became an international craze, Emmett and Pat staged Twist Contests. As the era of rock entered, bands led by David Clayton Thomas, Ronnie Hawkins, Robbie Lane and many others took over the stage. "Go-Go" Night was launched by The Paupers in 1965. A regular on Thursday night in the later 1960s was the popular Major Hoople's Boarding House. For nine summers the Casino rocked to the local sounds of Gordon Rhodes and the Swingin' Comets, featuring the McGrath's sons, Paul and Wayne.

Anne Ellis writes with her thoughts: "One of my fondest memories during the War years was the sounds of music wafting over the beach on Saturday nights from the Cedar Crescent Casino. I was too young to attend the dance, but the sight of the coloured lights and the music from the band were absolute magic to us kids."[1]

In 1968, Emmett and Pat decided to retire from the business and sold the pavilion. Two years later the pavilion burned to the ground. One week after the fire, Mrs. Helen Hammond composed a tribute to this pavilion. Here are excerpts from it:

To A Dance Hall

"Poor old Casino!"
"Dear old Friend!"
Numbly we watch, with unbelieving eyes—
The fierce, hot flame, so swift, so cruel—

Dumbly we watch, but through our sadness
Memories and the sound of music come
Crowding and dancing on the summer air.
Jazz music from the Twenties,
When you were young and gay—
Embassy's Ferde Mowry with the big band sound—
City glamour for a lakeside town—...
We voice a hope, a plea, to those
Who hold the doubtful future in their hands
That on you cold, dead ashes may soon rise
A new Casino, named the same.
To meet, to dance, to play—perchance, to dream.[2]

Top: Port Elgin's Cedar Crescent Casino, 1932. Cody and His Violin was one of the early entertainers, followed by the Wright Brothers. Emmett McGrath even played here for the summers of 1932-1934 with Ferde Mowry's band, fell in love with the town and the hall and later purchased the pavilion.

Bert Worth (*lower left*) and the orchestra at Port Elgin in 1945.

Dress styles varied from shirt and tie to casual wear for dancers in the 1940s at Port Elgin.

All photographs courtesy of Pat McGrath.

71

Helen's dreams were realized soon after the Casino burned. A new pavilion was constructed where dances and many other community events were run for about ten years. Unfortunately, this new hall was very soon condemned as being structurally unsafe on the sandy beach and was demolished. The site where both pavilions once sat is now a vast beach. On the bright side, Big Band music continues to draw music lovers every September to Port Elgin for the popular annual Big Band Celebration.

Inverhuron Pavilion

Long before the Bruce Nuclear Generating Station was even a glow in Ontario Hydro's eyes, the small community of Inverhuron had its own power plant in full operation as dancers created their own unique energy at the Inverhuron Dance Pavilion. The last dance was held here over 30 years ago, but the building—built in 1930—is a reminder of the exciting times that took place underneath the metal roof. George Scott, a musician himself, ran dances at the pavilion and still owns the building today. As he says, "I always liked playing dance halls. When I saw the ad for this hall in a London newspaper I took the plunge. As the crowds began to dwindle I closed the hall in 1964, renovated it and built apartments." The

only music you'll hear today in Inverhuron is the humming of electricity surging through the electrical transformers.

Kincardine Pavilion

For 80 years the Kincardine Pavilion has sat on the town's beach, surviving July's blistering heat and January's northwest gales. The Kincardine Pavilion is the only hall of its kind still operating along this stretch of Lake Huron. It has been partially renovated in recent years and hosts occasional functions, but requires further attention if it is to survive.

Resident George Conley designed and helped fund the new pavilion; in 1923 it was officially opened during the Old Boys and Girls Reunion. Pavilion owners have all leased this land from the town. As with all of the beach pavilions, couples would saunter along the beach during the evening, while others just sat and enjoyed the music floating through the open shutters and into the evening air. Inside the hall was a large circular light that looked like a moon when it was illuminated during a song with the word "moon" in the title, and also for the last dance of the night.

Music of every type from Big Band, to country, style to rock 'n' roll has been performed at the Kincardine Pavilion. One of the early local bands to play was Giles Merrymakers. Other orchestras who travelled to this resort community included Don Messer, Lionel Thornton, Mart Kenney and the John Brenan band. Jim Steele played sax with the Brenan band many years ago and remembers the Kincardine Pavilion with great affection. He says, "Our group was so well-known that

Ferde Mowry, seated in front centre, with members of his orchestra in the 1930s.
Courtesy of Pat McGrath.

The future of Lake Huron's only operating pavilion, located in Kincardine, is in doubt as politicians debate its future. The pavilion has been sitting on the shores of this Great Lake since 1923. This photo was taken in 1998.

Pavilion Dance News whetted dance fans' appetites for the upcoming season. "The Pav" was ready to open its doors! The lead article reads: "Overlooking the blue water of Lake Huron at Goderich, The Goderich Pavilion has long been the favourite dance spot with residents and visitors to 'The Prettiest Town in Canada.' " When you told somebody "See you at The Pav," they knew where you would be.

we developed quite a following of regular fans who would show up each week. Some of them were from London and owned cottages in the area. They all had their regular tables in the hall and responded enthusiastically, giving the band great support."

Another popular London band to perform at Kincardine was Johnny Downs and His Orchestra. In the summer of 1939 they persuaded owner Tony Campbell to book their newly formed band. Johnny remembers Tony as "a likeable old fellow with his trademark cigar stub in his mouth—and he made us work! We had to sign a contract that bound the band to rehearse every morning at ten a.m., start playing every night at nine and continue playing until Tony said the dance was finished."

In 2001, the town assumed ownership of the pavilion and changed the locks. At this point the future of Lake Huron's last operating pavilion is uncertain.

Even when owners Leah and Roy Breckenridge changed the name of the hall, which had been part of Goderich since 1920, to the Harbourlite Inn, people persisted in referring to it as The Pav.

Born in Goderich, Roy began managing the dance pavilion in 1940 and purchased it in 1947. "Everyone went to The Pav," Leah told me. It was the place to meet your friends and have a great time. And best of all, soon after Roy and Leah took over they winterized the pavilion so it could operate year-round. Many Goderich residents can still recall working part-time at The Pav for various functions. Leah recalls, "We hired a lot of young people when we catered various events over the years." One of those

The Pav by Mike Scott, sketched for Leah Breckenridge in 1980. *Courtesy of Leah Breckenridge.*

Goderich Pavilion/Harbourlite Inn

"Top Flight Bands Coming"

The headlines in the first 1947 issue of the *Goderich*

73

The first dance platform at Grand Bend, built in 1917, was converted into a picnic shelter after Lakeview Casino was built two years later. *Courtesy of Lambton Heritage Museum.*

people was Robert McKee, who writes, "For several years I worked part-time at the Harbourlite Inn, starting out in the coat-check room, sweeping floors, taking tickets, painting, cutting grass, etc. It was a fine old wooden building with a hardwood floor. A large curved bar was off to one side in a wing off the dance floor, and there were full kitchen facilities behind the bar."

Both Roy and Leah formed long-term friendships with many of the entertainers who played at the Harbourlite Inn such as Johnny and Dorothy Downs from London and Paul Cross from Stratford. London-area bands were extremely popular at The Pav, and included ones such as Lionel Thornton and the Casa Royal Orchestra, Neil McKay and his orchestra, Scott McLachlan, Ted Pudney and bands led by Johnny and Bobby Downs. Often a band

would be booked for the season such as Neil McKay's group. "They were just young fellows at the time," remembers Leah.

As time moved along, Wednesday night at The Pav was devoted to country and western music and drew some of the best crowds. Teen dances were big as well, with recorded music provided by a disc jockey from CKNX, the Wingham radio station. Roy kept the hall as busy as possible, with dances, bingos, service club dinners and other private receptions. The couple finally decided that it was time to retire from the business they had operated for 30 years.

New Year's Eve, 1972, was an emotional time for the 500-plus who turned out to say goodbye to The Pav—the Goderich dance pavilion which had been so much a part of their lives. In 1973, the land was sold and the contents of the hall were auctioned, including the dance floor. The building was then demolished.

74

Fred Elliott and his Orchestra *(far left).* **Taken at Grand Bend, circa 1932-33. Fred is standing by the pillar. Art Duncan and George Cairns were both members of the band.** *Courtesy of Art Duncan*

Emerson Gill poster courtesy of Lambton Heritage Museum.

This December 1972 charcoal sketch by Marlatt of the dance pavilion at Jowett's Grove is the only visual reminder that Margaret Garon has of the days when she and her husband, Red, ran the park and the hall. *Courtesy of Margaret Garon.*

Bayfield Pavilion: Jowett's Grove

Dances at Bayfield were well attended from the day the first round-shaped dance pavilion was opened at the turn of the century on the Bayfield River. Ethel (Jowett) Poth writes: "William Jowett operated Jowett's Grove at The Point on the north side of the river. The first dance pavilion here was a frame building with coal oil lamps along the sides and a raised platform for the musicians at one end. In 1920, William built a larger pavilion with a wide screened-in verandah where people could view the lake. Inside, a balcony allowed the spectators the pleasure of looking down at the dancers while listening to the music. At one time there was jitney dancing, and people could roam the beach or sit out in the picnic grounds between dances." One of the popular bands Ethel remembers performing at the pavilion was led by Harold Skinner.

In 1960, Clinton businessman Red Garon purchased the park from Lillian Jowett. Red's widow, Margaret says, "After we married in 1964, Red and I took over full management of the park and pavilion, and moved into the grounds for the summer months. We upgraded the park and it became a very popular tent and trailer camp. Red and I converted the large red barn into our living quarters upstairs, with a laundromat on the main level. The card nights became so popular that they were eventually moved to the dance hall. Of course the pavilion was the

main attraction for both campers and the general public who came from miles around to dance." A stairway with about 100 steps led down from the pavilion in Jowett's Grove to the beach, creating a very romantic setting for couples out on a moonlight stroll.

During the years previous to the Garon's ownership, Jowett's Grove had attracted primarily local orchestras. The couple changed the pavilion's music policy to reflect the tastes of the kids and rock bands brought in some of the largest crowds ever to the Bayfield Pavilion. Margaret observes, "We were saddened when the park was closed down for a housing development a few years after we sold it." There is still a Jowett's Grove cottage rental business at Bayfield, a reminder in name only of the summer dances that used to take place at the Bayfield Pavilion.

Grand Bend: Lakeview Casino

Saturday, June 6, 1981, was a memorable occasion in the community of Grand Bend. It was billed as "Eric McIlroy Day" in honour of the late businessman who owned and operated Lakeview Casino for 30 years. He was a driving force behind the growth of Grand Bend, nurturing it from a small holiday destination to a major summer resort with a large year-round

Jimmy Namaro, pictured here on the beach at Grand Bend, was a multi-instrumentalist, best known for his work as vibraphonist. He worked on CBC's The Happy Gang from 1943 to 1959 and wrote dozens of jingles and scores for TV shows before moving to the United States in the 1960s. *Courtesy of Lambton Heritage Museum.*

Art Hallman *(above)* was with Mart Kenney in the original Western Gentlemen. He then struck out on his own, forming one of the busiest bands in the province. For many years Art's band was a mainstay at Oshawa's Jubilee Pavilion. *Courtesy of Leah Breckenridge.*

Along with his work at the Palais Royale, Bert Niosi *(above right)* also performed throughout Ontario, including stints at Crystal Beach. This talented musician was asked several times to join Duke Ellington, and was friends with many of the other greats such as Tommy and Jimmy Dorsey, according to his daughter, Roberta Baldwin of Mississauga, in a letter to the author. However, Bert always wanted to stay in Canada. *Courtesy of Leah Breckenridge*

population. One significant reminder of that outstanding day rests at the southeast corner of Highways 81 and 21—a lovingly crafted fieldstone cairn with a bronze plaque featuring a carved likeness of Eric McIlroy, surrounded by the logos of the organizations he formed, led and/or belonged to. The engraved message is simple, but sums up the contribution he made to Grand Bend: "In Tribute to W. Eric McIlroy whose Lakeview Casino brought joy and music to thousands. Grand Bend remembers!"

Lakeview Casino was the major focal point of Grand Bend, being situated on the beach at the very end of the town's main street. From opening night with the then-unknown Lombardo brothers, to Rudy Vallee, to the Big Bands of the 1930s and '40s, right up to rock acts of the 1970s, Lakeview Casino booked in the biggest names in the business for special one-night engagements. But local bands from Ontario were also the ones who provided the steady danceable music that made the warm summer nights so enchanting for dancers.

Building a dance pavilion at Grand Bend was the brainchild of George and Ida Eccleston back in 1916 when they set up a temporary dance platform protected by canvas—really a dancing tent. Opening night was July 1, 1917, with the "London Italian Orchestra" (the Lombardos) performing at the official opening ceremony later that month. Some say that this was the Lombardos' first paid job. George and Ida then built a larger and more solid dance pavilion in 1919, constructed with wood and concrete that George poured himself. Some of the early bands to play the hall were McKinney's Cotton Pickers and McKinney's Chocolate Dandies—two Black bands from Detroit who were immensely popular wherever they played. Emerson Gill, Ted Burt's Nine Royal Collegians, Brian Farnan and His Boys, Gene Fritzley and the Fred Elliott Orchestra also played during the 1920s and '30s. Two surviving members of Fred's band shared their recollections of the Casino in letters to me.

George Cairns writes: "I well remember the dance pavilions. In fact, I played in some of them during the period 1931-1935, as a member of the

Fred Elliott Orchestra. This group was based in Hamilton, mostly from McMaster University. We played in 1933 in an extremely large pavilion at Grand Bend, where we followed by about five years a band from London, Ontario—Guy Lombardo!" Art Duncan of the Fred Elliott Orchestra echoed similar words to George.

When George Eccleston suddenly passed away in 1931, Ida chose to keep Lakeview Casino in her hands, which was fortuitous decision. George and Ida's daughter Ella, had married Eric McIlroy and, by 1937, the couple had purchased the hall from Ida. This turning point in the history of the hall would eventually lead to Ella and Eric McIlroy being called "Grand Bend's Mr. and Mrs. Music." From 1937 until they sold Lakeview in 1966, the couple worked long days every summer, operating a number of businesses underneath the hall during the day, and running the dances at night.

The Big Band era was in full swing when Eric came on board, and with his people skills, combined with the enjoyment of being an impresario, he brought people the best entertainment of the period in a relaxed holiday setting on one of Ontario's prime beach resorts. Along with stars like Tommy Dorsey and Louis Armstrong, Canadian music greats were featured every summer. Jimmy Namaro on his famous xylophone was a favourite, as were Juliette, Ellis McLintock, the Modernaires, Stan Patton, Bert Niosi, Len Hopkins, Joan Fairfax ... the list is long. With London being so close to Grand Bend, many of this city's best orchestras appeared at Lakeview. Eric's generosity and community spirit quickly became obvious to the area through the many local organizations and causes he helped out at Lakeview over the years. Through the mid-1950s and into the '60s Grand Bend was enjoying glorious days of summer fun. Beach parties, beauty contests, hootenanys all brought out enthusiastic crowds and Lakeview Casino was always front and centre at these events.

June 6, 1981, saw many of the people who had been touched in some way by Eric McIlroy pay tribute to him. Business people, musicians, politicians and friends all turned out for the unveiling of the plaque and the evening dance that followed.

Louis Armstrong, the "Father of Jazz," toured the world extensively during his long career. He performed in every major venue in Ontario, including Grand Bend. On a more personal note, he wished to be called "Louis," not "Louey." *Courtesy of Lambton Heritage Museum*

Twenty-five days later on July 1, the dance hall that Eric's father-in-law built in 1919 was destroyed by fire. The original Lakeview Casino site today remains simply a vast sandy expanse on the shore of Lake Huron, used in the summer as a parking lot.

Ipperwash Casino

The Casino at Ipperwash Beach was the centre of social life for many summers. Jeanette Ovens writes: "My husband John's uncle, Stuart Ovens, built the Ipperwash Casino at Ipperwash Beach on Lake Huron in 1929. Although John was just a small boy he remembers spending summers at the Ovens' cottages across the road from the Casino. To the best of his knowledge he believes dances were held nearly every night of the week at that time. Not being old enough to wait on customers, it was his job to sweep the floors and do some of the odd jobs. The Casino was destroyed by fire a number of years ago."

Sarnia: Rose Gardens

October 14th is a day when Dick and Elsie Rose usually pause for a moment to recall the years when they ran Sarnia's celebrated roller rink and dance hall—

77

For $1.75 one could purchase a ticket to enjoy Les Brown and the orchestra when they performed at Kenwick Terrace in Sarnia on Monday, May 26, 1946. *Courtesy of Douglas Kennedy.*

Rose Gardens. The final dance at their successful business was held this day in 1974, drawing over 2,000 people who came out to enjoy one last evening at their favourite place. Dick and Elsie purchased the Starlite Gardens in 1951 and immediately enlarged and re-surfaced the outdoor venue which they re-named Rose Gardens. Dick recalls, "We could see the demand from the kids for year-round roller skating and dancing so, in 1961, we completely enclosed the rink and opened every night during the year." Crowds of up to 1,800 were not unusual for an evening of roller skating and dancing afterwards. Record hops and dances with live bands were very popular during the 1950s and '60s. Many of Canada's name artists played at the Rose Gardens, including Ronnie Hawkins, Bobby Curtola, David

Clayton Thomas and The Staccatos (later the Five Man Electrical Band). Del Shannon also performed. Local bands were also hired for regular dances and included The Volcanoes, The Capers and Jays Raiders. The Rose Gardens was dismantled to make way for a high-rise apartment, but part of it lives on a few miles to the north. Dick and Elsie donated the steel supports and roofing material for the construction of the Lambton Heritage Museum's main building.

Sarnia: Kenwick Terrace

Kenwick Terrace in downtown Sarnia, and the romantic Kenwick-on-the-Lake in Bright's Grove were both owned by Jack and Genevieve Kennedy. The music store

Jack founded in 1966—today operated by son Douglas—continues to bear his name. "Dad always worked extremely hard and threw himself into every aspect of his work," says Doug. The name "Kenwick" was derived by combining part of Jack's last name with Gen's, which was Warwick. As the name suggests, Gen worked with Jack as an equal partner in their thriving businesses.

Louis Armstrong officially opened Kenwick Terrace on January 31, 1943. This hall held regular dances with Jack's orchestra, and booked in Big Bands and singers regularly. Weekly shows were broadcast across Canada on the CBC Radio network; William Boyd remembers those programs: "Cy Strange was a singer with the Jack Kennedy Orchestra ... Cy went on to become a figure at CBC radio." Kenwick Terrace was operated by Jack and Gen until 1978 when the couple decided to demolish the building and erect a large apartment and office complex.

Bill and Elizabeth Baldock have pleasant memories of Kenwick Terrace. "Many an evening was enjoyed with our friends here," writes Bill. "The flexible wooden dance floor allowed you to dance all night to the sounds of pop, jazz, big name bands and local ones.

Years later our oldest son, along with his friends, worked as busboys at Kenwick Terrace. I proposed to my wife at Kenwick-on-the-Lake many years ago. Les Brown and His Band of Renown were playing that warm summer evening on the shore of Lake Huron."

Bright's Grove: Kenwick-on-the-Lake

The location of Kenwick-on-the-Lake makes this hall the most unique summer venue in the area for people who came here to dance. Gen says, "We purchased the pavilion at Bright's Grove in March 1946, with the first dance scheduled for June 16 of the same year." During those three months Jack drove all over southwestern Ontario sourcing down building supplies. All the cement was dyed red. The grand opening on that June evening marked the beginning of a summer dancing tradition that lasted well into the 1950s for Jack Kennedy and his band. Kenwick-on-the-Lake was popular for its outdoor terrazzo dance floor as well as its indoor hardwood floor. The family planted trees, rock gardens, opened two dining rooms and a hairdressing salon. As Gen says, "We

In his early days as a musician, Jack Kennedy had three orchestras and travelled throughout Southern Ontario performing at various pavilions. For example, he would play two days at Collins Bay, move on to Hamilton for two more dates and then play the remainder of the week in Sarnia. Jack's orchestra also performed for dances throughout Lambton County, including places such as Wallaceburg's Primrose Gardens, The Pyranon in Chatham and, of course, at his own dance halls; Kenwick Terrace and Kenwick-on-the-Lake. *Courtesy of Gen Kennedy.*

79

Kenwick-on-the-Lake in Bright's Grove brought top entertainers to music fans in the Sarnia region for many years. Outdoor dancing under summer stars was a tradition for thousands of people, such as these dancers, shown circa 1950.
Courtesy of Doug Kennedy.

opened a bathhouse and stand to rent bathing suits, and then opened a concession booth. We also built an outdoor bowling alley, set up small shops and installed rides for the kids. The popcorn machine ran non-stop during those busy summer days."

Don Messer was the first country act to perform at Kenwick. Not being big fans of country music, Jack and Gen were amazed when people lined up hours early to see their idol. "Vaughn Monroe thought that Kenwick-on-the-Lake was the most beautiful place he had ever played," says Gen. Norm Harris played for one summer with his band and enjoyed the experience so much that he returned the following year by himself to sing with the band. Lawrence Welk became a personal friend of the Kennedys.

For many years Jack was a familiar face in local malls performing Christmas music on his electric organ, a tradition that many Sarnia residents still recall.

Chapter Six

FROM BRANTFORD NORTH TO THE GEORGIAN BAY AREA

Summer evenings at the Dard.

Brantford: Mohawk Park Pavilion and Area Halls

Mohawk Park Pavilion was one of this city's landmark dance halls. As Dorothy Young-Yeandle writes, "This was a particularly beautiful building inside and out, architecturally. It had a very springy floor. I knew very well at one time the people who ran the dances and I occasionally helped in the food booth. It was dismantled sometime in the 1950s."

Erwin Daniels disagrees slightly regarding the fate of this hall. "The Mohawk Park Pav on Mohawk Lake in Brantford was very popular during the War years, but was not used in cold weather. Area bands of ten or twelve members always played there. It burned down. We also danced at the Rainbow Ballroom and the Arcade Ballroom in Brantford, as well as Demont's in Burford."

June Nicholson provides some more information on Brantford's hot spots: "When I was 17 in 1942 during World War II, we danced three or four nights a week at the Arcade Ballroom, at the corner of Colborne and Queen Streets (the building is still standing but not occupied); the Rainbow Room on Darling Street (building destroyed); the Embassy Club on Colborne Street (building destroyed); the Coral Room of the old Hotel Kerby (demolished); and Mohawk Park, a summer dance pavilion with a wonderful floor (original hall torn down and replaced with a new pavilion). Other road houses and dance halls included Demont's in Burford, Lighthouse in Mt. Pleasant, Blue Haven on Highway #2 outside of Brantford (now an eating establishment), Everglades which had outdoor dancing in Galt and the Kos-Var in Brantford.

"Some of Brantford's dance bands were led by

81

Embassy Club on Colborne Street in Brantford, November 1943. This was a Wings Parade Dance. After the servicemen received their wings (graduated as pilots) in the Wings Parade Ceremony, a big dance was held for family and guests. This is graduating class #87. June Nicholson is seated on the left. "I wonder how many survived after going overseas, so many fine men were killed.

Courtesy of June Nicholson.

A celebration in Hotel Kerby in Brantford.

Courtesy of June Nicholson.

Archie Gray (with singer Raymond Hughes whom I knew well for over 50 years), Tim Eaton, Ronnie King and Al Gallager. Ted Pudney and Len Salie were popular at Port Dover's Summer Gardens.

"The dance halls were always packed during the War with servicemen. In fact, you seldom saw a male in 'civvies'—everyone was in uniform and sure danced up a storm. Number 5 S.F.T.S. (Service Flying Training School) was located seven miles from Brantford and trained pilots from Britain, Australia, New Zealand and, of course, Canadian boys. Number 20 Army Camp was in Brantford situated on the site of what is now the Pauline Johnson High School. Burtch Air Observer School was seven miles from town. In Port Dover the crowd came from Hagersville S.F.T.S., Jarvis Bombing and Gunnery School and the Simcoe Army Camp.

"In order to get to the dance in Port Dover we caught the electric train—The Lake Erie and Northern Railway (L.E. & N., or 'Late Every Night'). We went down to the dance after work about 6:30 and returned on the midnight trolley. What a wonderful time we had, even though the War was on. Life was much gentler then, drugs were unheard of and not too much booze floated around, perhaps because it was rationed—one 26-ounce bottle of liquor a month.

"I met my late husband at a dance at Mohawk Park in 1945. He was in the process of being discharged from the R.C.A.F. We were married in 1947."

Galt (Cambridge): The Highlands

The Highlands in Galt was this town's premier dance spot. In her letter Doreen Fraser notes, "The Highlands was close so we went there often to company parties and special dances. I think the name of the band was called the Highlanders with Anne Eadie as singer (another Guelph native). Mart Kenney also played there. As I recall many of these places were dry, so the ladies brought a 'mickie' in their purses if you wanted a

The Highlands in Galt (now Cambridge) was a popular dance hall for the area. This photo, taken in 1949, shows a group of friends enjoying their evening. From l to r: Keith and Gladys Rosebreegh, Bev and Doreen Fraser, Joyce and Earl Pfeffer, Jean and David Barnes and Bill and Marion Fraser. *Courtesy of Doreen Fraser.*

drink. The Matador on Hespler Road, Galt, also had a good following with live bands playing there."

Chester Kirk writes about The Highlands: "Since retiring from music one of my favourite dance halls was The Highlands. This was a lovely hall with a big eight-piece band called The Merrymakers."

Erwin Daniels remembers that along with his wife and close friends, they attended dances at many of the halls in southwestern Ontario. "We almost lived at The Highlands, though, in the winter. Located on Highway #8, it was the most popular in a wide area. Originally a tennis club, it became a night club from the 1940s to the mid-'80s when it closed. Our group of five couples were very frequent patrons—reservations were a must."

Preston (Cambridge): Leisure Lodge and the John Kostigian Orchestra

Certain halls, clubs and pavilions throughout the province evoke an immediate image of the house band, or the orchestra who was most frequently on stage over a long term. A perfect example of this partnership is Leisure Lodge in Preston and the John Kostigian Orchestra.

When Leisure Lodge opened in 1948, the young 23-year-old bandleader was on stage. Thirty-one years later, in 1979, John Kostigian was still performing on Saturday nights and New Year's Eves, and actually played his last gig there that year. Leisure Lodge burned down Friday, February 22, 1980.

Leisure Lodge was an integral part of the community, playing a large role in the social life of Galt and area residents. The club moved through many phases during its lifetime, trying to keep up with people's tastes in music and entertainment. In the beginning, of course, Big Band music was the main draw, and John's orchestra played the kind of swing people loved. Special guest artists were featured occasionally for one-nighters and included Stan Kenton, Count Basie, Woody Herman and Tommy Dorsey.

Built by Ollie Waimel on part of his mother's 100-acre farm which was located on a country

Joan Case, originally from Hamilton, was the featured vocalist. She was a seasoned radio and TV performer as well. *Courtesy of John Kostigian.*

83

Starting as a small group when Leisure Lodge first opened, the John Kostigian Orchestra grew with the lodge to ultimately include five saxophones, three trombones, trumpet, piano, base, drums and vocalists. John Kostigian played the lead trumpet. *Courtesy of John Kostigan.*

road east of Preston, years before the 401 sliced through the property, Leisure Lodge initially was a great success. The original structure was built from scratch by Ollie and his brother Hants during any spare time they had from their full-time day jobs. They chopped and chipped stones used in the complex. In the early years people brown-bagged it to Leisure Lodge, dressing up in their best for the dance. The big attraction during the good weather months was dancing under the stars on the patio. Doreen Fraser writes: "What a romantic place to dine and dance outdoors in the summer to John Kostigian's band with his wife Joan Case as singer. It was wonderful, except, as I recall, for the mosquitoes."

Ollie decided to sell the business after 20 years of providing great music in a beautiful setting. After Ollie, followed a long parade of owners who experienced financial challenges as they enlarged the premises and tried to fine-tune the operation for a new generation of people. From rock music to disco and even to hosting a Miss Nude World Pageant, Leisure Lodge made every attempt to turn a buck.

The real memories of Leisure Lodge, however, were created during the John Kostigian years. Born in Owen Sound of Armenian parents, Johnny Kostigian began his musical career at a very young age. Starting out as a bugler in a cadet band, he soon purchased his own trumpet and began taking lessons. He formed his first band at 13 and was playing in dance halls by his late teens. From 1943-45 he played trumpet in an army corps band in Nova Scotia. After he returned, John formed a seven-piece group in 1946, the same orchestra he would take to Leisure Lodge three years later. As the band grew in the early 1950s, Joan Case began singing with John, about a year after the couple were married.

Using many arrangements by Eddie Graf, John's band broke into local television in 1957-58 with its own show, "Sunday Serenade," on CKCO, Kitchener. Many members of the orchestra were with John for over 20 years, a testament to the friendship and respect the men had for each other. Along with their regular engagement at Leisure Lodge, the band played numerous high school and university proms, along with many jazz concerts in Waterloo and Guelph.

John Kostigian has always put great stock in traditions and family, the existence of places parents can show to their children as they pass on the stories of the old days. That's why he and Joan were both so sad to see Leisure Lodge go up in flames. The many Saturday night jam sessions around the lodge's fireplace that would go on until three or four the next morning over a huge pot of coffee are just some of the wonderful thoughts that the Leisure Lodge brings back. He said that the lodge was part of the community, part of the heritage, because it had so many memories. "Without nostalgia, without memories, without something to look back on, then a community is very shallow."

Puslinch Lake: Butler's Pavilion, Barber's Beach Pavilion

Tragedy is rarely associated with a dance pavilion, but Frank A. Smith has a rather sad anecdote associated with one of the pavilions at Puslinch Lake, in the Guelph/Cambridge area.

"This would be in the 1930s and '40s at Butler's Pavilion when Friday and Saturday night dancing (long gowns for the women, smart suits for the men) was probably the highlight of a young person's social life. It was located right on the edge of the lake and was somewhat long and narrow. It had glass-paned doors along both sides which opened onto an open-air verandah, for cuddly dances, a breath of cool air, whatever. I can still picture us small kids with our noses looking in on the glamorous couples gliding and swaying to the music of Merv Himes and his orchestra.

"One late summer evening, when the moon was full and the night was warm, the three of us had driven over to Galt and taken in a movie. Afterwards we drove back to the lake with the intention of enjoying the last hour or so of music from the pavilion. As we pulled up to the hall, we noticed a police car parked at the side and an area nearby was roped off. The pavilion was built over the water, so a boathouse was constructed underneath the structure, and it was this lower area which was being investigated by the police. Inside the boathouse was a canoe the police had pulled from the lake. Lying on the bottom of the canoe were two bodies—a husband and wife who had drowned earlier. They had young children at home. To this day that image has remained with me. Up in the pavilion were hundreds of dancers having a wonderful time on a warm summer night, and a few feet below, unknown to the dancers, was the contrasting tragedy."

Doreen (Hall) Fraser recalls the other pavilion at Puslinch Lake. "The one place that is dear to my heart and brings back many very pleasant days is the Barber's Beach Pavilion," she writes. "We only had a jukebox but this was family fun at its best. We used to dance all day with family and friends. We had a cottage at the lake for many years and always enjoyed the dancing; my sister had her wedding reception there. I can still manage to dance today with my husband, children and grandchildren."

Guelph: Paradise Gardens

Paradise Gardens on Woodlawn Road was built and owned by Joe Contini. Johnny Downs led one of the first bands to play here and helped the owner develop a musical policy that would eventually bring in the crowds. According to Johnny, "It was a great place

but initially couldn't attract a sizeable audience." Joe contacted the London musician and arranged to start a series of Sunday night concerts, which many of the province's clubs and halls were discovering to be very popular with people. There was a good variety of general entertainment involving lots of audience participation. "Gordie Tapp played here often and had his jokes written on paper which he rolled up his arm," recalls Johnny. Once word about Paradise Gardens spread, up to 800 people would arrive on a Sunday night for these concerts. Johnny's orchestra was part of this entertainment for three years. Paradise Gardens eventually became a very successful banquet and convention hall with dances on Saturday nights.

Gloria Ferringo writes that Paradise Gardens is now known as the Desert Inn. "It was a good spot to book a banquet or have a wedding reception. Don Singular and the Twi-Lights played Friday and Saturday nights for dancing."

Guelph: Ryan's

Having grown up in Guelph, Gloria remembers the "very, very popular" Ryan's Dance Hall, located downtown on Wyndham Street." The hall was above Ryan's Clothing Store. There was popular music on Wednesday and Saturday, and on Friday it was country music. The Kidd Baker Band played on Fridays. Dalt Gibson and Don Singular played pop music on the other two nights. The store was sold and it all stopped." Gloria "found her husband at Ryan's"— they've been married now for over 43 years.

Other Guelph Area Halls/The Frank Family Band

Gloria names a few other dance halls where people went dancing "They had dances in Eden Mills, Aberfoyle and Elora. In the first two towns the dances were often held in the schoolhouses. In Elora the dance was held at Charlie Hills' barn. Local bands played, such as Galbraith Fletcher's Orchestra. "We danced at the Olde Mill on Speedvale Avenue, by the river—the Al Watson Orchestra played there every Friday and Saturday night, both country and popular

85

music, with lots of square dancing."

For over a decade Chester Kirk played in another Elora hall. "I played saxophone in a small orchestra (violin, piano, drums and myself) for ten years in the same hall every Saturday night with an average attendance of 150-300 people," he writes. "It was a beautiful stone building then called the Old Elora Armouries. Admission in the early 1950s was 50 cents and we were paid $6 each for three hours work, 9 to 12. I've seen many many people meet their spouses-to-be and I've had the chance to see many marriages develop. Not only have we played for several of their weddings but since retiring I have also played for some of their children's weddings. At that time there was no bar; ironically, this same stone building is still there, but it is now a liquor store."

Jean Somerville published a book in 1995 in which she wrote about the band her father and grandfather led in the region of Halton County from 1890 to 1960. In the Foreword of *The Bands Played On: The Story Of The Frank Family And Their Music*, Jean writes: "Community musicians provided entertainment and played an important part in the social life of the residents in rural Ontario before the days of radio and television .... At first, the Frank family entertained in the vicinity of their home in Nassagaweya township, in Halton County. Over a period of time, their popularity broadened the geographic area of their performance. Their weekly radio program over station CKOC in Hamilton in the early 1930s lead to engagements in more distant centres of southern Ontario."[1]

Warren Ovens and His Orchestra. *Courtesy of Warren Ovens.*

Kitchener-Waterloo: Summer Gardens

Chances are if you danced in the Kitchener-Waterloo area at any one of the many favourite places like the Summer Gardens you moved to the music of Warren Ovens and his band. The group was also popular out of town at summer pavilions in places like Hanover and Sauble Beach.

Warren was not only recognized as a superb trumpet player—he was one of those few musicians who also had the talent to write great musical arrangements. It was during Warren's membership in the Swing Patrol during World War II, when he had the opportunity to perform with some of Canada's best talent, that he became interested in arranging and was started on his way with the help of head army arranger-musician Tony Braiden. "I played with CBC musicians like Murray Ginsberg, Teddy Roderman and Murray Lauder," he says. "In May 1945, we were the first organized band to play a concert in Amsterdam and we did a command performance for Queen Wilhelmina in that city." Warren also played with Peterborough bandleader Bobby Kinsman.

After the War, Warren integrated himself back into the musical community, joining Wilber Ott's 13-piece house band at the Summer Gardens on Queen Street South in 1946. "We had some wonderful times there for more than two years until the disastrous fire wiped out the building, including all the band's music and instruments."

The Summer Gardens was set up in an arena which was converted into a dance hall and had been operating as such since 1940. This was the hall where the big bands from the U.S. would give concerts when they were passing through on tour. Writes Doreen (Hall) Fraser: "The Summer Gardens was the place to go in the '40s during the time of the big bands. We would go there to listen and dance to Tex Beneke with the Glenn Miller Band, Vaughn Munroe, Tommy Dorsey, Gene Krupa, Woody Herman and many others."

Dorothy Jones remembers the Summer Gardens and writes: "On Saturday nights during the War men in the various services came from their camps to dance and meet the local girls. An area was cordoned off for Jitterbugs, to ensure the safety of more conventional dancers. Dances were held there Wednesday, Friday and Saturday nights and I think we paid 75 cents for regular admission and $4.50 for name bands. During intermission we headed down to the Walper House for a refreshing glass of beer."

Margo Kerber writes that the Summer Gardens was a great dance spot. "We took the trolley from Preston to get there. I shrieked at a skinny Frank Sinatra there and danced to some of the biggest names around in the 1940s."

To give the arena hall a homey atmosphere, a number of chesterfields and easy chairs were spread around the dance floor. Although this furniture gave the Summer Gardens a more intimate feel, it proved to be the venue's downfall; the fire was apparently caused by a cigarette butt that had fallen between the cushions. The night it burned, London musician Johnny Downs and his orchestra were on their way home after performing at the Gardens.

Warren Ovens formed his own orchestra after the disastrous arena fire, writing all his own arrangements. "My bass player also sang," he says. "I also made sure that I kept my music current." Some of the band members included Bill Weber (drums), Keith Fancett (bass), Art Harris (alto sax), Matt Reiner (tenor sax), Stan Schreiter (piano), and Warren on trumpet. The band immediately landed a steady weekend job at Conestoga (Trail's End Hotel) and soon was heard on radio. "C.A. Pollock had one of the first FM stations in Canada, and for nearly a year we played a weekly half hour show from the stage of the Capitol Theatre. They stopped the movie while the broadcast was on and then continued it afterwards."

Warren recalls some of the many places in Kitchener-Waterloo where people went dancing. "The Rubberworkers' Union Hall was a great place for new bands to get their start—they would play Monday and Tuesday, with the bigger bands coming in for the rest of the week. Also, the top floor of the Dunker Building had regular dances on weekends during the 1940s."

Kitchener-Waterloo: Victoria Park Pavilion/Rosslyn Grove

The Victoria Park Pavilion, where the Little Theatre later staged their performances, was a favourite of many people. Dorothy Jones writes about Victoria Park: "When I was a very young child I played on the swings and slides at Victoria Park. Time went on, but we were oblivious to the fact that it got dark. We were attracted by the lights and people gathering at the Pavilion and soon the dancing started. At that time we were fascinated by the couples dancing with the ladies in long gowns ... when I was sufficiently grown up an mature enough I went dancing at the Pavilion myself."

Rosslyn Grove was another landmark dance hall in the area during the 1950s and '60s, and is generally considered to be one of the three most popular night spots, the other two being Leisure Lodge and The Highlands which were in the Galt area. "It was large and rather barn-like with a good floor designed in concentric squares," recalls Warren Ovens. "Rosslyn Grove was operated by Ross Bullis, who owned a glass-cutting business; he always had good house bands, such as Merv Himes." It burned in 1964 and the Tu-Lane Restaurant now sits on the site.

Bingeman Park today is a "camping resort and family playground" complex, but for many years dances were staged in the large arena. During the 1960s and '70s it was customary for popular Ontario rock bands to play as people roller skated for part of the evening. Then, for the last hour or so, the kids doffed the skates and danced to the band. With the

87

An early postcard of Wasaga Beach with the Dardanella in the background left, circa 1920s.

bandstand being located in the centre of the rink, the biggest challenge for band members was to safely cross the roller rink during intermission without being creamed by speeding skaters.

Wasaga Beach: The Dardanella

Wasaga Beach has a number of constants—the long sandy beach, clear blue water, hot summer days and tourists. There is also another constant at Wasaga Beach. It has stood at the corner of Beach and First for over 80 years, enduring summer heat and winter blasts. Hundreds of thousands of tourists and residents know this location well, for it has brought people together for generations.

The Dardanella or, as most people call it, The Dard, has the distinction of being one of the longest surviving dance halls and gathering places in the province of Ontario. John McLean built the Dardanella in 1918, across the street from his Capstan Inn. It's still as exciting and vibrant today as it was then, when many people travelled here by

horse and buggy. The reason for The Dard's longevity lies much deeper than location. The Dardanella gives people what they want in a holiday setting. The present owners, Michelle and Rick Seip, know the key to The Dard's endurance has meant that they, and the two previous owners, have had to move with the times. "We're 'hands-on' people," says Michelle. "We look forward to coming in to work every day and we're here for many hours each day, seven days per week during our season. We have many employees and we run The Dard very much like a family."

People still recall dancing to the Redjackets or Trump Davidson forty or fifty years ago, or to Frank Evans' orchestra in 1964. Today, rock music is what The Dard's customers enjoy, and the Seips are there to provide just that. Some of the biggest names in the business have set up on The Dard's main stage including Burton Cummings, Allanah Myles and

Early bands performed at the The Dardanella travelled by auto, as seen in this 1920s shot. Note the tuba which played bass notes before the string bass became the norm.
Courtesy of Michelle Seip.

from the 1918 to the '50s, followed by a successful 30-year run under the Timlock family. Michelle and Rick became associated with The Dard in 1985 and, in 1990, they obtained full title to both the land and the business. "The name has never changed, and that in itself has given our business a long-term association with the beach," says Michelle. The Dard has housed a tea room, a beauty parlour, bowling alley and a lunch counter. Owners have rented bikes and rafts. It has featured dinner theatre and fashion shows, and Michelle has co-ordinated Miss Wasaga Beach pageants. The Timlock's downstairs bowling alleys have been converted into a bar area with tables, chairs and music replacing lanes, gutters and the clatter of old

April Wine. At other times a popular DJ takes over the musical reins for the Dance Club. The downstairs bar features live rock also, seven nights per week during July and August. Over 90% of The Dard's business comes from the Greater Toronto Area, just an hour and a half away.

The Dardanella has also done well because of the longevity of tenure. The McLean family ran the business

When Billy Nelson and the Varsity Collegians performed at The Dardanella in the 1930s, patrons would come to the dance in dresses and jackets and ties. The piano was rented from Heintzman's of Toronto.
Courtesy of Jack Lomas.

A typical dance scene *(above)* **of the time. The orchestra is not identified.** *Courtesy of Geoff Hewittson.*

Howdy Brown *(left)* **and his orchestra members line up on the beach at Wasaga for the group shot, circa 1930s.** *Courtesy of Michelle Seip.*

90

bowling pins. A 2000-square-foot outdoor deck the length of the complete building faces the beach where you can sit under a colourful umbrella, have a bite and a drink and watch Wasaga have fun.

The purpose and focus of The Dard has also remained constant. Michelle notes, "It's a meeting place, and that's what brings people to The Dard." On the exterior, today's building scarcely resembles the original structure, but the interior still retains many reminders of the early days. The upstairs dance hall has the original floor where many pairs of feet have fox-trotted, tangoed, twisted, and moved in all manner of dance styles over the years. Originally the

Dardanella's upstairs dance floor was round, surrounded by a railing for jitney dancing. This upper level was reached by climbing a set of stairs which were later enclosed.

Alan Waters worked at the Honeydew stand, about 150 yards from The Dard in 1939-40. He recalls the romantic summer evenings listening to the music of Trump Davidson wafting over the beach from the open windows of The Dard. He'd often take a few minutes and watch the dancers through these windows.[2]

Vi (Marsh) Hoare was also vacationing at Wasaga and going to The Dard: "The number 1 spot in my life was the Dardanella Pavilion at Wasaga Beach from 1935 to 1939. Each night we dressed in our best and off we went to dance to Joe Wallace's orchestra. They were immaculate in white suits and they played the sweetest music one ever heard. Wasaga Beach and the dear old Dardanella seemed destined to bring romance into my life and in 1939 I met my husband-to-be. In 1994, we celebrated our 54th anniversary. We will always remember the good times we had at the CNE tent, Woodbridge Pavilion and the Dardanella."

With the proximity of Camp Borden, Wasaga Beach boomed during the War years. Thousands of enlisted men spent their leave at the resort area in the summer months and, as a result, there was a tremendous surge of construction—cabins, cottages, campgrounds, amusements and dance halls sprung up to give these new visitors a place to stay and a place to party. After the roof of The Dard collapsed one year, it was volunteers from Base Borden who showed up to help with the repairs.

When Michelle and Rick were renovating the stage area a few years ago, they discovered a trunk containing packages of old receipts, cancelled cheques and other historical papers from the years the McLeans owned the Dardanella. Original blueprints for the building, a 1927 Musicians' Association contract, a piano purchase/rental agreement with Heintzman and Company dated 1923 and a handwritten note signed by Alex, covering the subject of installing a beauty parlour at The Dard. These were just some of the fascinating papers. More recent archaeological findings have included similar treasures from the 1950s and '60s.

Just as the McLeans and the Timlocks updated, renovated and added attractions to the business, Michelle and Rick continue the practice. They have invested in modifications and upgrades to keep the business viable—the downstairs street level facing the beach is comprised of a number of beachwear and fast food shops which lease space from The Dard's owners. The Dard promotes beach activities throughout the year such as the annual Corvette weekend, volleyball tournaments and band competitions.

Helicopter rides, jet ski rentals, teeny weeny bikinis, fast food ... John McLean would probably have a hard time visualizing Wasaga Beach of today—over 80 years after he built The Dardanella, but he would no doubt be happy to know that Michelle and Rick Seip are continuing the tradition that he likely had in mind himself. In Michelle's words, "The Dard is doing today what it has been doing since its inception, and that is providing fun and entertainment for young people at an ultimate beachfront location."

Other Wasaga Dance Halls

Wasaga has been home to dozens of dance halls; some lasted a few years while a few, such as the Beacon, survived much longer. The Strathcona featured both dancing and roller skating. So did Watson's Pavilion, built on the beach, in 1912, just across the river from the old wooden bridge. Wasaga also had its own Silver Slipper, famous for Sunday jam sessions. Davie's Club, operated by Milt and Orel Davies was another favourite dance place. Other than the Beacon, none is in existence today.

Woodland Beach: Ship-A-Hoy Pavilion

Margaret Renton writes with some background on Woodland Beach's Ship-A-Hoy pavilion: "Built in 1932 by Mr. Whelan, it was originally called the Sunset Pavilion. The opening dance of the season was held in May on the long weekend. The music was provided by the Johnstone family band from Midland, with a dance held every Wednesday throughout the summer. In the 1940s there was a square dance on the weekends, also a weekly song and dance evening with Mrs. Rutherford playing the piano. Proceeds from the admission to that event were sent to the *Toronto Telegram* newspaper's War Fund. In the 1950s, the pavilion was sold to Mr. and Mrs. Jack Tocher, and renamed the Ship-a-Hoy. On Saturday nights there was bingo at 7 p.m. The teenagers then helped clean up the hall so a dance could be held until midnight. On long weekends there was a Midnight Dance on Sunday nights until 3:00 a.m. Music was provided by a disc jockey named Nick—he eventually married the Tocher's daughter, Julie.

In the late 1960s, the pavilion was sold again to the Ellisons. They in turn sold it, and it is now the

91

Bayshore Seniors Club."

The pavilion has been completely renovated and totally upgraded into a modern hall. The old wooden chairs have been replaced with chrome and plastic seats, and the juke box has long since disappeared in favour of a wall-mounted speaker

The Ship-A-Hoy *(above)* at Woodland Beach had a popular dance floor. The spot was also a centre for bingo. In 1959, the author split $4.00 bingo pot with another winner. *Courtesy of Margaret Renton.*

This photograph of the Beauchamp family band, known as the Georgian Swingsters, was taken in the old Chateau Gae Pavilion at Balm Beach in 1945. Today the bass drum sits on display in Midland's Johnstone Music Centre. Shown are, left to right: Jeanne Beauchamp, accordion; Jack Cowan, trumpet; Jack Beauchamp, alto sax; Alex Larmond, drums and old-time violin; Herb Beauchamp, tenor sax & drums; Alice Beauchamp, piano; Audrey Desroches, vocalist. *Courtesy of Jack Beauchamp.*

92

system, but one feature still remains – the portholes.

Balm Beach, Midland: Chateau Gae, Wagon Wheel & Circle B Dance Pavilions

If you would like to see Alex Larmond's old bass drum, it is on display at Johnstone's Music Centre in Midland. Alex played drums with the Beauchamp family orchestra, known as The Georgian Swingsters. The Beauchamp name, printed in large block letters on the front skin of the bass drum, is a name that represents many years of musical history this family gave to the town, beginning at the Chateau Gae dance pavilion on Balm Beach a few miles west of Midland.

Four of The Georgian Swingsters who began playing here were Beauchamp family members, including Jack Beauchamp: "My father (Herb) operated a successful radio parts and repair shop in downtown Midland for many years." Jack continued in his father's path, and was an RCA dealer for 30 years. Herb's love of music resulted in his decision to open the Wagon Wheel dance pavilion at Balm Beach. With the Chateau Gae experience to guide him, Herb purchased a plot of land at the beach in the mid 1940s and built the dance hall, booking his own band on a regular basis.

"It was an immediate success," says Jack, who was 15 when he took over alto sax duties. "Cottagers and people from Midland/Penetang came to the pavilion all summer long. We played a variety of music, modern and old-time, but the folks really loved barn dances, square dances and the very popular schottisches (a round dance). It was a great way for people to get to know one another. The popularity of the Wagon Wheel was so strong that people were sad to see the end of the season. "People kept asking Dad to set up something for the cold weather months."

Enter the Circle "B" Dance Pavilion—that's "B" for Beauchamp. Herb constructed this new pavilion in 1952, just outside of Midland on the road to Penetanguishene, using logs to give the structure a rustic appearance. And just who provided the entertainment? Naturally it was the Beauchamp family. The Circle "B" operated during the fall and winter until the long May weekend, at which time the

The original Wagon Wheel dance pavilion built by Herb Beauchamp in the mid-40s. Dances were held here during the summer months until the structure burned in 1956. A new hall was constructed with cement blocks.
Courtesy of Jack Beauchamp.

Wagon Wheel rolled to life. The family suffered a setback on Easter Sunday, 1956, when the original Wagon Wheel burned due to a problem with the hydro system. A new building was erected, this time constructed with cement blocks. As the popularity of dancing began to decline, Herb decided to sell the pavilions and turned his sight to politics. He served as mayor of Midland from 1962 to 1967.

Both the new Wagon Wheel and Circle B buildings still stand and have housed various businesses over the years.

Midland: Blue Room/Bayview Dance Hall

When Ted Johnstone settled in Midland, his name quickly became associated with entertainment and music. Ted's son, Guy and his wife, Kathy, operate the popular Johnstone Music Centre in the downtown area. There you can see the numerous reminders in the store of the musical contribution that his family and others, such as the Beauchamps, have made to Midland. In his office Guy has a number of pictures of his family's band performing in various halls around Midland. Many old instruments, such as an old tuba and autoharp, rest comfortably on the wall of the music store, along with Alex Larmond's bass drum. "The Johnstone family band would set up an outdoor stage down at the town

93

Charlie Parker's well-known Parkside Dance Pavilion in Midland (left) was located across the road from Little Lake, 1941. *Courtesy of Bruce Taylor.*

Whenever the urge struck to wash or brush their teeth, Johnny Downs and his Band (right) visited St. Margaret's Cemetery across the street from the Parkside Pavilion, photo 1941. *Courtesy of Johnny Downs.*

dock to welcome tourists from the U.S.," recalls Guy. "These performances would promote the band's dances at the Blue Room, above the Dynasty Chinese Food Restaurant." This hall was closed at the end of the War, and another opened above Preston's Meat Market (now the Bowling Lanes), named Bayview. Guy Johnstone remembers the "friendly competition" with the Beauchamps' dance halls, but there was plenty of business for everyone.

Midland: Parkside Dance Pavilion

North America's first canonized saints are recognized at the Martyrs' Shrine near Midland. Unfortunately for the musical martyrs who performed around Midland in more recent times, there is nothing to commemorate their contribution to the area, except perhaps the water taps in St. Margaret's Cemetery, across from the old Parkside Pavilion! These taps memorialize the presence of the orchestras who had to use this graveside water source to brush their teeth and wash their weary bodies. The young men slept in crude quarters at the Parkside, but the dance hall did not supply bathing facilities. At least, not in 1941 when London musician Johnny Downs and his band played there for the summer. "Charlie had a little

cabin built on the back of the pavilion where the band stayed," describes Johnny. "Washroom facilities were in the pavilion and across the street the town's largest cemetery provided us with the running water we needed." The "Charlie" to whom Johnny is referring was Charlie Parker, owner and operator of the Parkside. More than one musician has remembered Charlie as a spiritualist who regularly saw ghosts. Charlie was also mayor of Midland for a few years.

Johnny Downs came to Midland three years later by way of Peterborough. His orchestra had started the summer at Rye's Pavilion in that city, but the notorious owner decided to chop their wages and increase their workload. The band left for Parkside Gardens where Johnny and his group were amazed at the large crowd and the warm reception they received. With straight admission, rather than jitney dancing, the group was able to stretch a little on stage and get into some of their novelty numbers and generally "ham it up a bit."

Beside the cemetery across the street from the dance hall was the town's popular park—Little Lake (Midland Park Lake)—which drew hundreds of people for picnics and swimming on summer days. Jack McGrattan, who later settled in Kingston and enjoyed a lengthy musical career in that city, was born in Midland and performed with the Mark Wolf Perry Band, the house orchestra at the Parkside Pavilion during 1938. Jack says that during the Depression, hundreds of people would go to this park and camp in tents. "They'd sit and listen to the concerts and then we'd play in the Parkside afterwards."

Dances began to go downhill as Charlie seemed to lose touch with the youth of the town, according to one resident. Ownership changed and the building stood vacant and unused for a few years. In 1995, the dance hall, which had been left attached to a large newer addition, was demolished. There is one part of the general landscape that hasn't changed, however, and that's St. Margaret's Cemetery just across the street, complete with running water.

Anten Mills: Pine Crest Dance Centre

The former Pine Crest Dance Centre is no more, but I was fortunate to photograph the old building before new owners began renovations on the Anten Mills area hall.

Pine Crest opened September 10, 1948, the brainchild of Charles Miller. This Barrie-area man had a love of music and enjoyed all forms of entertainment so he and his wife, Barbara, decided to erect a dance hall next to their home, where they could run regular dances for people in the area. Pine Crest soon became a destination for people from all over the area. A Teen Town began on Friday nights and, as with similar Teen Towns in both nearby Orillia and Barrie, this one was also successful. Adult dances took place on Saturday nights featuring orchestras who played

the popular Big Band hits. In the later 1970s, Charles' daughter, Gayle Collins and her husband Ray, purchased the hall and held country and western music dances on Saturday nights into the mid-'90s.[3]

Orr Lake Dance Hall

South of Midland on Highway 93 is the Orr Lake Golf Club where just a few steps beyond the pro shop you enter an entirely different world: The Orr Lake Dance Hall. The first pavilion was built by Clarence Crowe in 1929, a simple open-air dance floor with no roof. Clarence's son Tom, and his wife, Goldie, now operate the business. "My father decided to move the dance floor from across the road to its present site," explains Tom. "At this time a roof was constructed and screening was installed with flaps to fold down—it gave the dancers the feel of the

The original Orr Lake dance floor *(top)* **built in 1929 by Clarence Crowe still gleams and is in use today.**

The Pine Crest Dance Centre at Anten Mills closed in the mid-1990s.

95

evening air, while still protecting them from the elements." Clarence enlarged the hall over the years as the crowds increased to make more room on the dance floor. Goldie says that years ago there used to be ropes around the floor for jitney dancing.

Down through the generations, many members of the Crowe family have been quite musical. Clarence himself played fiddle in the pavilion's first orchestra—the banjo and organ duties were shared by other relatives. Tom Crowe now leads the house band at the hall, playing trumpet and keyboards. The Orr Lake Orchestra numbers anywhere from six to eleven instruments, depending upon who is available to play on dance nights. As Tom says, "The people who show up to hear our live band play music from the 1930s to the present claim it's the best entertainment around." Tom's son, Stephen Crowe, is a well-respected trumpet player and, if he has a free Saturday evening between gigs, Stephen will occasionally sit in with his dad's band at the pavilion.

Orr Lake Pavilion became a very popular destination for dancers during the War years. "We ran dances Tuesday, Thursday, Friday and Saturday nights," said Tom. "Midnight dances on long weekends were also big." The pavilion was insulated and heated in 1961 when Tom and wife Goldie took over business. They built the nine-hole golf course in 1967 and added their family home, which is attached to the pavilion and golf course pro shop, six years later. Today, the hall at Orr Lake operates monthly dances on a year-round basis and is also rented out for special occasions. Tom respects the history that the dance floor his father built represents: "Although the old wooden walls have been replaced by brick walls and the interior has been spruced up to keep up with the times, the hall still has the original wooden floor which is smooth as glass."

Chapter Seven

AROUND LAKE SIMCOE

Orillia: The Pavalon (The Pav)

Many images come to mind when you mention the city of Orillia: Stephen Leacock, Gordon Lightfoot, the Opera House .... But another highlight of the city should be added, The Pavalon, also known as Couchiching Park Pavilion, Club Pavalon, or simply The Pav. It had everything a dance hall required for success—it overlooked the water of Lake Couchiching, was within walking distance of downtown Orillia and was close enough to cottage country to attract thousands of dancers during the summer months.

During the War there was plenty of business for all the dance halls in the general vicinity of Orillia, Barrie and Wasaga Beach with Camp Borden filled with young recruits in search of weekend fun.

A Club Pavalon advertisement, circa 1960.
Courtesy of Ray Cockburn.

The Pavalon continued to prosper. Bill Burridge played bass here with a band during the summer of 1946: "Archie Hudson owned the Pav at this time and brought in orchestras for the summer season. We played four nights a week with Russ Waters fronting

the band. In Orillia we stayed with our trumpet player's mother, Mrs. Milligan. Denzel [Denny] played alto sax and was a Julliard grad; in his class photo there was a picture of a young Les Brown. Denny was also a popular photographer in town and his wife ran the snack bar in the Pav; their daughter would also help out, making the Pav activities a family affair." [1]

Vera Battalia writes about The Pav: "I danced at The Pav from 1942 until its demolition—it was the most elegant place to celebrate New Year's Eve! Everyone seemed to have a wonderful time. Some of the managers and owners I knew were Archie Hudson, Larry Parrott and Ray Cockburn." Anne Reeves' husband played here: "He was with the Moonglowers who played Orillia's pavilion during the summers from about 1950 to '56." "The Pav in Orillia will always hold special memories for me," writes Dorothy Forsythe. "My husband spent most of his youth in Orillia and, when we were married in July 1949, we spent our week's honeymoon in a little cabin near the edge of the park and very close to The Pav. Every night was spent dancing here, and I met all his old girlfriends!"

Pat Langman sends these words: "I had my first date with Dave my (now) husband at The Pav. We danced there from 1958 to the early '60s. After the dance it was a tradition to go to the Shangri-La Restaurant for a coffee." So did Jean Jardin: "We always went for a Chinese lunch after the dance. I had come to Canada from Scotland in 1957 at age 21, and The Pav was one of the first pavilions I went dancing at after meeting my future husband. It was dresses and suits at The Pav, which was unlicensed and sold soft drinks and ice, but we brown-bagged a bottle under the table!"

As The Pav moved into the 1950s and '60s, teens came out in larger numbers than ever before as one of Ontario's most vibrant Teen Towns was established. Terry Ann (Lee) Elliott was part of the crowd who made a weekly trip to The Pav. She writes: "As a teen I worked the ice cream stand for banquets and on Teen Town nights when Ray Cockburn owned it.

Russ Waters and his band at The Pav. As a member of this orchestra, Orval Fleetham played quite often at The Pavalon in Orillia; they became the house band at The Pav for three years, performing three or four nights per week during the 1940s. This photo was taken in 1946. Orval later joined the McNeilly Orchestra. One of this group's memorable jobs was performing on the opening broadcast of the newly established radio station, CKBB. *Courtesy of Orval Fleetham.*

Everybody in Orillia loved The Pav, photo circa early 1960s. *Courtesy of the Orillia Public Library.*

Archie Hudson, standing with his New Year's Eve hat in his hand, owned the local bowling alley and ran The Pav in Orillia. During the winter months he would rent the Oddfellows Hall for dances such as this New Year's party, **1945.** *Courtesy of Orval Fleetham.*

I was lucky to meet some of the groups that played there, and enjoyed a friendship with Bobby Curtola over the years. It was rocking and rolling—a super place to go and meet lots of kids." Dan Bonner knew The Pav well: "As an almost life-long resident of Orillia, The Pav was a big part of my young adult life. From 1959 to '65 I attended dances every weekend. During my high school years I helped play the music. Again in the late '60s and early '70s, I deejayed at The Pav with my own disc jockey business."

Teen Town was a group of Orillia teenagers formed about 1960, when Ray Cockburn ran The Pav. Following one remote CFOR radio broadcast by Hap (Taylor) Parnaby, Ray said, "Teen Town caught on like fire." Bob Matiuska, who was on the Teen Town executive, describes the crowds at The Pav during these years as "huge, sometimes close to 1,000." The music was the drawing card and all the big rock bands from cities around Ontario and beyond played—Little Caesar, the Mandala, Stitch 'n Tyme and The Guess Who. Clothes were also important when you went dancing during Bob Matiuska's years: "I made sure my footwear was the latest fashion… as were the stove-top pants and suspenders all the boys wore." In 1986, a reunion of 350 Teen Towners saw dozens of acquaintances being renewed as

Bobby Curtola and the Martels were hot young stars of the early 1960s. They played all over Canada, in arenas, dance halls and pavilions, including The Pav in Orillia in 1963.
Courtesy of Terry Lee Elliott.

Robbie Lane and the Disciples played on stage.

The *Packet and Times* (Orillia) reporter Jamie Lamb wrote a piece about life at The Pav in 1976: "You could find places of light or places of darkness. Somewhere, somebody was sneaking a drink, kids were hanging out and a couple was necking. You can't really explain it but anyone who hit The Pav in the mid-'60s can understand it. It's the summer nights that most of us remember. Out of the house, lacquered and scented, and down to the park. At The Pav … you felt like you had the world by the tail. The girl you wanted to dance with was usually found crowded into a booth … to walk to The Pav alone, and come out holding hands … there was a lot of pride in that."

Why did The Pav become one of the hottest dance halls during the 1960s? Location was significant, but it is still the operator of a hall who ultimately controls the pavilion's destiny. Ray Cockburn was at The Pav's helm during this time and he looked to Teen Town for advice. Ray had purchased the hall in 1958 and developed a relationship of mutual respect with the kids who came to both The Pav and The Kee to Bala (formerly Dunn's Pavilion), which he later acquired. Hootenanys at The Pav were very popular for a period of time in the mid-'60s, and Ray has Gordon Lightfoot to thank for this. Lightfoot suggested that Ray install a revolving stage around the fountain and have folk singers and singalongs.

In 1973, the pavilion became available and Carl McDaid bought it with the hope of rejuvenating the hall. "We put in a $7,000 stereo system with Cerwin-Vega speakers for records and matched it with a very creative lighting system, designed by my manager at the time, Don Mathias," says Carl. About 450 people came the first night to check it out. Many well-known groups continued to play The Pav. Carl adds, "I booked Triumph in the early days before their rise to fame, Downchild Blues Band played, Little Caesar and the Consuls were regulars, and many other groups." It was not an easy task, pleasing the fickle tastes of kids, and Carl made a point of listening to his customers' suggestions for groups.

Ultimately, Carl decided to sell the property to Mike Smith, who then had The Pav torn down.

99

The Pav's physical condition was actually in excellent shape due to the many costly renovations Carl had undertaken over the years. However, he had to be pragmatic about the dance hall: "People were simply not coming out to dances in the numbers required to continue to make The Pav a viable business investment." A condominium housing project which was to be fittingly labelled The Pavalon By The Lake was planned for the site, but this project did not materialize.

Many people will always remember The Pav as very special. In her letter, Andrea Kostek writes

Poster courtesy of Ray Cockburn.

Originally from eastern Canada, this talented rock group moved to Toronto and introduced exceptional vocal harmonies into their music, enjoying success with their recording of The Beatles' song "Got To Get You Into My Life."

with her own personal feelings about The Pav: "During my teen years in Orillia I spent every Saturday night at The Pav dancing to bands like the Stitch 'n Tyme, Major Hooples Boarding House and Lighthouse. Some of my memories include the atmosphere as we walked outside on a hot summer's night, the sound of the band playing, people mingling, young lovers walking down to the water across the park—or walking down Bay Street in the wintertime with my girlfriends on a cold night filled with the anticipation of another wonderful night, as snowflakes fell and clung to our coats and the trees. One night in November of '68 I stood at the front of the hall near the stage watching the band, and from the corner of my eye I saw a boy I had danced with a few weeks earlier. He said, 'I really want to see you—will you meet me here next Saturday night?' To this day I remember the exhilaration I felt that night. For two years after that first night, Jim and I went to The Pav every weekend and danced to the music of those favourite bands. It makes me smile just to remember those days. Every once in a while when a song comes on the radio I will remember Jim. My mind races back to those days when I was in my teens dancing every week to those same songs. I am very happily married, have a successful career and two beautiful daughters. I sometimes think of those days, my first love and how my life revolved around the bands and the music at The Pav. It was a wonderful time in my life—I hope my children have such fond memories of their teen years."

Jamie Lamb has the last word on The Pav: "Every generation has its hot spots. Everybody grew up with a place that was the focal point for a Friday or Saturday night. The place to go. For many Orillians, and a large contingent of area cottagers, The Pav was our spot. It's the symbol to many of us of a past that can never be recaptured."

Oro Beach: Lucky Star Pavilion

Donald Hills was not the type of man who would let the Depression keep him down. In 1934, this energetic Toronto electrical contractor constructed a dance pavilion at Oro Beach near Lake Simcoe. His son, Norman, was just a young fellow at the time, but remembers the busy dance hall was an immediate success. Norman says his dad coined the name of the hall from two unrelated areas—a song of the times, and the pavilion's large coloured lamp shade with paper spears which resembled a star: "That's how he came up with The Lucky Star." Norman often emceed dance nights, which gave him experience on stage in front of large numbers of people. [2]

By the 1950s the pavilion was sitting unused, a victim of strong competition from other Lake Simcoe pavilions. But that did not deter two young Barrie entrepreneurs who were looking for a profitable business venture. Jack Phillips and his good friend, Alvin Norrena, revived dancing at the Lucky Star Pavilion in 1958: "Alvin and I offered to give

Activity at the Lucky Star's soda fountain: From the left, Beverly Norrena, Peter Myers and Alvin Norrena serve friends Linda Winter, Norman Ineson and Harold Parker in July 1959. *Courtesy of Jack Phillips*

Mrs. Hills one-half of the proceeds we took in if we could re-open the hall and concession booth." The boys promoted their new dances extensively. The old music format of country and western was quickly nixed in favour of rock 'n' roll music of the late 1950s. "It was strictly records," says Jack, who had wired numerous large speakers around the hall and attached them to the juke box, "We billed the place as Simcoe County's First 'Stereophonic' Dance Hall and the sound was terrific." The dance hall had a unique design with a rounded front facing the street. Coloured lights were strung around the parking lot, giving the hall an 'American Graffiti' atmos-

phere: "We were busy every night. The snack bar was also open during most days of the week for cottagers and picnickers on the beach."

In the autumn of 1960, Jack received a telephone call that he'll never forget: "Someone had broken into the small office we had beside the stage. We think they were searching for the large collection of records we had accumulated over the years. A fire started and completely destroyed the pavilion." It was never re-built, and Mrs. Donald Hills later sold the property.

Barrie Area: Minet's Point Pavilion

The slogan in the old ads for Minet's Point read "Something New Doing Every Dance Night." Maybe that's why just about everyone from Barrie who is old enough to remember this summer pavilion can look back to fun times. And half the fun was getting there. Most people hopped aboard the small ferry boat that whisked you across Kempenfelt Bay to Minet's Point, a trip that took just a few minutes.

Else McConachie writes with her recollections: "I've been wanting for years to tell about Minet's Point Pavilion. I guess it was built in the 1920s with a hardwood floor that was great for gliding around. The band used to be in the centre of the floor, then they moved the stage to the far end of the building, leaving the glass ball of tiny mirrors glittering with the dim lights. Being a young girl of 11 when I first danced there, we did not have to pay— the young men paid for each set of three dances. There was a refreshment booth where you could buy pop, chocolate bars, etc., from either outside or inside the pavilion. There was also a screened porch where you could look out over Kempenfelt Bay. Bob Powell and his orchestra was the band. It was wonderful."

Audrey Fettes and her family used to spend weekends and summer vacations at the cottage on Minet's Point. She writes: "Before we were old enough to dance away our evenings, we would lie in bed at night and hear the music wafting up from the waterfront, wishing we were old enough to be there."

Doug Brown, whose family cottage was close

101

to the pavilion in the 1950s, and writes: "An older man named Sammy owned the hall—he'd let a group of us play records in the afternoon on the jukebox in the corner and dance to songs like "Rock Around The Clock." The full wooden dance floor, always waxed to a very high shine, was surrounded by a

Poster courtesy of Orval Fleetham.

wooden railing. The interior of the pavilion was lit by lights covered with the large Chinese paper lanterns. The pavilion was sold by Sam. One hot summer day when this new owner was sitting on the old grey wooden covered deck, a storm blew up. Lightning hit the very same deck throwing the man clear, but the hall caught fire. In all the excitement, the fire hose was just thrown into the shallow water of the lake and it sucked up sand and gravel. The complete structure burned to the ground and the hall was never rebuilt. Perhaps that's just as well—as some things never age when we store them in our memories."

Else captures the emotional attachment that Minet's Point created for so many people: "I met my first love there and my last love. I'll never forget him, a soldier in the Tank Corps in the pay office. I still have a picture of him in his uniform. Bob Powell played 'I'll Be Seeing You' every night at the pavilion, and this song will forever remind me of Ernest Harbin. I will never forget Minet's Point till the day I die. What a wonderful place!"

Orval Fleetham has been making music in Barrie venues—including Minet's Point—for over 60 years. This well-known musician has worked part-time in many orchestras from as far back as the early 1930s, playing trumpet, trombone and violin. Orval and his wife, Mary, made many friends during the many years they operated a large grocery store in Barrie. As a member of the Russ Waters Orchestra, Orval played at The Pavalon in Orillia with this house band for three years. He later joined the McNeilly Orchestra. Minet's Point was another home for Orval as a musician and was particularly enjoyable for him since Mary also worked at the pavilion running the coat check booth for many years.

Barrie: The Embassy

The hall on 386 Blake Street is now the property of the Barrie Lions Club. Forty years ago when it was built, people in town knew it as the Embassy. Barrie Teen Town, which used local schools until the Embassy was built, began staging their regular dances here; most people remember that the biggest act to grace the stage in those years was Roy Orbison.

Alcona Beach Club

The Alcona Beach Club's hall has a long history of association in the community as both a dance hall and an all-purpose facility, used regularly by members. The pavilion has been renovated but still retains some of its original shape. Muriel (David) McDermott recording early memories:

"Beginning History of Alcona Beach Club"

The Alcona Beach Club was originated in 1927 when Percy David and Roly Gemmell decided that the cottage owners needed an organization to provide recreation and entertainment for the community during the summer months .... The first activities were all outdoor events such as concerts, dances and sing-songs around campfires on the beach ....

In 1929, the hall was built by John Adams .... A band was formed by Vic David, Percy's nephew, who invited some fine musicians from Toronto to play for the Saturday night dances. Admission was ten cents a dance. Vic played the drums and there were usually four other members playing saxophone, clarinet, banjo and piano. The band played every Saturday night during July and August from 1929 to 1940 .... It was not unusual for four generations from one family to attend dances. That is where a lot of the children learned to dance ....

The Sunday sing-song was emceed by Percy David who was a well-known baritone/comedian on the entertainment scene in and around Toronto. Over the years he invited many popular entertainers to appear—Billy Meek, Zena Cheevers, Tom Hamilton, Nancy McCague and Violet Murray. Joe Hailey was his faithful accompanist. These programs continued until about 1955." [3]

Bill O'Neill worked at the hall: "During the years 1940 to 1944 I was in charge at the Alcona Beach Community Hall. My job was to clean the hall, set up seats and benches, set up card tables and to supervise dances during the week. During my time, Monday, Thursday and Friday evenings were dance nights to the recorded music of the Big Bands. We used a Roccola jukebox—I would open the front and trip the switch, allowing dancers to press their favourite selections. Saturday evening was the Big Dance Night with a live band, if available. Labour Day Saturday evening they had a big dance with balloons and lots of other stuff. It was a lot of fun during this time; I learned to dance. There was lots of jiving and swing dancing."

Stroud: Peggy's Pavilion/Peggy's Place

If you're familiar with the corner of Concession 10 and the 25th Sideroad near Stroud, then you'll likely remember the famous Lake Simcoe dance hall which was the site of music and good times for close to four decades. Parsons' Dance Hall. Peggy's Place. Peggy's Pavilion. Or just plain Peggy's!

Back in the 1930s, George and Peggy Parsons purchased this land, cleared the brush and used the logs to construct a general store. George then added a dance hall to the rear portion of the store and, by the early 1940s, dancing at Peggy's was in full swing. Unlike many pavilions which hired live orchestras, the Big Band music at Peggy's boomed from the hall's juke box. The opening of the hall coincided with World War II, which meant that soldiers training at nearby Camp Borden would arrive at Parsons' Dance Hall ready to jive with the local girls. The pavilion was also the site of a giant homecoming party at the end of the War—hundreds of people showed up and celebrated.

Shortly after the pavilion was finished, George added a two-lane bowling alley to the west side of the building and, for a couple of winters, he flooded an area of the grounds so local people cold come and ice skate. The name Peggy's Place, and Peggy's Pavilion, gradually evolved as so many people who lived and holidayed in the area came to know and love Peggy Parsons, an outgoing woman whose business became a landmark on this part of the lake. "Through the week during the summer there were a number of activities at the hall, including card games, roller skating twice a week, and movies," Peggy's daughter Barb told me. During the Queen's Coronation, Peggy brought in her television and set it up on the dance floor. People came from miles around, since this was virtually the only TV set in the area.

Many of the teenagers who came to Peggy's hailed from various parts of Toronto, and danced regularly at halls like Fallingbrook and Balmy Beach, bringing their own unique dance styles with them. Jack Phillips lived in Barrie and says that Peggy's was *the* place to go. He also remembers the various dance fads including "The Drop where everyone would lift a leg, turn slightly and slam their foot down on the dance floor. The whole building shook when dancers' feet hit the floor at the same time—it was great!"

The Parsons knew they couldn't remain

103

static—they had to be prepared to make changes and move with the times. As early rock 'n' roll music made its mark Barb finally convinced her mom and dad to book Toronto's Richie Knight and the Midnites, who were just becoming well-known with their hit, "Charlena." As it turned out, the night was a giant success, and Peggy's Place never looked back. "Once we made the switch to live bands, we were packed every Saturday," says Barb.

When the 1970s arrived, George and Peggy were ready to retire from the business, and rented out the hall to another party who ran dances. The property was then sold and converted into various business for a few years until it was finally demolished in 1990, but not before a few people gathered mementos of one of the hottest summer dance spots on the west side of Lake Simcoe—Peggy's Place.

Jacksons Point: The Royal Casino/Jacksons Point Casino/Peppermint Lounge

With so many dance halls in such a relatively small community, competition was fierce for the dancing dollar at Jacksons Point, a booming summer resort area drawing thousands of people during the summer. During the 1930s, '40s and '50s people jammed the streets of Jacksons Point on hot summer nights. Music floated through the air from the dance halls as people sauntered around stopping at ice cream parlours, the Honey Dew stand, Dog House, Red Spot and the famous "Lav's"—the traditional eatery for people after the dance.

Vita Epstein gives us an overall feel for those wonderful summer days and nights at Jacksons Point. She writes: "Many families had a summer cottage at Jacksons Point in those days. I remember all us teenagers eagerly getting dressed up for the Saturday night dance. As I recall the bands were good and we danced all evening in our youthful energy. It was very enjoyable and we all went home at 12 o'clock."

Depending on the years you visited Jacksons

Parson's Dance Hall as it looked in the 1950s. The music of Elvis was big by the mid-1950s, as were other artists like Paul Anka. Peggy's daughter Barb played the records on the house jukebox, pacing the songs so that there were enough slow songs interspersed with the faster ones.

Peggy Parsons standing in front of her business circa 1950.

Both photos courtesy of Barb Parsons.

(Stroud)

PEGGY'S PAVILION
Presents
THE FUGITIVES
Friday, July 29th
BARRY ALLEN, WES DAKUS
& HIS REBELS
SATURDAY, JULY 30th
LENARDS BEACH, LAKE SIMCOE
45 MILES NORTH OF TORONTO

Point, you'll remember this pavilion by one of its names, the latter coined from the popular New York twist club. It was located on the northwest corner of Jacksons Point Avenue and Lake, in the hub of downtown activity and always busy. Early dances were five cents to get in the door and then five or ten cents for each dance, with dancing contests to liven up the evening.

Jack Bissett was associated with The Royal Casino in the early years and writes about his experience: "In 1933, while the country was still in the Great Depression, I had a friend who had collected a group of musicians together to play at dances in southwestern Ontario. It was brought to his attention that there was a dance pavilion available for rent at Jacksons Point; he located the owners of the property and we opened the pavilion for business. The members of the orchestra each contributed a few dollars, and I was elected to be manager of the pavilion as well. When we arrived at Jacksons Point, we found what looked like a pile of badly weathered shingles, but the rest of the building was in pretty fair condition. There was a good-sized living quarters attached to the building which was to become our home for the next few weeks. We opened for business on May 24th, and stayed open five nights a week until Labour Day. The pavilion was called The Royal Casino and we returned for the next two or three years."

Betty Shillinger's parents owned the Royal for some years. "The orchestra for many years at the Royal Casino was led by Rudy Toth." His band played six nights per week throughout the summer season. "I recall the coloured lights inside the hall, strung along the beams. Four to five hundred people danced here on weekend nights. There were other places to dance at Jacksons Point but ours attracted all the boys and girls—it was just a fun place to go," says Betty. Marlene Phillips has lived in Jacksons Point most of her life and has some memories of the Casino. "Around 1948 people by the name of Newtons purchased the Casino," she writes. "I remember it had a beautiful hardwood floor to dance on; sometimes a live band would play, other times we'd use the jukebox. Later the Casino was sold and renamed to the Peppermint Lounge and was often

used for roller skating." [4]

Ruth Beeforth worked in the Peppermint Lounge from 1959-62 while in her mid-teens: "It was operated at that time by Jack and Millie McMillan and the music was supplied by their son Gord. "It was done by records and the last song he played at every dance was 'Goodnight Sweetheart, Goodnight.' My brother Raymond often helped Gord do the dances. Whenever anyone had a problem they could always count on Millie to listen and try to help. She was like a Den Mother to everyone but was also strict and wouldn't stand for any nonsense from anyone."

The Peppermint Lounge eventually fell into disuse and was torn down.

Jacksons Point: Edgewater Park Dance Pavilion

The Edgewater was "classiest pavilion in Jacksons Point," according to Marlene Phillips: "People always dressed up to dance at The Edgewater Dance Pavilion—it was a special place to take a date." Stephen Sellers constructed the Edgewater in 1934, right on Lake Simcoe near the present site of Bonnie Boats. Along with The Briars, the Edgewater was considered to be a gracious spot to dance. Tables were set around the large dance floor, but on most summer evenings you would find dozens of couples holding hands on the outdoor verandah overlooking the water. Women often wore long dresses with the men in jackets and ties. A large area was set aside for food and soft drinks and, in another section, pinball machines were installed for kids to use during the week. In 1963, the Edgewater Pavilion was torn down, but as a staff member at the marina told me, "The wood from that pavilion ended up all over the area in various structures from the marina here, to barns in the country." [5]

Jacksons Point: Mossington Park Pavilion

Travelling a couple of miles east from the centre of town you could see—until recently—the remains of what was a vibrant and popular summer playground known as Mossington Park. Named after Thomas Mossington (1780-1864), one of early settlers to the

105

The old Mossington Park Pavilion along the banks of the Black River, July 17, 1995, long after its heyday. Unlike nearby dance halls in Jacksons Point, Mossington was a more casual place to dance. This building was torn down in the late 1990s.

area, the park's pavilion was so dilapidated that it was condemned and completely fenced off to protect curiosity seekers from falling through the rotted boards into the Black River. Oshawa musician Tommy Cinnamon played here many times when the hall was filled with dancers. In the Sutton Library, one of the librarians whose aunt owned the combination boathouse/cottage just to the south of the pavilion shared her memories. Her family would stay upstairs while on their holidays: "I can still remember drifting off to sleep to the strains of 'Lipstick on Your Collar' on a warm summer night."[6]

Franklin Beach: The Lighthouse Dance Hall

A drive west from Jacksons Point downtown, takes me to Franklin Beach, home of the once-popular Lighthouse Dance Hall. The *Georgina Advocate* newspaper reported that in 1965 local teenagers marched in protest after the hall was closed down by council "after incidents of fighting and drunkenness." Council must have had a change of heart at some point because the hall continued operations under the ownership of Mrs. Anna Ebner for eight more years until disaster struck. Vale Clark writes about the incident: "On Sunday, February 25, 1973, my husband and I were ice fishing about two miles southwest from Jacksons Point on Lake Simcoe. We had the door of the fish hut open when my husband

Dennis—a member of the Sutton Volunteer Fire Department—noticed a concentration of smoke arising to the east of us along the shore of the lake. He set out towards it on our snowmobile. I remember it well for two reasons: firstly our daughter Jenna Lanette Clark was born during the early hours of the following morning and secondly, that was the day that The Lighthouse burned to the ground." The hall was not rebuilt.

Port Bolster: Roni-Vern Dance Hall

In the early 1940s, Verna Scott-Creber's father, Cyril Scott, purchased a small business in Port Bolster on eastern Lake Simcoe, which consisted of a few cabins. "In 1944, Dad built the dance hall and constructed a restaurant in the front portion of the building," says Verna. "Our family ran dances every Friday and Saturday nights from May to October, bringing in anywhere from 300 to 350 people. The music was provided by a five-piece orchestra from the Oshawa area led by Rudy Spratt, and another band led by Wilf Miller." Cyril began to grow restless with the dance hall and cabin business, and looked for new opportunities in the area. "We sold the pavilion after 1950 and Dad built the drive-in theatre," recalls Verna.

The original building in Port Bolster still stands and has been used by several owners for a variety of purposes over the years. It currently stands unused.

Beaverton: The Commodore

The sign on the rustic log building today still reads The Commodore, but instead of dancing inside, the owners are selling gifts and antiques. At one time this dance hall drew large crowds from nearby Beaverton and the surrounding area. As a poster indicates, there was "Tourist Accommodation" available as well, with "comfortable spring filled mattresses." An anonymous writer gives some great details about The Commodore: "I was a teenager in 1949 and remember the fun we used to have at dance halls. The Commodore was my favourite pavilion on the south

The Roni-Vern Hall, located near Port Bolster and shown here in 1995, was once a dance hall. Over the years it has been home to a number of different business ventures. Currently the building is vacant.

end of Maple Beach. The owners I knew were Mr. and Mrs. Peter Bistrey who ran dances from May to Thanksgiving. Tourists and locals would pack the place. They had a lovely hardwood floor that would be cleaned and waxed weekly. The entrance would be crammed with people for hot dogs with warm buns and pop during intermission. There was no bar, so of course some would cheat outside. Mrs. Bistrey was a big strong lady and watched her crowd closely. Mrs. Carl St. John sold tickets. Many people from far and wide had romances and later marriages from The Commodore. The orchestra was a 10-piece band directed by Charlie Andrews of Orillia. It was wonderful. His son, Ross Andrews, played sax. Mrs. Andrews played piano and Charlie was on bass. The Andrews family owned the Rainbow Room in Orillia

where they played in the winter."

Ross Brethour played sax with Charlie Andrews' orchestra at The Commodore. Ross extended his love of Big Band music a few years ago and became a record producer, establishing his own record company—Nomadic Records—to preserve some very rare live recordings of Canadian Big Bands. The retired public schoolteacher has also written a bio/discography of Mart Kenney and is currently compiling one on Rosemary Clooney.

Today's Commodore Antique and Gift Shop was the site of many memorable dances near Beaverton. People often still stop in and reminisce with the current owners about their dance hall days here. This photo was taken in 1995.

Poster courtesy of Ross Brethour.

Chapter Eight

THROUGH THE HALIBURTON HIGHLANDS INTO THE KAWARTHAS

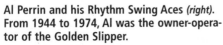

Al Perrin and his Rhythm Swing Aces *(right)*. From 1944 to 1974, Al was the owner-operator of the Golden Slipper. *Courtesy of the* Haliburton Echo.

The Golden Slipper *(left)* on the shore of Kashagawigamog Lake, a dance pavilion for **43 years.** *Courtesy of the* Haliburton Echo.

Haliburton: The Golden Slipper

At its peak, more than 600 people would jam into Haliburton's Golden Slipper nightly, dancing to bands like Al Perrin and His Rhythm Swing Aces. Al wrote an article for the *Haliburton County Echo*, not long after the last owners, Haliburton Youth Development, demolished the building. Here are some of Al's words:

"Friday, February 18th, 1977, was the last of what has been a landmark, a place of recreation and dancing—where people of all ages for the past 43 years gathered, met and danced. The guideline was 'Where friends meet friends and make friends,' dancing at the Golden Slipper. Back in 1934, Roy LaBoutillier built the dance pavilion on the north shore of Kashagawigamog Lake. He decided on the

name from the square dance number, 'Oh Those Golden Slippers.' Al Perrin, with his dance band, joined Roy to supply the music and continued playing until 1944 when Al took the Slipper over, operating it until 1974. Al then sold it to Wren Blair. The Slipper will always be remembered for the smooth, highly polished hardwood, easy-to-dance-on floor. On some evenings there would be as many as 12 square dancing sets on the floor.

"The bands who performed will no doubt be remembered by a good many. One musician in particular, Frank Faulkner, will be remembered for his laughing saxophone and as a gold medallist square dance fiddler. Other musicians who at different times played the Slipper were Chris Young, Al Blanchard, Claude Wade, Marshal Leighton, Eddy Oscopella, Bob White, Red Greer, Carl Holmstrom and Gordon

108

Kennedy. One piano player in particular, in the early days of the Slipper, was the late Mary Wood who was admired and liked by everybody. From 1950 until 1966, Fred Clements took charge of the band and will be remembered for both his good principles, as well as being a good musician and master of the piano. Other accomplished musicians included Harold Broadhagen on violin, Harold Moore on sax and clarinet and Harry Bagshaw on bass. Harold Broadhagen also owned and captained the *Queen Mary*, a passenger boat that made trips to the Slipper on Kashagawigamog Lake.

"In 1966, the young people demanded rock music, so a band was contracted to play modern, square and rock dance music to please everybody. They were called The Telstars: later they changed their name to the Bad Habits. The group proved to be a wonderful band that drew people from as far away as Lindsay, Peterborough and Huntsville on a Saturday night. When the parking lot filled up, cars were lined for a half mile in both directions from the Slipper.

"After 40 years of owning and being associated with the Slipper, Al decided to sell the pavilion. So for a good many people, we say with deep feelings of nostalgia, so ended a most colourful, popular and widely known dance pavilion in the Highlands of Haliburton—The Golden Slipper."

Carnarvon: Medley's Dance and Bowl

Carnarvon Lanes sits at the southeast corner of Highways 35 and 118, two busy highways threading their way into Ontario's cottage country. The building has been refaced with brickwork and siding and a full-length verandah has recently been added along one side. These are only cosmetic changes, though; the underlying handiwork of Bud Medley is to be found in the basic structure, for it was he and his wife, Muriel, who constructed this building which was known for miles around as Medley's Dance and Bowl.

In 1946, Bud and Muriel were busy developing their idea for a dance hall and bowling alley in Carnarvon, about nine miles north of Minden. "My

father owned the four corners of highways 35 and 118," Muriel told me. Bud purchased the southeast corner from his father-in-law with the intention of building their business and home on the site. As with many innovative hall owners, Bud designed and constructed it himself. The couple felt that while the dance portion of the business upstairs would be great for the summer season, the bowling action would last year-round. May 24, 1948, saw the first dance at Medley's and the place was a hit. Many organizations and church groups throughout the area started bowling leagues, meeting at Medley's. Bud says one attraction that really brought the crowds in, especially in the afternoons, was Muriel's home baking.

The official opening of Medley's took place on the Monday of the Civic Holiday in 1948 and, as a special presentation, the Medleys hired Mart

109

Medley's Dance and Bowl at Carnavon, under construction. *Courtesy of Bud and Muriel Medley.*

Stan Pederson practises his barbering skills on Mart Kenney's band members while on the road, circa 1930. *Courtesy of Mart Kenney.*

Kenney, an engagement which was one to remember for Bud and Muriel. Bud explains. "When the dance was over the party began. One of Mart's band members gave shaves and haircuts to a half dozen of the band members up on the stage, the old Wurlitzer was turned up and our staff joined other band members on the dance floor. Meanwhile, Mart was discussing blueprints with me in the kitchen over hamburgers." At this time Mart Kenney was planning his Ranch in Woodbridge and was very interested in Bud's design.

By the 1960s, the Medleys could see that rock 'n' roll was the music of choice for a whole new generation. The couple advertised their dances extensively in local newspapers and put up posters all over the area. Bud added an extra: "I'd also put a speaker on our car and drive around to all the lodges and beach areas broadcasting that evening's event or attraction."

Bud and Muriel were very involved with their community: "We gave various organizations a free day on the lanes in the spring so they could raise money." Muriel was one of the driving forces with her U.C.W. group to establish a nursing/seniors home in Minden in mid-'60s. When the doors of Hyland Crest were officially opened, the event represented a very satisfying conclusion to a campaign in which Muriel had been involved every step of the way.

After investing close to 30 years of their life in the business, they were ready to move on to a quieter pace. "We sold the business in February 1976," says Muriel. Bud adds, "We've never looked back—we certainly enjoyed our years but we were glad to retire." The hall has changed hands a number of times since then.

Coboconk: Wonderland Pavilion

If one word could describe Nathan Pearce, the Coboconk man who built Wonderland in 1939, that word would be "innovative." He was an individual who could solve problems and make an idea work through his uncanny ability to create solutions. A welder at General Motors for many years, the owner of the local White Rose service station in Coboconk

and a farmer as well, "Natie" designed and built the pavilion just outside of Coboconk at the northern tip of Balsam Lake. His wife, Gertrude, also worked with him running the dances.

Gertude and Nathan Pearce, circa 1960s. *Courtesy of Annie Robertson.*

Nathan's daughter Annie and her teenaged friends were beginning to dance at some of the local pavilions, so Nathan decided to check out these halls and see just what the attraction was for the younger people. As Annie remembers, "Dad thought that there would be enough demand in this area to support another dance pavilion, and he decided to proceed with the project on his property." Wonderland's name came about quite naturally. As Natie was constructing the hall, people would often stop by and ask him about his new building. "Since people were continually wondering what he was doing, he just decided to call the pavilion 'Wonderland,'" explains Annie. "After dance night, the floor was first cleaned with a push broom to remove any debris. The next step was to polish the floor. My father designed his own polisher to maintain this surface from a thick piece of raw fleece shorn from his sheep on the farm. He then attached the fleece to a unique two-by-four frame. Powdered wax was always sprinkled on the floor, to be worked in by the dancers."

At this time there was no hydro near the pavilion site, so Natie acquired an old gas generator that had once been used to run the street lights in Coboconk, to juice up the lighting system in the hall.

From time to time the generator would cut out, leaving the pavilion in darkness, but not for too long. Nathan would pull out his trusty coal oil lanterns until power could be restored, and the band would just play some instrumental music. Hydro was installed in the later 1940s.

The crowds were so large that after one year Nathan had to build a walkway around the perimeter of the hall to extend space on the dance floor. The rails were constructed with cedar branches cut and peeled from his property. The PA system for the stage was another Natie Pearce design, powered by a series of large batteries. "You could always hear the square dance caller at our hall," says Annie. "We had three squares per night at Wonderland, along with a good variety of modern music as well."

Winters can be fierce in Coboconk. A young Nathan Pearce shovels snow from the roof of Wonderland.
Courtesy of Annie Robertson.

People would be turned away some nights, it was so full. Annie recalls a dance that took place towards the end of the summer in 1939. "One of the band members had gone out to his car and turned on the radio. He returned to the stage and announced that World War II had just been declared. The crowd was very sombre that evening." Annie explains that there was no final dance. "Dad had suffered a heart attack in 1966 and didn't open up the next year; that was the end of Wonderland." The building then sat on the family's property until the early 1980s.

Kinmount: Crystal Pier Marina Dance Hall

Like a lonely sentry, the Crystal Pier Marina dance pavilion sits on the shore of Crystal Lake, reminding passing boaters of the days when many cottagers looked forward to the lively Saturday night dances that Ken and Ida Young held here for many years. These happy Saturday nights will be forever engraved in the refreshment stand counter where dancers carved their names, dates, favourite band or love interest. Ken and Ida retired from the business as their eight kids grew up and started cutting their own paths in life, but it wasn't so very many years ago when the Crystal Pier Marina was the centre of activity on the lake, where cottagers gassed up, bought supplies, stored their boats and, of course, came to dance.

From the year it was built, the dance hall at Crystal Pier Marina was a beacon that could be seen from far out on the lake. The single story wooden pavilion was set 70% out on the water. The building is over 50 years old, constructed originally by a fellow named Thoms who established a marina and lodge business. "Thoms began a tradition of having a smorgasbord on Sunday night—people would stop off to eat before heading home," says Ida. The Youngs began their own special annual affair on the lake. Every Civic Holiday weekend they opened up their grounds for an annual pig roast. Hundreds would attend this free mid-summer celebration.

"We never hired live bands here," says Ken. Instead, the Seabreeze jukebox was filled with current

The dance hall at Crystal Pier Marina was set well over the water. Today it is used for storage.

111

hit songs: "The kids would bring in their own records for the jukebox, and then they'd pay to listen to them during the week, or when our disc jockey, Glenn Elliott, was taking a break on a Saturday night." There were also some arcade machines in the hall which would be played by kids from the lake during the week: "The parents would always know where their kids were, and we kept a close eye on them." Many couples first met here recalls Ken: "One man drove his girlfriend into the driveway a few years ago and presented her with a diamond engagement ring—he felt it was romantic to propose on the site where they met and had their first dance together."

"When the family finally shut down the business in 1983, there was a general sadness that

Carving one's name into the counter became a Crystal Pier tradition.

crept over the lake that year," says Ida. Even though they have retired from the business, the Youngs will always be very special people on Crystal Lake, especially evident throughout the summer months as boaters continually wave and shout greetings to the family as they motor by.

Fenelon Falls: The Cameo

Hope (McPhee) O'Rourke writes about the Cameo Pavilion's early days in Fenelon Falls: "It was built by my father, Edward McPhee, who had a decorating business in Lindsay and was well known in the area .... We had many good bands play at the Cameo and among them was Gilbert Watson. Luigi Romanelli from the King Edward Hotel played for one night, which was very special for me as it was my 16th birthday. Many people came in evening dress and drove 40 or 50 miles. My father later sold the

business to Jack Marshall from Peterborough who then had a band of his own."

Jack Marshall's son, Jim, lives in Fenelon Falls where he and his wife operate a business not far from the old dance hall. Jim also has good memories of growing up around the pavilion which his father purchased in the mid-1940s. "I remember listening to Buddy Holly and the Crickets doing 'That'll Be The Day' on an old 78 rpm record in the Wurlitzer jukebox we had in the hall—I guess I was about 11 at the time," he says. "The hall was open during the week all summer long so kids could come in, play records and the pin-ball machines and get a soda." Jack ran a pretty tight ship, forbidding alcohol in his hall. As a result, the drinking crowd would often head over to one of the other nearby halls: "There was never much worry about fights at the Cameo." Jim thinks the only blood spilled on the dance floor might have been his own, thanks to a bite he suffered from his pet hamster which he carried around the hall in a blue Seagram's bag.

Jack was known throughout the area as an accomplished musician. "My dad started his own

Jack Marshall, a veteran musician and bandleader, acquired the Cameo about 1944.
Courtesy of Jim Marshall.

band very early—I can recall a shot of a 1929 Chev with the name 'Jack Marshall' on the spare tire. Dad would often play the American Hotel on a Saturday night and was at the organ in church the next morning." Jack would also tour for the Rotary Club playing the Hammond organ and was given the title of life member of the Musicians' Union. In the mid-

The dance pavilion overlooking Cameron Lake on Fenelon Falls. *Courtesy of Hope (McPhee) O'Rourke.*

The 2500 square feet of floor space combined with great music made the Cameo a popular dance hall.

1950s, Jack was asked to manage the Edgewater Pavilion in Bobcaygeon. Jim remembers, "For a couple of years dad was commuting between the two pavilions during the summer."

Jim says that Mart Kenney played the Cameo, a night that Mart covers in his book: "After the bomb was dropped on Japan, the war was over. When the celebrations for V.J. Day started, we happened to be at the Cameo Pavilion in Fenelon Falls. The people at the dance were obviously buoyed up by the news, but the atmosphere was one of happy relief rather than wild celebration."[1]

Marge Lucas remembers going to the Cameo when she was about 15. "My first dance date was at the Cameo and Mart Kenney played," she writes. "Both my date and I spent the afternoon arguing with our parents to get permission to go—we were at last able to be part of what up until then we had only seen from the boat out in the lake. The Cameo was a typical frame pavilion, built right on the water's edge. There were just benches along the walls. But with music like Jack Marshall's, who wanted to sit anyway? Every time I hear the 'Johnstone Rag' I think of those nights. The dance floor was huge and beautifully maintained. Hanging in the centre was a mirrored globe which revolved during waltzes. Three sides of the building were surrounded with a verandah—very dimly lit—real romantic, with a great view of the lake and the boats of people who had come to hear the music which seems to take on a special magic when heard coming across the water. Tradition was that the Cameo opened Easter weekend. One year around 1950 the ice was barely out of the lake and there was no heat in the building. But Jack rigged up some form of temporary heating and we bundled up in our coats and gloves and danced. I will always remember the delightful fun evenings spent at the Cameo."

Jack sold the business around 1960, at which

113

time dancing ceased and a marina was established. Today a new restaurant is located on this site.

Sturgeon Lake: Greenhurst Dance Pavilion

It was late April when I drove down the hill leading to Sturgeon Lake and stopped to gaze at one of the few original dance halls remaining in Ontario. The green-and-white clapboard barn-shaped building with its sign sandwiched between two red "Drink Coca-Cola" globes said it all—Greenhurst Dance Pavilion, one of the oldest operating dance pavilions in Ontario, the exterior basically unchanged from the day Martin Thurston opened his hall in 1932.

Before my eyes I was looking at not just a building, but history. Musical history. Romantic history. Social history. I tried to visualize the years when patrons would arrive here by horse and buggy and in Model T's, dressed in their finest clothes to dine and dance to orchestras. My mind then went over what only could be described as Greenhurst's "Golden Era" through the 1960s when Toronto's famous Little Caesar and the Consuls filled the pavilion with dancers almost every Saturday night of the summer. I then thought about some of the more recent years as different owners tried so hard to keep Greenhurst viable.

As I walked through the pavilion doors where tens of thousands of people had gone before me, the old wooden floor squeaked with each step I took, as if the old hall was welcoming me.

The Greenhurst Dance Pavilion shortly after it opened in 1932. *Courtesy of Joe Kondyjowski.*

Immediately on my right, I noticed an old set of Toledo "No Springs, Honest Weight" scales. Martin Thurston bought these brand new when he opened his hall, and charged one penny per use. A little further into this tongue-and-groove panelled entrance room was a bank of arcade machines—high-tech video games for today's players, but still reminders of the old five-cent pinball games that once stood in their place.

The larger inner chamber on the ground floor is a games room, with a small bar and stools, tables, dart boards and billiard tables set up for leisure time pursuits. Advertising posters from previous years adorn the wall, a testament to the recent bands who have hauled their equipment up the stairs to the stage, located on the second floor. The wide stairway leading up to the dance floor level has felt so many pairs of feet over the years that the wood has been worn down at least an inch and a half, leaving a visible hump in the middle. The large second storey of Greenhurst Pavilion is the focal point of the pavilion and its reason for being—the dance floor. The post and beam construction exposes rafters from which a few signs, coloured lights and speakers are hung. Dancers take in whatever summer breeze manages to find its way through the windows where shutters are propped open for the evening. The large dance floor surrounds a semi-circular raised stage, a podium where every imaginable form of dance music has been performed by orchestras and bands for over 65 years.

"Dancing in the area started back in 1917 when Martin Thurston returned from World War I and started a regular dance in a large barn-like structure just behind the present site of Greenhurst," explains Helen Lines, who purchased the business with her husband from Martin in 1952. "Martin decided to build a new hall in the late '20s, and opened the present pavilion around 1932."

Edna Templeton writes about the early years at Greenhurst: "From 1924 to 1933 we spent part of the summer at Thurstonia Park and in the evenings we would go to the pavilion. Before I was old enough to go dancing I'd go with the other kids and help spread the dance floor wax by sliding around the floor. The orchestra I remember best was led by Ferde Mowry. Our mothers walked us to the dance hall and sat at the side on benches or in the ice cream parlour on the lower floor. We could walk back to our cottages with our date, or our mothers would wait for us."

Peggy (Reynolds) Challice has her own recollections of Greenhurst: "The summer of 1939 was the beginning of the best ten summers of my life. My parents rented a cottage in Greenhurst and my mother and father became instant friends of Martin and Vi Thurston, owners of the pavilion. Mr. Thurston suggested that my father might like to help out on dance nights, selling tickets for jitney dancing. My sister and I were allowed to sit on a bench near my dad and listen to the music and watch the dancers. The orchestra was conducted by Jack Galloway. I can still see that band, the men with their white jackets and black pants, and oh, the music! It left quite an impression on a six-year-old. The summers at Greenhurst, with the moon over the lake and the music, the men in their white flannels and the gals with their gorgeous strapless dresses is something I will never forget."

Florence Reynolds writes that she still retains the "great memories of Greenhurst Pavilion. A student at Oakwood Collegiate, I was working at the Thurstonia Lodge Hotel as a waitress. Away from home for the first time, a summer romance bloomed with a student from Bloor Collegiate who was working on a farm near Bobcaygeon. We met at Greenhurst and dance nights were 'the nights' to be remembered. The Summer of '42! Although it was during World War II, it didn't seem to touch any of us that summer. Great music, great summers—the memories live on!"

Joan Olesuk writes that she had great fun times and experiences at dance pavilions: "I was a waitress at Thurstonia Park, Dunsford, and remember hearing 'Blue Moon' for the first time in my life, played by Paul Minacola and His Orchestra."

It was at Greenhurst that Gord Daniels met his future wife, Betty, in July 1955: "She was staying at a cabin almost directly across from the pavilion, my friend and I drove past in our '50 Merc, we waved

at each other and the rest is history. I was 17 and could not dance very well. She was 18 and could dance real good, so I learned to dance that summer of

The Don Hopkins Orchestra on stage at Greenhurst in 1940. Back row (l-r): Keith Hesselton (Moose Jaw) drums; Harry Positsky (Ottawa) bass. Centre (l-r): Ted Donaldson (Ottawa) piano; Bob Robinson (Leamington) trumpet; Ted Everet (Peterborough) trombone; Buck Positsky (Ottawa) trombone; Don Hopkins (St. Thomas) trumpet & vocals. Front (l-r): Don (Pooky) Cowan (Winnipeg) tenor sax; Norm Bigras (Ottawa) alto sax lead; Jack Ellison (Port Stanley) alto 3rd. *Courtesy of Freda Hopkins.*

'55 at Greenhurst. We've been together ever since, and it all started in Greenhurst."

Freda Hopkins has a musical connection with Greenhurst, as well as an astute observation of the times. "In 1940, my husband's band played here—he was Don Hopkins," writes Freda. "That summer Italy went into the War on Germany's side. Martin Thurston was afraid locals might burn down his dance hall because we had two Italian men in the orchestra (second-generation Canadians, by the way!). The dance finished at 12 o'clock and we drove our two musicians back to London, Ontario—they were enlisted men waiting to be called up by the Canadian Military. That memory will stay with me forever."

Fred and Helen Lines' move to Greenhurst began one of the most dynamic periods in Ontario dance pavilion history. With Fred taking care of the "behind the scenes" responsibilities, Helen was the person everybody came to know, and associate with Greenhurst. Honest, fair, no-nonsense, respected and loved by almost everybody who had the pleasure of meeting her, Helen Lines soon became affectionately

115

known by patrons as "Mom," and even "Ma." When the Lines first took over Greenhurst, the music was mainly Big Band style, with Paul Minacola from Peterborough being the usual summer house orchestra. Says Helen, "As rock 'n' roll began to take roots, I felt the new brand of music would draw far more— I could see the movement, so one day I decided to hire the Lincolnaires from Oshawa. It was the right

An aerial view of Greenhurst in 1954. *Courtesy of Pat McEachern.*

time for change and the crowds began to increase in size immediately."

Steve Macko, who was a member of Lincolnaires in the late 1950s and who later went on to play with Little Caesar, remembers coming into Green-

hurst as the first rock band. He says that Mrs. Lines was a very knowledgeable and astute business person: "She could see trends in the music business and was not afraid to move in the direction she felt would bring in more people and subsequently more money. Greenhurst was busy every weekend—from 800 to 1000 kids would show up on a Saturday night." But the weight of the crowd, combined with raunchier dancing, put immense strain on the upstairs floor, especially when Steve's band would blast into its finale with the rock anthem of the day, 'Shout.' The dance floor could actually be seen moving with the rhythm of the music." The owners had to double joist every second joist to support the movement of the dance floor.

Helen had a strict dress code for the bands and that included her favourites—Little Caesar: "They usually wore suits and ties, even during the hottest summer nights. The band once told me, 'If we're not sweating, we're not working!' " The group would often stay after the dance concluded, talking, playing pinball and generally having a good time. Helen's great affection for all the guys in Little Caesar is evident as she talks about them by name—Bruce (Morsehead), Tommy (Wilson), Ken (Pernokis),

The original Little Caesar and the Consuls in the early 1960s. They were the house band at Greenhurst for countless Saturday-night dances and were still performing around Ontario as recently as the late 1990s.
Courtesy of Joe Kondyjowski.

Steve (Macko). "They were almost like sons or nephews to me."

Joanne Farrell remembers Little Caesar and The Consuls at Greenhurst. She writes: "Every weekend during the summer in 1965 when I was 15, a gang of us would drive from Streetsville up to my girlfriend's cottage on Sturgeon Lake. Excitement and anticipation ran high! We would arrive, have a swim then set our hair in rollers, primping and preparing for the Greenhurst dance that night. We danced to Little Caesar and the Consuls—remember the song 'Poison Ivy?' What a thrill!"

The time eventually came when Mr. and Mrs. Lines decided to sell Greenhurst. Helen says they both agreed that they had reached the end of their tenure at the hall: "I did love our time at Greenhurst and didn't consider it work—the days were long, but it was a labour of love." A subsequent owner of the landmark pavilion was Lawrence Schurman who took over around 1982. He carried out some remodelling and repairs and a liquor licence was obtained.

Adam Parry learned the business of running a dance pavilion from the broomstick up during the years his family ran The Kee to Bala (formerly Dunn's Pavilion). The Kee was also where Adam met Andrea Smith of Bala, when she came to work at the dance hall. Years later, when the couple learned that Greenhurst was on the market, they decided to fulfill a dream they shared. "We purchased Greenhurst in 1990," Adam says. "We booked in bands that appealed to a wide variety of people." In addition to Little Caesar making an annual appearance, the Parrys hired many bands covering material by popular artists. "We had a good cross-section of music with rock and country—something for everybody."

In the summer of 1994, a very emotional band reunion took place at Greenhurst. Janette Parker from Lindsay explains: "I have older sisters who attended Greenhurst years ago and enjoyed the Big Band sounds of Paul Minacola. When it was my turn in the '60s I went to hear Little Caesar and the Consuls. Way back then I also sang in a band. In 1982, a friend of mine thought it would be fun to do a big reunion of the four bands that had been around

Lindsay in the '60s. We called ourselves Elbow Room and have played in and around Lindsay for the past ten years, doing all '50s and '60s music. We played our last dance on the August 1st long weekend 1994, but the great part about that was the fact we did it at Greenhurst. The night was sold out and we had a marvellous time, seeing friends we hadn't seen in years. We have all wanted to play Greenhurst, but never got the chance until the very last dance."

Greenhurst changed hands once again in 1997. Oshawa businessman Lucky Sodhi purchased the hall and tried to inject new life into the venerable pavilion. Tragically, Greenhurst Pavilion was torched by an arsonist in October 1998, causing heavy damage to the great hall. By order of the local Fire Marshall, Greenhurst was torn down in the summer of 1999.

Bobcaygeon: Edgewater Pavilion

April and Ric Scott wanted a descriptive name for their newly purchased cottage rental business in Bobcaygeon and finally decided upon Water's Edge—Cottages For All Seasons. What they did not realize at the time of their choice was that the property was once the site of Bobcaygeon's popular summer dance hall, built 60 years previously and named—ironically—the Edgewater Pavilion.

Author Stanley Redman, who resides in Midland, recalls his experiences during the early years of the Edgewater. "When I finished high school at Runnymede in 1933 and had no job, my family heard that a dance hall was to be built in Bobcaygeon," he writes. "We all thought it might be an idea for me to open a boat livery adjacent, so I ended up with 100 feet of Sturgeon Lake shoreline next to the pavilion." Stan's business was called Kawartha Craft Boats. "The Saturday night of the grand opening there were massive crowds and gridlock on the parking lot and nearby roads. But attendance began to sag and the crowds turned to Greenhurst near Sturgeon Point. I had rigged up a sound system in my boathouse and used to play sentimental records for those who left the dance to rent canoes from me. They drifted around the lake until I

117

The Edgewater Dance Pavilion at Bobcaygeon, about 1945.

Jack Brown's Band from Welland pose on the steps of the Edgewater, circa 1934.

Both photos courtesy of Stanley Redman.

played Ted Lewis' recording of 'Goodnight.' My dad bought me a 28-foot launch and I was able to augment my income by picking up passengers at the Bobcaygeon town dock and bringing them to the dance hall for five cents. Next summer they hired Jack Brown and his band from the Welland House in St. Catharines—a great bunch and nice music. A couple of seasons later they hired Ferde Mowry, who played at the famed Embassy Club in Toronto."

After Stan left this part of the country the pavilion continued under new owners, Skip Vaughn and Mike Kubnicki, who provided new energy and great music. "We brought in other musicians from Oshawa and Peterborough and put together a good orchestra, which brought back the dancers," says Skip. The men also booked in many well-known orchestras as guest bands during the years they owned the Edgewater. For a couple of years after Skip's departure, Jack Marshall from Fenelon Falls also managed the Edgewater in Bobcaygeon. Hoteliers Eugene Sheedy and his brother followed Jack into the

Edgewater, feeling that the business would be a good investment along with their hotel interests in Peterborough. Unfortunately, the brothers were unable to attract large crowds to the dance hall. "By this time people were going to drive-in movies and bingo games," says Eugene. Eventually the pavilion's property was sold and the dance pavilion dismantled.

Margaret Dobbie and her husband moved to Bobcaygeon in 1965 and purchased the property adjacent to the site of the pavilion. She writes: "The Edgewater was no longer there, just an empty field, but I know quite a few people born and raised and still living in Bobcaygeon who remember it well."

On a warm moonlit night, if you listen very carefully, you might just pick up a few strains of 'Goodnight,' signalling to the couples romantically drifting in their canoes on the still water that it is time to return to shore.

Chapter Nine

PETERBOROUGH AND ENVIRONS

Juniper Island Pavilion and Sunset Pavilion are landmarks in the Stony Lake region.

Peterborough: Rye's Pavilion

One pavilion in Peterborough with a reputation for swinging times, hot music, big crowds and a fun atmosphere was Rye's. Located near a small public park on the Otonabee River, the old wooden building was torn down long ago. Affectionately known by some as the local "Bucket of Blood," Rye's was also the meeting place for hundreds of young couples during its time, couples who can look back to their first shy dances with each other.

Son of the original owner, Herb Rye was in his 80s and lived with his wife just across the river from where his dad ran the boat business that made the Rye name quite well known in Peterborough. "My dad, Harold, ran a canoe and paddle manufacturing enterprise and boat livery on the Otonabee

River," says Herb. "In the '19-teens', Dad invented a unique paddle-making machine which improved the contours of the paddle, and also cut the time it took to make a paddle to one minute per oar." When Harold received a small inheritance in 1922, he decided to expand his business. "So Dad hired Mr. Sloan, a local contractor, to oversee the construction of a dance pavilion, wood frame, set up on a foundation of posts."

The hall operated six nights per week during the summer months and year-round in later years when furnaces were added. Some of the orchestras who set up on Rye's stage included Ferde Mowry, Bert Niosi, Eddie Stroud, Mose Yokum, Benny Kline, Gordon Picard and His Girls' Band and Roy Locksley. Jitney dancing was popular in the early years of the pavilion. Harold actually approached

Harold Rye, *(above left)* **the originator of the dance pavilion bearing his name, photo circa 1930s.**

The Roy Locksley's Orchestra on stage at Rye's Pavilion circa 1920s. From left to right: Gord Robertson, sax; Sammy Silvarstein, trumpet; Curley Rosen, drums; Roy Locksley, leader; ___, piano. *Both photos courtesy of Herb Rye.*

Ovaltine to see if they would be interested in placing an ad on the back of the tickets—this was one of the early forms of corporate advertising on event tickets.

By the end of the 1930s, Harold's summers were busy with his boat business and dance hall both thriving. When a local truck fleet owner, Herb Payne, approached him about running dances there, Harold decided to rent the hall to him. Herb Payne later purchased the pavilion but retained the name Rye's. Payne operated the pavilion for a number of years and eventually opened another pavilion in Bridgenorth—The Pines. Rye's was sold and the next owner demolished the pavilion. A house was later erected on the site.

Well-known Peterborough resident and historian Marlow Banks recalled one particular evening when a few of the local lads were not happy with the calibre of music being played by a band which had been brought in from the States. "These fellows decided to show their displeasure with the music by tossing a couple of stink bombs under the pavilion floor, effectively stopping the music and clearing out the crowd for the remainder of the evening."

Jack Ainslie was part of the "south end gang"

and lived near Rye's. "I made my first dollar working at Rye's sweeping floors, and taking tickets" says Jack. "It was pretty good pickings for a young sweeper in those days. There were a lot of 'Fancy Dans' who'd walk around with a long strip of dance tickets hanging out of their breast pocket, so when a fellow wanted to get out on the dance floor with a young lady he had his eye on, he'd simply put out his cigarette, even if he had just lit it." One vivid recollection Jack has is the large chimney at Rye's where a sign was posted that read "Stop, Smile, Dance A While." Harold Rye ran a good hall, according to Jack who echoes the words of many other people who recall the early days of this pavilion. However, under the management of Herb Payne, the personality of the dance hall changed. Bands were encouraged to shorten their three-song sets so that more tickets could be sold. "No sooner had a song ended than the rope boys had them hustled off the floor so a new group of dancers could start," says Jack.

Molly McNaughton in Peterborough met her husband through Rye's Pavilion. "He took tickets at the dance and would also come up to Dean's Cafe with other staff members and the band. I would often

One of Andy Rutter's early bands included Del Crary (far right) and both Minacola brothers, posing on a Dodge Phaeton sometime in the late 1930s. *Courtesy of Andy Rutter.*

help my sister at the cafe and this is where I met my future husband." Mr. and Mrs. McNaughton were married for 43 years.

Perhaps the most eerie story about Rye's comes from a friend of mine—singer, musician and songwriter Geoff Hewittson, whose house is very close to the old site of Rye's. "One summer night I awoke and, through the open window, I swear I could hear faint strains of Big Band music and the noise you associate with crowds dancing and having a good time. I went back to sleep, woke up a little later, and the same sounds were still there. It was very strange." Very strange indeed, because at that time Geoff had no idea that Rye's Dance Pavilion had ever existed. Had the ghosts of Rye's decided to make one last appearance?

Peterborough: Brock Street Arena/Brock Summer Gardens/Brock Ballroom

If buildings could talk, then the old Brock Street Arena in downtown Peterborough would have many tales to tell. From the early days as a natural ice arena, through its many years as the city's premier ballroom, right up to the present where it houses a giant food market, Brock Street Arena has always been able to draw a crowd. To learn just how an old arena built in the late 1800s had new life injected into its soul, a visit with Andy Rutter, who was there when the transformation began to take place, proved to be most informative:

"The owners in the early '30s were Rolly Glover, publisher of the *Peterborough Examiner*, politician and general entrepreneur, E. V. Warn, who owned a piano store, and Sarsh Sheedy, a local builder," said Andy. According to him, the Brock Arena began running dances in the summer of 1934, and these events were originally managed by a relative of Andy's, Osias LaPlante. In the winter a natural ice rink was maintained for hockey games and other ice activities.

In the early 1930s, Andy was playing the

121

The Mose Yokum Orchestra of 1934 to 1940. From left to right: Al Phfifer, Gord Robertson, Andy Rutter, Emmett McGrath, George Gatfield, Mose Yokum, Hal McFarlane, Curly Gibson, Tap Thornbeck, Pat Connell, Jack Thackery. *Courtesy of Andy Rutter.*

violin and bass as a young man; he also sang, MC'd, and generally organized entertainment for many affairs in Peterborough. He joined the Mose Yokum Orchestra, a popular Peterborough band. In 1936, the owners of the Brock called Andy and asked if he would take over management duties back in Peterborough after Osias died. "I wanted to really make the arena a special place for dancing during the non-hockey months but transforming a huge arena into an elegant dance hall was no easy task," Andy said. So he put his flair for music and atmosphere to work: "I had a good 4,000-square-foot parquet hardwood floor laid down for the dancing months, and a 2,000-square-foot boardwalk with railing going around the perimeter of dance area. Ropes surrounded the floor so that tickets could be collected from the dancers." Walls were refurbished, chairs painted, a dozen colourful eight-foot-square crepe paper chandeliers treated with fireproof material were hung 12 feet down from the ceiling and a large stage with a capacity for 20 musicians was built. Andy put the Brock in the black for the owners.

In 1937, Andy was offered the chance to buy the arena for $8,500, a considerable sum in those years of hardship. He then worked feverishly to complete his project of creating beauty and a feeling of intimacy out of the cavernous arena by adding areas of white stone pebbles, a fountain, a pool and a flowering arbour just inside the front entrance. "The stage was redecorated as well with a background of royal colours and photos of the King and Queen, and I had soft lighting installed throughout the building. Once I was owner I decided to build a very classy dance hall." Eddie Stroud and Norman Harris were two of the original house bands to play the Brock during Andy's tenure. Later, bands led by Peterborough musicians Hal McFarlane and Del Crary were hired. Andy had more than two good years at the Brock. The dances closed in early October at which time the dance floor and decorations were dismantled to make way for the winter OHA hockey. "About 1938 I decided to sell the building after I was accepted at Quaker Oats," says Andy. He sold the business in 1939 to Mr. Brown, who also owned the Port Hope pavilion.

The magical Summer Gardens had the best entertainment in town says Marlow Banks. "We had most of the big names like Benny Goodman, Tommy Dorsey, Stan Kenton, Eddie Spivak, Count Basie and Guy Lombardo. At the time I don't think we

An early view of Club Aragon, circa late 1940s.
Courtesy of Fran Domenic.

Jack and Gertrude Wineberg ran Club Aragon from 1946 to the early 1970s.
Courtesy of Fran Domenic.

appreciated the widespread fame of these bands."

Sylvia Ducharme writes about her brother's association with music in Peterborough: "Back in the 1930s my late brother Jack 'Curly' Gibson was the singer with Mose Yokum's band at Rye's, and then with Hal McFarlane at the Brock Street Summer Gardens. He later went to Niagara Falls and sang at the General Brock Hotel and then to London before coming back to Peterborough as assistant manager of the old Centre Theatre on George Street."

In the 1960s, the Brock Ballroom began booking rock 'n' roll acts for the teens in Peterborough. The Lincolnaires from Oshawa played here many times; former band member Steve Macko remembers the Brock. "The hall held at least 1000 dancers and featured a two-tiered stage with a gleaming white grand piano," he says. The Brock was also the first place that Steve saw Ronnie Hawkins play live. As the years rolled by it became obvious that dancing could no longer sustain the cavernous building. Today, the only music you're likely to hear at the old Brock Arena is the beeping from check-out scanners and the squeaking wheels of grocery carts.

Peterborough: Club Aragon

"It's nice to be seen at the Aragon." This was the

phrase coined by the owners of the establishment, and it seemed to take hold from Day One. As Fran Domenic says, "We were busy from the day we opened up—it was a very successful business." Fran is the daughter of Jack and Gert Wineberg who ran the Aragon.

In 1986, a short blurb in the *Peterborough Examiner* looked back 40 years to August 30, 1946. "An eager dance crowd of more than 1,500 was on hand to launch the dance ship Club Aragon, the Kawarthas' ultra-modern night-spot." Club Aragon was the result of Jack Wineberg and his brother-in-law, Joe Halpert, pooling their business ideas together in 1946 and coming up with a dance hall/restaurant to be built on what is now called Landsdowne Road. As the business grew, Jack moved further into the hospitality trade, and built a set of motel units and added the Fiesta Lounge upstairs.

Bobby Kinsman and his orchestra were hired as the house band, providing excellent dance music for the regular Saturday night dances. "We got to know the musicians very well, and they became just like family," says Fran. In addition to the popular Saturday dances, Club Aragon was also busy on Sunday evenings for the weekly variety shows. As house photographers Don and Winnifred McIndoe

123

Duke Ellington, one of the greats to play at the Aragon.
Courtesy of Don McIndoe.

recall, customers were given a bottle of pop and a plate of cookies or cake and were charged 75 cents for this snack as they watched singers, dancers, comedians, hypnotists, magicians and even bell players.

Club Aragon was also known for bringing big-name talent to Peterborough. Nat King Cole, Duke Ellington, Robert Goulet and many other stars were booked in by Jack. Unlike summer dance pavilions, which operated mostly between May and October and were active during this period, the Aragon's busy season began in the fall and continued throughout the winter. Jack Wineberg was also a talented musician. Many times after the crowd left on a Saturday night, Jack would climb up on stage with the band for an informal jam session. Fran says, "Dad would often sit in on piano with Bobby Kinsman and the orchestra until the early hours of the morning."

After the Winebergs sold the business the restaurant facility was enlarged and a name change was in order—Miss Diana Motor Hotel was born. In 1991, Tom Malakos took over and changed the name once again, this time to Trentwinds International Centre and Motor Hotel. As Peterborough has expanded, the Aragon's setting, originally surrounded by farmers' fields, has also changed dramatically. Restaurants, hotels, donut shops, plazas and numerous small businesses have sprouted up. It's getting a

124

little tougher to be seen at the Aragon these days.

The name Bobby Kinsman is synonymous with music in Peterborough. When the request for "One O'clock Jump" was shouted at the band, Bobby was not surprised—he had been getting requests for songs since the 1930s. Some of the band members were a little amused, however. The request was delivered from the street outside Bobby's house, through the open window of his rehearsal room. It was Sunday afternoon (about one o'clock) and his 12-piece band was crammed into the music room, grand piano and all, playing the music they love—Big Band. The passersby couldn't get enough of this great swing music either, and were standing in the street enjoying every moment.

Bobby is known best for his 25-year association with Club Aragon as leader of the house band, starting in 1947. He became almost like a member of the family to the Winebergs. Bobby's first gig in the Peterborough area was in 1934 at the pavilion in Lakefield known as the Melody Inn, commencing the May long weekend until the end of the summer. Born in Fonthill, Bobby's introduction to music was from his aunt, a classical piano teacher. After taking up the sax which would become his main instrument, Bob put together a band in the Niagara Peninsula. As his musical talent grew, Bobby's orchestras became increasingly more sophisticated to the point where they were hired at many of the famous dance halls on Lake Erie, including Crystal Beach, Morgan's Point and Long Beach. In the summer of 1995, Port Colborne columnist and historian Ruby Conway reminisced about the wonderful summer evenings she spent at the Morgan's Point pavilion: "One band in particular I enjoyed so much was Bobby Kinsman and his seven-piece orchestra, including Del Crary."

Bobby's wife Elsa, an accomplished musician

Best known for his 25-year stint of leading the house band at Club Aragon, beginning in 1947, Bobby Kinsman and his band were well-known in Peterborough and beyond. This 1935 photograph is from his early days at Peterborough's Melody Manor. Rear (l-r): Tap Thornbeck, trumpet; Jimmie Duffus, drums; Lloyd "Cookie" Cook, bass. Front (l-r): Del Crary; Hal McFarlane and Bobby Kinsman, sax; Don Rathbone at the piano.
Courtesy of Bobby Kinsman.

herself, has often sat in with Bob when her piano skills were needed. By the time Bobby had moved to Peterborough, he had played just about every pavilion and dance hall within 50 miles of the city at least once. Bobby also played for three summers at Greenhurst, before Paul Minacola took over as house band.

During the War, Bobby was part of the Canadian Army Show, a group of talented servicemen and women who performed for the troops both in Canada and overseas. Coincidentally, he found himself in the same unit as his friend and fellow musician, Del Crary. Bobby met many musicians during this period, many of whom have remained life-long friends. One of these close friends is respected Toronto musician, arranger and composer Eddie Graf, who still leads his own band in Toronto. A couple of years after the War, when Bobby was con-

templating packing his musical life away with his tenor sax, it was Del who suggested that Bob investigate the new Club Aragon which had just opened. Del's idea kept Bobby Kinsman busy for the next quarter century. Bobby and Elsa also owned and operated the Pines Pavilion in Bridgenorth for many years.

Bob has always maintained a keen interest in keeping Big Band Music alive and well, and has introduced this "new" music to younger generations over the years through the dozens of nostalgia dances he has played.

Bridgenorth: Chemong Park Pavilions

At the intersection of Communication Road, Hatton and Hunter streets in Bridgenorth, four dance pavilions were to make their mark in Chemong Park.

125

The small bronze plaque in the quiet picnic grounds of Chemong Park gives a glimpse into the long history of this seventy-acre parcel of land. Established originally as a park for private cottages in 1881, Chemong Park was one of the first planned recreational subdivisions in Ontario. Early pictures of the first pavilion, likely constructed in the late 1800s, show a water tower at one end, which operated on gravity. Bridgenorth historian Helen Willcox says that this tank was for the pavilion's use as well as the picnickers. The building was moved in 1907 to the northwest corner of Hatton and Communication Road and it became known as Dan Sullivan's Pavilion, after the name of the man who operated the business. The pavilion attracted both cottagers as well as groups of people from nearby towns such as Peterborough and Lakefield who would travel by horse and carriage to the dances.

Unfortunately, Dan's pavilion burned down in August, 1926. Even though The Rendezvous pavilion had been operating across the street from Dan's since 1922, the loss of this building saddened many people, and moved one anonymous individual to compose a poem about the event, which was discovered in the Bridgenorth Fire Hall years later. The few lines of the poem that follow give some idea of the impact of the fire.

Chemong Park Fire

Sunday morning at 1 a.m. the cottagers all retired
Suddenly voices rang through the Park and gave the alarm of "Fire!"
Arise ye sleepers one and all the weak, the brave, the strong
The old Pavilion is all ablaze in dear old Park Chemong.

Bill Bradburn he was all dressed up with a diamond pin and tie
And said, "Boy if there was a wind we would all speed up on high
But if the Lord will keep it calm I promise you as man's M.P.
A brigade that's action quick and strong will be installed in dear old Park Chemong." [1]

Just north of The Pines' parking lot lies a small grove of trees. In the middle of this thicket, you'll see the towering ruins of a large stone fireplace—the only evidence remaining today of The Rendezvous Pavilion. This octagonal-shaped building was originally operated by Nick Douras and Peter Gettas, and later by Harry Forler. The Rendezvous also burned, but not to worry. The Palace—pavilion number three in Chemong Park—was constructed on the southwest corner of Hatton and

126

A rendition of Dan Sullivan's Pavilion of the early 1900s.
Courtesy of Helen Willcox.

The Pines, one of the few dance pavilions remaining in Ontario past the 1970s, was closed in 2001.

Communication Road by John Douglas in 1940. Helen Willcox says that although its official name was The Palace, the pavilion was also referred to as The Barn by many.

Bridgenorth resident Joyce Turner—whose father and brother helped to build The Pines and also laid the dance floor themselves in that building—sold strips of jitney dance tickets at The Palace, and recalls that the bands usually stayed in the house next to The Palace. The building was later painted green and made into apartments, but deteriorated so badly it had to be demolished by the Bridgenorth and Area Ratepayer's Association in 1970.

Author Stanley Redman's family cottage was in Chemong Park. "I remember Dan Sullivan's Pavilion which was used for sing-songs and other forms of entertainment," he writes. "I also recall The Rendezvous where on a Regatta prize night I was presented with a flashlight for coming in third in the cross-Chemong Lake swim. Robert Farnon was there one summer, and also Don Wright and his Western University Orchestra. They used to give concerts on Sunday evenings after church, and one of them had a member who made beautiful music on a one-stringed Chinese fiddle."

Of the four pavilions in Chemong Park, The Pines was the largest, and has enjoyed the longest run. The Pines is also one of the few dance pavilions still remaining in the province. Constructed in 1946, it has brought music to the people from bands such as Bill Thompson and the Red Jackets, and Jimmy Duffus and His Music (who opened the hall over 50 years ago), to Blue Rodeo and Kim Mitchell who have played here in recent years. The Pines was originally a group of army drill halls that owner Herb Payne incorporated into a dance hall. A number of people have been at the helm since the doors opened 50 years ago. Herb sold the business to Douglas MacPherson in 1956. Popular Peterborough musician and orchestra leader Bobby Kinsman and partner Jeff Purvey ran The Pines for some time, later selling to Sandy Myers. The local Lions Club followed, staging regular dances and special events for a few years. Chris Black then purchased the business from the Lions Club, and continued the tradition of showcasing some of the most popular entertainment in Ontario.

Bobby, his wife Elsa, and Jeff Purvey carefully guided The Pines through the early years of rock 'n' roll era. With Bobby's expertise in music and building renovations, along with Jeff's knowledge of the food business, the partners brought new blood into The Pines. "We completely winterized the building," says Bobby. "A full water system was installed including indoor washroom facilities, and we built a new kitchen." A bar was also constructed, using marble

127

The Cedar Junction Band played locally in the Stony Lake area for a number of years. One of their annual gigs was on Labour Day weekend when they would ship their gear over by barge to the Juniper Island Pavilion.
Courtesy of Sean Pennylegion.

slabs from the old MET store in Peterborough. Bobby and Elsa booked in many of the popular rock acts of the '60s, including Edward Bear, Truck, Lighthouse and Major Hooples Boarding House. Bobby also began running Big Band nostalgia dances with his orchestra for Saturday night dances.

The durable dance floor installed by Joyce Turner's father and brother so many years ago still gleams inside The Pines, but the music in Chemong Park has been silent for a few years as The Pines and

the large lot on which it sits await development.

Stoney Lake: Viamede

Of the four dance pavilions built on Stoney Lake, all of them are still standing and two are still used during the summer. In the latter part of the last century tourists discovered a pristine location near Peterborough—the Kawartha Lakes. The most popular lake in the area has always been Stoney Lake (also spelled "Stony"), often referred to as The Jewel of the Kawarthas.

Steamships were responsible for opening up the area to tourism, transporting passengers and bringing supplies. Many of these vacationers would stay at Viamede Resort, owned for many years by Bea and William Ianson. At night guests enjoyed themselves down at the resort's pavilion where they would dance and stage masquerade and toga parties. Bea recalls, "We had dances usually at least once a week to live bands. Both our guests as well as people from towns in the area came by car and boat to dance. Dress at the dances was very informal—bare feet, shorts and other summer wear." The boathouse, where dances were held upstairs, was torn down in the 1950s with most of the original wooden dance floor being carefully removed, scraped, cleaned and installed in the new facility, with new wood added where necessary. "We reused as much of the tongue and groove floor as possible because it was still in good shape since most people danced in bare feet," says Bea.

At Viamede, people danced upstairs in the boathouse. This photo was taken circa 1920.
Courtesy of Bea Ianson.

Juniper Island Pavilion was reopened on July 11, 1992, by Margaret Anderson and dedicated in memory of her husband, Don. In the background to the left is the historic Juniper Island Store.

Often guests would take a turn with the band—one summer a band member with Benny Goodman was staying at Viamede and sat in on dance night. Groups such as the Firehouse Five and George Novotny's orchestra were regulars in the boathouse hall. Ferde Mowry also did a few jobs at Viamede in his early years.

Stony Lake: Juniper Island Pavillion

The year 1997 marked the 100th anniversary of Juniper Island Pavilion on Stony Lake.[2] This building has a rich past associated with the lake's summer life and was recently fully restored. The original hardwood floor was refinished, new shutters were built, and the exterior was stained. All of the lumber for the renovation was acquired and milled locally. It's a true open-air pavilion used daily throughout the summer months for a variety of activities such as exercise and aerobics classes, movie nights and square dancing. A little different perhaps, from the days of afternoon teas and bridge parties that took place in the earlier part of the century, but Juniper Island Pavilion still

provides a strong bond between the cottagers on the lake, many of whom can boast with pride that their families have been coming to Stony for generations.

Originally built for church services, Juniper Island Pavilion soon became a central meeting place for just about everyone. "The branch of the Red Cross Society held weekly meetings during the summers of 1915/16," says Katharine Hooke, a Peterborough writer and historian and long-time cottager at Stony Lake. "Other activities have included masquerade parties, art classes, fitness classes and concerts. There were also dances with various orchestras mostly from local towns." The pavilion is also used for meetings, banquets and wedding receptions. It is very much a family affair to boat over to the island, pick up some ice cream at the 100-year-old island store and take in some of the activities.

Ronnie Hawkins performed at the annual July 1st weekend barbecue in 1995, setting up his band on the store's verandah. (Ronnie has lived on a farm for many years on Stony Lake.) "There were so many people here to see Ronnie that we knew there would not be enough room for everyone if

129

The historic Juniper Island Store as shown in 1906. The store sits near the restored Pavilion and is still in operation.
Courtesy of the Roy Studio Collection.

the band played right inside the pavilion," says one cottager.

For many years an annual end-of-summer dance was held at Juniper Island Pavilion on Labour Day weekend with the Cedar Junction Band providing the music. The group was led by Sean Pennylegion, who, along with his wife, used to run the busy Woodview General Store out on Highway #28.

"We had huge crowds for the dance on Labour Day," says Sean. "Over 400 would come out, all by boat, and the overflow would have to dance on the pier. People had a great time. Playing the Juniper

Island Pavilion was particularly beautiful with the moon reflecting over the lake, and the distant lights of Viamede twinkling in the distance."

Crowe's Landing Pavilion

It's painted white and sits on a small rise at Crowe's Landing. On the north side facing the water there's a picture of an outboard motor, followed by the simple word "Mercury," indicating the building is part of a small marina. At one time this old clapboard structure was a pavilion, the centre of activity at Crowe's

Today the Sunset Pavilion, built by the Whetungs, belongs to the Upper Stoney Lake Association.

Landing for many years.

Within the main door is a smaller entry, cut in the shape of an enormous keyhole. This, and the old upright piano (painted sky blue) inside the hall, are the only indications that long ago something very special happened here. At one time this pavilion was called The Keyhole where people came to dance and bands came to play, and the only way to get in was through the unique opening. But long before curious doorways were cut and modern orchestras performed, this building was used for much more sombre purposes. Marjorie Armstrong remembers the very early days at Crowe's Landing. Interviewed by my wife when Marjorie was in her late 90s, she says she was there with her family when cottagers were called "campers."

"My grandfather was 15 when he first visited the lake," says Marjorie. "He and his two brothers canoed up from Peterborough." Stoney Lake became part of Marjorie's life when she turned five and her family built a cottage here. The pavilion at Crowe's Landing was built in 1906, primarily to hold church services for the cottagers in the area. "The congregation was a good size and there was always a minister available who would take a service." Dances and social gatherings were also organized after the pavilion was constructed. Marjorie started attending some

of these functions when she was 12 or 13. "We rarely had to hire anyone to perform unless a special occasion was scheduled because there was always someone who could play the piano. I loved those evenings."

Adjacent to the old pavilion at Crowe's Landing is the former Belvidere Hotel. Betty Knox still lives in the historical building and says that in later years, brothers Greg and Herb Knox continued to let the community use the pavilion for meetings, church services, regatta celebrations and dances. "The men also supplied the music for dances from the mid-'50s to the mid-'60s. The music was modern—Big Band style." When the pavilion finally ceased operations and was put into use as a storage shed, Betty Knox gathered up the hymn books and the brass collection plates (which she had engraved) and donated them to the nearby United Church.

Meanwhile, at the same time as The Keyhole was in full swing, Sonny and Leonard Whetung built Sunset Pavilion, up the road and literally a long stone's throw from the lake. The construction took place in the late 1940s or early '50s, according to various residents in the area. When the Whetungs operated the hall it was used for a variety of purposes including regular dances during the summer months. In the mid-1960s, favourite Peterborough entertainers, Geoff Hewittson and The Fugitives were booked

131

The original pavilion at Crowe's Landing was in full use every summer for the annual regatta. This photo, from the Dorfman Collection, was in the *1995 Stoney Lake Vacation Guide*.

An inside entrance, cut in the shape of a large keyhole, is a reminder of the days when this pavilion, known as The Keyhole, was a popular dance hall.

132

regularly on Saturday nights for rock dances, with The King Bees doing the honours on Fridays.

Today, Sunset Pavilion is the property of the Upper Stoney Lake Association, a strong group of residents and cottagers who own property in this area. The hall is used practically every day during the summer for wedding receptions, meetings, classes of all types, craft sales, movie nights and dances. Events at the pavilion are run by volunteers from the USLA—the cottagers.

SUNSET PAVILION
CROWE'S LANDING
STONY LAKE
EVERY FRI. NITE
Vocals by Marg. Raymond and Gary Knight
EVERY SAT. NITE
Jeff Hewitson and The
FABULOUS FUGITIVES

The KING BEES

Chapter Ten

THROUGH THE OTTAWA VALLEY
TO THE SEAWAY VALLEY

Lakeside Gardens emerged as a dance pavilion in 1920. *Courtesy Ottawa City Archives #18289.*

Ottawa: Lakeside Gardens

"During the '30s and '40s Britannia Park was the centre for Big Band dances in Lakeside Gardens, large enough to hold 1200 people. For a nickel people boarded the streetcar and rode to the end of the line at Britannia Park for a day at the beach or an evening dance."[1]

In 1905, this pavilion (originally called The Auditorium) was dismantled from its original location and re-assembled in Britannia Park beside the water as a vaudeville theatre and playhouse. It was later turned into a movie theatre before ultimately being converted into a dance hall in the 1920s. When dancing was introduced in 1920, the name was changed to Lakeside Gardens. During the years of World War II attendance peaked; on July 24, 1946,

some 800 veterans and their families were honoured at a Homecoming Reception. Many Ottawa musicians provided the entertainment at Lakeside Gardens. Charlie Quail's Orchestra, Berkley Kidd's Orchestra, the Alex Dawson Band, Larry Carrigan and Mel Johnston were just a few.

Iona Skuce attended dances here with her cousin, Margaret, in 1944. She writes: "The pavilion had a huge reflecting ball hanging from the rafters, sending down a circle of hundreds of coloured lights. The inside walls were beautifully decorated with coloured lanterns, streamers, balloons and other panels. We could watch the moonlight on Britannia Bay from the patio doors. The band played a lot of jive and jitterbug dance tunes, as well as romantic ballads. It was very exciting. Marg's high school beau was a talented local pianist named Mel Johnston who

133

Berkley Kidd and His Orchestra were regulars at Lakeside. From left to right: Woody Hill, guitar; Herb Fairchild, trombone; Vince Alexander, sax; Harold Swerdfefer, vocalist; "Bert" Kidd, piano and leader; Jack Sterling, sax; Charley Wimperis, bass; Percy Beer, drums; Willie Fairchild, trumpet; a 1938 photo. *Courtesy Ottawa City Archives 18288.*

composed arrangements for the band that played regularly at Lakeside pavilion. Marg and Mel became engaged, they married and had five children." Barbara Logsdail also remembers Mel's band. "The regular orchestra in my day was Orville and Mel Johnston, brothers from Ottawa. They had the sweetest sound this side of heaven! As the crooner, Orv's theme song was 'Blue Moon.'"

The city of Ottawa had leased the building to the Westboro Kiwanas Club who managed the dances. In later years the hall had been renovated extensively and was touted as one of the most modern dance halls in the country. After the pavilion burned down on July 3, 1955, Mayor Charlotte Whiton indicated that Lakeside Gardens was very special to her, recalling that she came down from Renfrew to

The Château Laurier Dance Orchestra of the Canadian National Railway Radio Station CNRO, the forerunner to CBC. From left to right: F.H. Leduc, N. Ivimey, J. McIntyre (conductor), A.C. McGuirl, A. Lewis, R. Wimperis, J. Brown.

attend her very first dance here when she was just 13 years of age.[2]

Hull: The Aylmer Road Pavilions

Imagine living in a city that rolled up its sidewalks at dusk and where searching for a dance hall or night club was about as futile as asking for free samples from the Canadian Mint. Other than Lakeside Gardens and the Canadian Grill in the Chateau Laurier, there were few places in Ottawa to dance and enjoy live music. But only five minutes away in Hull,

Quebec, the seven-mile stretch of highway between Hull and Aylmer, known as the Aylmer Road, featured a number of clubs and showplaces, ranging "from the sleaziest of dives to the most glamorous of supper clubs offering dining and dancing to the strains of the best bands in North America," according to Diane Aldred in her book, *The Aylmer Road: An Illustrated History*.[3] Crossing the bridge was like Pinocchio visiting the Land of the Lost Boys because Quebec's liquor laws were also much looser.

One of the earliest and most popular venues to open in 1929 was Standish Hall, once the home of

Standish Hall, originally the home of E.P. Eddy, became a popular spot for dancing, circa 1950.
Courtesy of Ed Hall.

In 1951, Standish Hall Hotel was consumed by fire, but, almost immediately, a replacement structure was constructed and the fans returned.

135

lumber magnate E.P. Eddy. In her letter, Marion Mills calls it "a piece of paradise with a beautiful large dance floor with doors opening to a large enclosed garden where we sat on warm nights. There was also a large balcony area where people could sit and look down on the dance floor." During a fire in 1951 which destroyed the building, one of the victims to suffer injuries was Louis Armstrong's bassist Dale Jones, who had to leap from a window. A new Standish arose from the ashes and soon all the top names in the Big Band field were back, as well as local orchestras led by Harry Pozy, Norm Richards and Alex Dawson. The Campeau Corporation levelled Standish Hall in 1975.

By the 1930s, the Gatineau, Glenlea and Chaudière golf clubs had all opened dining and dancing lounges with Big Bands appearing every night. After fire destroyed the original Chaudière building in 1949, its replacement quickly became known for the Rose Room supper club. The bizarre mural of a giant matron in a hooped skirt painted on the rear wall of the stage set the floral atmosphere for the room. Tables were painted with roses and the carpet had roses woven into the fabric. The crowds that filled the club when it re-opened in 1953 (capacity of 1200) agreed that this was one room you would never forget. The hall booked in many local house bands who performed for dances and backed up international stars. The Rose Room also featured hour-long variety shows, not unlike a live Ed Sullivan production with comics, singers, dancers and acrobats. It was torn down in the 1980s.

The Gatineau Golf Club cashed in on the booming night life scene when the owners added a huge barn behind the old stone clubhouse and turned it into a cavernous dance hall in 1926, holding over 1000. Billed as "The Showplace of the Stars," practically every major singer and orchestra stepped on stage at this club, as well as comics and chorus girls. For years the Gatineau held the reputation of being one of the top supper clubs in the area. When the first club burned in 1960, a new all-purpose banquet hall was built in its place, only to be torn down in 1990.

Ed Hall is a long-time Ottawa musician (trumpet) and former President of Local 180 of the Musicians' Association. Over the years he gigged at most every hall in Ottawa/Hull and was often in the house band when the stars came to perform. Ed could see the impact that television was beginning to have on clubs like the Aylmer Road spots: "People began staying home when TV arrived—for example, quite a few of the acts that we backed up as musicians at places like the Gatineau Club turned up on the Ed Sullivan television show a few years later." The Hull clubs provided great music while they lasted. With Ottawa being such a sedate government city, the Aylmer Road offered music fans another side of life that was not always "politically correct."

Osgoode: The Lighthouse

The triangular-shaped beacon on the Rideau River near Osgoode, south of Ottawa, is now a storage shed. Still, it is a reminder of the days when this symbol welcomed people to The Lighthouse—a public park and dance pavilion. The original pavilion also

The Lighthouse was a beacon on the Rideau River.
Courtesy of Vera Boyd.

sits beside the small lighthouse, although it was transformed into a low rambling house overlooking the Rideau.

Vera Boyd, who ran the pavilion for many years with her husband Alfred, still lives beside the old Lighthouse property. "Our business consisted of a park and beach, along with the dance pavilion and concession stand," recalls Vera. The original idea of creating this park and dance pavilion was the brainchild of Harry Boyd, Alfred's father, and his friend Doug Wallace. "The business ran from spring 'til fall," says Vera, who took over the park with Alfred a few years after its creation. "We'd often have over 500 people on a Saturday night." Throughout the week the pavilion would often be rented to other groups such as a square dancing club from Ottawa. A bridge was built over the old railroad so dancers would have easy access from the parking area over the gully to the hall. According to Vera, "They'd be parked all up and down the road."

John Ferguson has lived his whole life near The Lighthouse and writes about the pavilion: "It was built about 1935. Before World War II started, there were three dances a week—one was all square dancing. I started going to dances around 1945. The Lighthouse was constructed to appear like an authentic lighthouse; at that time its use was a refreshment booth. The actual dance pavilion was a one-story building made with one-ply clapboards, strictly a summer building. About 1946 there was a cement slab put outside for dancing. A large Hallowe'en party finished the season, then the crowd would then go to the Harmony Hall in Manotick and in later years to the community centre in Richmond for the winter months until The Lighthouse opened in the spring."

John Gordier's recollections about this hall are particularly sharp. "I was there twice in the 1930s, and the occasion I remember best of all was when Toby Hall and his Hawaiian Orchestra played for our pleasure. Toby was from Morrisburg and I knew him personally. It would be another 40 years before I heard any other Hawaiian Orchestra which would inspire me to the same degree, and that was in Hawaii!"

Pembroke: The Cedars & the Town Hall

Two Pembroke residents have very fond memories of a couple of notable dance halls in this upper Ottawa Valley Ontario city. Helen (Chaput) Clouthier writes about The Cedars:

"During the late 1930s and the War years, Pembroke had a dance pavilion built and owned by a local businessman named Williard Whitmore, now deceased. The Cedars was a lovely two-story building situated partially on land and on peers over the beautiful Ottawa River. It was located about two miles east of Pembroke off Highway #17. There were few people with cars then so we had to walk there, east on the highway, left onto a dirt road, over the CPR tracks, and there it stood amidst all the cedar trees, so numerous in that vicinity.

"The Cedars was just the place to be for our favourite pastime—dancing. Sometimes we would have bands made up of local musicians, and other times army musicians formed the band since we were close to the military Camp Petawawa. The music was always the big band sound and it was so good! With so many military personnel, there were lots of partners—the best dancers in the world, from all parts of Canada.

"The dance floor was smooth with the dance area surrounded by a screened verandah on two sides. The entrance-way contained a refreshment bar and the dance ticket sales; the men gave a ticket for each dance. There were chest-high windows looking in to the dance floor, and when not dancing you could watch the partners gliding, jiving or jitterbugging on the dimly lit floor. When there was a full moon on the Ottawa River it certainly was a very romantic setting. The building was demolished some years ago but the memories of our happiest dancing times will live on forever."

By the time Teresa Halpenny attended dances at The Cedars, ownership of the hall had changed. "The Cedars, owned by Mr. A. Campbell Sr., was located half a block from my parents' homestead. At the age of 14 in 1944, I recall stalling for time with my parents in an attempt to linger outside and listen to the night's entertainment. Most of the

137

patrons were servicemen. My parents prohibited any visiting during the evening, however, my eldest sister worked during the day cleaning the establishment for the next night. I would often be given the chance to 'trail' along, provided I pitch in with the work. This arrangement provided an excellent opportunity to enjoy the atmosphere of the building and the view of the beautiful Ottawa River, often leading me to dance around as I recalled the music of the previous night."

Teresa also writes about another hall. "Town Hall, now called Victoria Hall, has a very special place in my heart. In the year of 1950, I was asked to dance by a young gentleman new to the Pembroke area. As we enjoyed and danced the night away in this local hall, we would never have thought that our lives would be changed forever. That night was followed with a further five years of dating each other before our marriage. We are happily celebrating our 40th wedding anniversary this year. I often visit the hall now used as a drop-in centre for seniors. Although the band music and dancing have long gone, the hall will always bring back these fond memories."

Lake Dore (Eganville): Sunny Dale Acres

Music, dancing, the Ottawa Valley ... the people in this part of the province always loved a good time on a Saturday night at the local pavilion, hall or hotel. The dance pavilion probably most representative of the good times where you could hear and dance to the "down home" country music that was, and still is, revered in the Ottawa Valley, was the hall on Lake Dore, called Sunny Dale Acres.

Whenever the name Sunny Dale Acres is mentioned, people automatically think of the late musician and songwriter Mac Beattie who led the house band here for years. Sunny Dale Acres was so dear to Mac's heart that he wrote at least three songs relating to the pavilion: "The Big Dance hall," "Lake Dore Waltz" and "Tribute To Frank Martin."

Teri Lyn Martin's grandparents were Frank and Lillian Martin, who built and operated Sunny Dale Acres. Although Teri is too young to have memories of her own, she does write with some background on the hall: "After both my grandparents passed away, their youngest son (my father, Terry C. Martin), ran the dance hall on a weekend-only basis. When my father moved away from Lake Dore, Art Deighton held dances at Sunny Dale Acres on the long weekends during the summer. When he retired, the pavilion ceased functioning. It was recently demolished by the current owner of the property on which the hall was situated, my uncle Jack Martin. Mac Beattie and the Ottawa Valley Melodiers were the most popular band to have played at the hall and recorded songs pertaining to Sunny Dale Acres. It was not uncommon to see children dancing on stage in the pavilion and wearing shirts with 'Sunny Dale Acres' emblazoned on the back. I believe that they were a group of young people who competed in either step dancing or square dancing competitions."

Barry's Bay: Lakeside Pavilion

Barry's Bay is located on the north shore of

Kamaniskeg Lake at the western fringe of the Ottawa Valley. Part of the uniqueness of this area is the music and dance which is so indigenous to the Valley. Fiddling and step dancing—people of the Ottawa Valley take this custom very seriously. This music and dance has developed from the very deep roots the region has in logging. As musician Ed Hall from Ottawa explains, although the cities featured primarily Big Band music, once you left the urban boundaries and visited the small town and country dance halls, "fiddlin" music was virtually all that you would hear.

Ambrose Plebon knew the people of Barry's Bay loved to dance and constructed his Lakeside Pavilion in 1947. "He drew up the plans and built

The Madawaska Valley Ramblers at the Lakeside Pavilion, Barry's Bay, 1964. **From l to r: Lawrence Dombroskie, Joe (Fiddlin' Joe) Peplinskie, Clifford Hoare, Ed Peplinskie, Ernie Peplinskie. In front: Don Peplinskie and Cy Peplinskie.** *Courtesy of Dave Peplinskie.*

most of the pavilion himself," says his wife Bernadette, who worked hand in hand with Ambrose once the hall was erected. As Ambrose and Bernadette's children grew up they too became involved with the operation of the business. Daughter Joanne sold tickets at the door for many years, and it was here she met her future husband, Dave Peplinskie from nearby Combermere. Dave just happened to play in Lakeside Pavilion's house band,

the Madawaska Valley Ramblers.

When this group wasn't supplying the music, other bands and entertainers were booked into the hall. Dave elaborates: "The CFRA Happy Ramblers played here and were a very good group. Mac Beattie occasionally got over this way. Don Messer and His Islanders were really popular and played at Lakeside when they were on tour, as did a number of acts from the U.S., like Wilf Carter and Doc Williams and family."

After Ambrose's untimely passing in 1967, Bernadette continued to operate the pavilion for four more years, aided by members of her family. Finally, in 1971 Bernadette made the decision to sell the pavilion. Although now a private residence, it is one of the few original dance hall buildings remaining in the Ottawa Valley. Bernadette says, "There are a lot of memories in that building both for me and for the many people I run into who still like to tell me that they met their wife or husband at Lakeside Pavilion."

One of the best known country music players in the Ottawa Valley was Mac Beattie. His full name was John McNab Beattie, but most folks just called him Mac because, as he describes himself in one of his many songs, he was just "an ordinary Joe." As a singer/songwriter, his poems and music describe the stories, places and people in his life. Born in 1916, Mac formed the first version of his Melodiers in his early teens in Braeside with washboard, harmonica, accordion and Spanish guitar. His first introduction to dancing was attending the Dew Drop Inn where Gilmour's dance platform operated. With roots like these it's no surprise that Mac was devoted to "breakdown" music featuring fiddles, banjo, guitar and square dance callers. By the late 1930s Mac and his band were busy playing town halls in many small communities.

Mac Beattie *(above)* and his Ottawa Valley Melodiers were known throughout the area, particularly in the rural dance halls. *Courtesy of Teri Lyn Martin.*

En route between gigs, circa 1950s. *Courtesy of Karen Shaw.*

5,000. Just like many couples who can say they met at a dance pavilion, Mac Beattie was no different. He was introduced originally to Marie MacMunn at Sunny Dale Acres and the rest is history.

Mac's radio career really received a boost when his show went national across the CBC network on Saturday nights. Their first Canadian television appearance was on Don Messer's show in 1962 live from Halifax. "Charlie Chamberlain said we were his kind of people," writes Mac.

In 1948, Mac re-formed the Melodiers in Arnprior and approached Pembroke radio station CHOV to do some live performances—they agreed, and a 25-year association was born. The Melodiers' career really took off as people heard their music on the radio and began requesting the group for dances. This year held many "firsts" for the band, including their premier engagement in October at Lake Dore's Sunny Dale Acres Dance hall, owned by the Martin family. The hall was powered by Delco batteries.

As the band's popularity grew, they started playing live shows and dances on Ottawa radio station CFRA for the Friday Night Dance at the Playhouse show. "Often while on the road in the valley we would do remote broadcasts for CFRA," writes Mac in his autobiography. The best part of the CFRA association was working the annual Ottawa Exhibition where the Melodiers played to crowds of

Locally, Mac arranged appearances for the group and various other acts on Ottawa's CJOH-TV. "We were given the distinction of having the first old-tyme country music series to appear on Channel 13; the show was called 'The Haylofters.' " Eventually the CTV network picked up a show, "Cross Canada Barndance," which ran for 26 weeks and featured the Melodiers in each show.[4]

Mac died in 1982, before he could complete his book. The conclusion was created with a series of essays from Mac's friends including a tribute from friend and broadcaster Max Keeping: "The Ottawa Valley returned some of his love in April 1981, when Mac was made the first inductee of the Ottawa Valley

Country Music Hall of Fame. Close to 500 people attended the inauguration dinner at the Renfrew Armouries, as more than a dozen people praised his five decades of song and poetry .... I can think of no better way to remember him than to try and live my life in his mould. Mac: thanks, ol' friend."

Westport: Scott's Ballroom

Until 1997 an old Quonset hut sat in the middle of the picturesque village of Westport, 30 miles north of Kingston. Wild vegetation covered much of the grey corrugated metal structure. The building's final use was a storage warehouse, but not too many years ago this half-moon shaped edifice was the hottest place in Westport. On the walking tour of Westport it was listed as Number Five: Scott's Ballroom.

Ellie Stuart moved away from Westport some time ago and writes: "Westport is a small town at the top of the Big Rideau Lake where I grew up, and many hours were spent at dances in Scott's Ballroom. Once we paid at the entrance and were stamped, there was a little booth type area at the entrance to the right where soft drinks and chips and chocolate bars could be purchased. There were no tables or chairs in this hall—only a long bench running the length of the hall."

A visit with Florence Scott at her cottage rental business reveals more about the popular ballroom she and her late husband, George, operated: "In 1933 George and his partner, Harman King, built an open-air dance platform near the centre of town. The men felt that there was little entertainment in the general vicinity for both the permanent population as well as the people who visited the surrounding lakes during the summer." The obvious problem with an outdoor facility was the weather.

The best solution, decided George, was to build a covered dance hall. By this time he was operating all alone. "He visited an exhibition in Peterborough which featured corrugated metal Quonset huts and decided to purchase one of these buildings," says Florence. After the shell was erected, George completed the interior himself, including planing and installing the dance floor. "We advertised

Ellie Stuart, under the arbour at dance hall, Scott's Ballroom, circa 1958. *Courtesy of Ellie Stuart.*

it as a 'non-tiring floor.' The stage was about two and a half feet high, down at the south end." Scott's Ballroom was officially opened early in May 1948, with the Stardusters from Carleton Place performing. It was a success from the first dance. "People travelled from all over the territory to dance in Westport," Florence remembers. "Perth, Cornwall, Brockville, Kingston, Napanee ... they thought nothing of travelling 50 miles or more for a dance."

In the beginning, the hall operated on Fridays only, and featured western music, but the Scotts soon added a Saturday dance with modern music and then later, rock music. Most musicians from the general area, including Kingston, can recall

141

performing at Scott's more than once in their careers. Live remotes were done from Scott's Ballroom on CKLC during the summer with Don Johnson and his band providing the music on these occasions. Scott's Ballroom originally operated from May until October, but after George installed heating the hall ran dances year round: "Our New Year's dances were really special—I recall making a lunch for those dances myself." Florence also rented the hall to many private individuals for weddings and other functions.

Ellie Stuart recalls the dance nights when girls sat on the long benches waiting to be asked to dance. "We sat like ducks in a row on the benches and the boys stood around the entrance in clusters. Whenever the band started to play, the boys—like robots—would all start to drift towards the benches to pick the girl of choice to dance. If you were a bit of a 'wallflower' it could be a pretty disheartening experience. However, we Westport girls were generally considered to be a pretty lot, so I think we were a 'calling card' for all of the towns around for the Saturday night dance at Scott's Ballroom." The last dance at Scott's Ballroom was held in late 1972. Early the next year George passed away and Florence decided to end the dances. For the next 25 years it sat as a reminder of the wonderful times that Westport and area residents enjoyed at dances provided by George and Florence Scott. "People often talk to me about the dances; it still means a lot to them," says Florence.

By the time I visited the old hut, George's non-tiring dance floor was beginning to show severe signs of wear due to the heavy equipment being stored and dragged around. But on that stifling July afternoon the faint odour of musty wood, a couple of ancient speakers suspended from the ceiling, four or five patio lights dangling from the wall, the long wooden bench where the girls anxiously waited to be asked to dance, and the painted pink piano all came alive and took me back to a breezy summer evening

DANCE
At
Scott's Ballroom
WESTPORT.
EVERY FRIDAY NIGHT
Music by Don Johnson and His
Serenaders
EVERY SATURDAY NIGHT
To Gordie Durant's Orchestra
(You Always Have a Good Time
at Westport)
ADMISSION 75c EACH

forty years ago when the music was grand and romance filled the air in Westport.

Merrickville: Merrickville Armouries

Although not a dedicated dance hall, the Merrickville Armouries was the site of many dances. John Boyd writes that this building "boasted the largest dance floor in eastern Ontario. The music was provided by such bands as Leo Beauvais and his band from Brockville, George Warmington from Kingston and on occasion such name bands as Don Messer and His Islanders."

Today the remodelled and newly-sided armouries building is now the community centre on the outskirts of town.

Rideau Ferry Inn Pavilion

About halfway between Smiths Falls and Perth lies the small, tranquil community of Rideau Ferry on the Rideau Canal system, the site of a dance pavilion that drew people from as far away as Ottawa and Kingston. One of the best people to turn to for some early background on the Rideau Ferry Inn is a fellow who played many of the halls as a younger man, Gord Durant from Smiths Falls.

"When I was in my early teens a friend and I used to go to the Rideau Ferry Inn on any Saturday night we could hitch a ride. This was a typical dance hall in those days, constructed mainly of wood with windows that were screened all around. I used to stand behind the screens to the rear of the bandstand and watch the trumpet player in particular. This Inn burned to the ground and a new Inn was built in its place, a two-storey building of grey granite blocks with a large dance area on the second floor with screens opening on all sides and with seating on three sides. This was a very popular dance hall in the area. It was built by a man named Doug Wallace. When we played at the Ferry in Jim McNishes' Band on Saturday and Wednesday in the early 1940s, men paid one dollar to get in. With a band of my own we played at Scott's Ballroom in Westport for several years on Saturday nights. We also played at the Rustic Inn adjoining the Carleton Place Canoe Club on the Mississippi River. This was also a favourite Friday night dance spot featuring various area bands. I played with Brockville area bands at such places as the Colonial in Prescott named after a bus stop, and also at another place outside of Brockville called the Barn. With the advent of rock 'n' roll and the demise of the Big Band era in the 1950s and '60s, many of these summer dance halls just slowly faded away. The Rideau Ferry Inn, after catering to the Rock crowd, burned down and was never replaced."

Stan Wiggins, part of The Commodores' Orchestra from Belleville played at the Rideau Ferry Inn, and said that the last big band to play here was Stan Kenton in the late '70s.

Today the site of the Rideau Ferry Inn Pavilion holds only the memories. *Courtesy of Jack McGrattan.*

Antler Lodge

Just down the road from the Rideau Ferry Inn was a smaller and more intimate dance spot, with a definite woodsy atmosphere. Frederick Joyce elaborates. "Less than a mile from Rideau Ferry was Antler Lodge," he writes. "We had danced at the Ferry pavilion but it went rock 'n' roll so we moved on to Antler Lodge. It wasn't too big a place but it had a huge fireplace with moose antlers over the mantle. It was a much more homey place and the same bunch of people used to dance there. Antler Lodge was like a big house party where everybody knew everybody. We used to drive from Kingston on Saturday night, about 65 miles one way—that's how good the time was."

Antler Lodge is also just a memory, having been destroyed by flames many years ago.

Kingston: Lake Ontario Park Pavilion

A stroll through Kingston's Lake Ontario Park in late September will tell you that it's time to say goodbye to many of the activities and good times that have filled the park over the summer. Many years ago on the site where The Longhouse refreshment building now stands, the Lake Ontario Park Pavilion would also mark the end of summer as the popular dances finished for another year. The pavilion itself was constructed around 1920. A canteen ran full length along the east side of the building, with the dance floor facing north. A balcony was located above the

143

Many years ago, on the site where The Longhouse snack bar now stands, Kingston's Lake Ontario Park Pavilion would welcome summer as they opened for another season of dancing.

canteen where people could watch the dancers and the band. There were no tables or chairs inside the hall, enabling the rope boys to do their job herding crowds on and off the hardwood floor when jitney dancing was in vogue.

When park manager Bert Revell passed away in 1944, his son and daughter-in-law, Hiram and Val Revell, took over management duties, and held this position until 1973. After Hiram died, Val (last name now McEwen) continued running the campground at the park until she retired in 1980: "We looked after the grounds, ran the camping portion of the business and completely oversaw the pavilion's operation during the season from May 1 until September 30." Hiram and Val lived in the pavilion's apartment during the summer.

Val says many local bands played at the pavilion. "We generally booked bands in for a season. Dances ran on Tuesday, Friday and Saturday. Some of the groups included Al Smith and the Rocky

Mountain Ramblers, Nick Hamlet and His Orchestra, Eric Truman, Eric James Band, Riders of the Southern Trails, the Brown Brothers, Sid Fox and the North Country Ramblers from Watertown, New York. Western dancing was really popular here— there would usually be three squares in an evening, with the rest of the dances being modern. After jitney dancing finished we charged straight admission of fifty cents initially." The pavilion was demolished in late 1963, says Val, making way for The Longhouse.

Val and Hiram were so successful running dances for the city at Lake Ontario Park that they started their own enterprise on the side, running Thursday and Saturday dances at the Oddfellows Hall from 1950 until 1967. "We had a regular crowd, many of the same people came every week. In those days Kingston was more of a small town where everybody knew one another. Folks came to the dances in groups and would often pair up during the night." Val became affectionately known as "Ma" to everyone.

James Reid writes: "Gordon Keele, Jack Elliott and myself used to go to Lake Ontario Park every Saturday night. Cuth Knowlton's band had Joe Sheets and Bernie Parent on saxophone. Lots of people went out there to hear this real good band. They always started off with 'I Left My Love In Avalon.'" Cuth Knowlton Jr. writes about his father's orchestra: "Dad's band was very popular at the pavilion during the 1950s; he also played for a band at London's Wonderland in earlier years." Ann McCahill remembers the pavilion as a real hot spot during the War years: "It was popular at this time because of the army base and the British training facilities at Norman Rogers airport. I remember musicians Sid Fox and Don McCallum. Part of the pavilion's history includes a murder which happened there sometime during the 1950s. A Kingston man was fatally stabbed and an American sailor was tried and acquitted."

Music has been important to Jack McGrattan for his whole life. He played tuba in the Vimy Army Band, switching to string bass which he played in many of his bands. From performing classical music with the Kingston Symphony, to jazz in the Limestone Jazz Band, Jack's talents have taken him through all musical forms. Along with a partner, Jack opened the Harmony Hall music store which he operated for a number of years, providing instruction and instruments for many budding Kingston musicians. Also during this same time, Jack performed five days per week for many years on a live noon-hour local television show. "I'd just leave the store and walk over to the studio at noon," he says. "We did a total of 639 shows." Jack also was a well-known piano tuner in town. As President of the Musicians' Union, local 518, for five years he oversaw the business of this large local, which represented musicians from Kingston to Peterborough. Jack played all the local pavilions, such as the Golden Slipper, Lake Ontario Park Pavilion, the Rideau Ferry Inn and Gananoque Canoe Club. "We were the house band for one summer at Rideau, playing every Saturday night." Although there are many familiar names in Kingston's musical community, Jack McGrattan will always be regarded as one of the city's versatile, hard-working members.

Herb Simmons began studying music as a youngster in Kingston, and became familiar with some of the local musicians, such as Jack Telgmann

and Cuth Knowlton. "Cuth was possibly Kingston's best jazz musician, playing drums and vocals. He was also a great showman and promoter." Herb developed his own unique style of piano playing. "I sat in with many of the bands in town and got to be part of the music community." His first paying job was with the Jack Telgmann orchestra at the La Salle Hotel in Kingston in 1936. The next job was with Cuth's group as the house band at Lake Ontario Park Pavilion for the 1937 season. "I do remember one thing about that hall—the piano was murder to play, with many of the white keys missing their ivory tops!" Herb then formed his own band and rehearsed in the Park Pavilion during off hours. "We actually competed a bit with Cuth, and played many Queen's University dances. Charlie Leduc of the Fairmount Club in Hull contacted us and offered a job at his place for one summer." After serving with the RAF on Canadian bases, Herb settled in London where he played with a number of the local musicians such as Benny Vanuta at the London Hotel, Lionel Thornton at Wonderland, Alf Tibbs and the Originals at the London Arena and Don Wright's Choir and Chorus. He also played many of the southwestern halls such as the Chatham Chateau-Gae, Rondeau Park and the Stratford Pavilion. Music is still a large part of Herb's life; he uses a portable Roland piano for gigs, but his real treasure is his gleaming baby grand piano which sits majestically in his home.

Bath: Masonic Hall

Although Masonic Halls are considered to be multifunctional and really beyond the scope of dedicated dance pavilions, there were certainly memorable dances held at many of these buildings around the province. One such historic hall is still standing in the community of Bath.

Olive (Clement) Hogan has some special memories about the Masonic Hall in this town and writes: "This is the town where I grew up and where I spent many many evenings of dancing. My husband William and I had our first date at one of these occasions. A few years later we were given a community shower in the Masonic Hall after we were married.

There were two old box stoves, one on each side of the hall, and oh my, how cold it was until things got under way. There was always a hearty lunch with coffee made in the old copper boilers.

"The most popular orchestra that played there was the Aces. It was our favourite, and always drew a big crowd. It was a big band, with all the brass instruments. As long as dancers were held there, my husband and I attended. The hall is still in use, but the days of dances with big bands have long gone."

The Masonic Hall in Bath. Dances were popular here, with The Aces being one of the crowd's favourite bands.

Amherst Island: Stella Dance Hall

The only access to Amherst Island is by ferry, but that didn't stop people from the mainland from travelling year round to the dances in the hamlet of Stella which held Amherst Island's one and only community centre. One nearby resident remembers the "outhouses" were located on the second floor of the building where dances were held. The township offices and library are presently located in this old hall.

Olive Hogan also attended dances in Stella and writes about her experiences just getting there. "On Amherst Island there was a small hall in the village of Stella. We lived on the mainland in Bath, opposite the island and there was a three mile stretch of water to cross, sometimes by ferry, sometimes by small boat and sometimes on the ice. The Brown Brothers from Wilton often played on Amherst Island as well as in some of the small villages. They drove a big old car with three seats. The drums and some of the instruments that wouldn't fit inside were strapped on the roof. The Amherst Island ferry would make an extra late night trip for these special occasions. Amherst Island also had a small band of their own—The Glenns.

"One time four of us went across the lake to the island in our friend's motorboat. After the dance there was a beautiful full moon on the water, the perfect romantic scene. We were all settled down for a special crossing when suddenly our friend told every-

body to get up and sit on the side of the boat. He had neglected to put gas in the boat and the only hope we had was to tip the boat so the gas in the gas line could get to the motor. It worked, and we reached the opposite shore without much romance in that trip.

"We had a few frightening trips both by boat and on the frozen lake, until I finally refused to go over there to the dances. My husband and I loved dancing and still do; we recently celebrated our 50th anniversary."

Jack Grant's Deseronto-based band, The Aces, had a memorable gig on this island. It was in early spring and the bay was still frozen so the boys drove across the ice. During the dance a ferocious snow storm developed, stranding the band on Amherst Island for several days. The warmth in the hearts of island residents was apparent in the hospitality they showed the orchestra, billeting the members during their unexpected stay.

Collins Bay: Bayside Gardens

People who wish an evening of fine dining in the Kingston area often visit Clark's-By-The-Bay, situated in Collins Bay just west of Kingston proper. The land on which the present homestead and award-winning restaurant is located has been in Frances

Day's family since 1785—it was originally a United Empire Loyalist grant. The limestone block house was built with materials recovered from the property itself, and over the years many additions have been made.

Not only have hospitality businesses been operated from this location, but the family heritage on this land is deep. "Part of who we are is this land," says Frances.

George and Helena Clark, Frances' grandparents, founded Loyalist Lodge on their farm property in the early part of this century, providing vacation accommodation for guests on the shore of Collins Bay. Ken Reid still resides within walking distance of the Clark's property where he worked as a youth. "I specifically remember the beautifully manicured tennis courts of Loyalist Lodge," he says. "The Clark family farmed, ran the lodge and eventually built the pavilion." While they were busy taking care of tourists, the Clark's son, Harold and his wife Harriett (Frances' father and mother), felt that the business would be enhanced if another feature was added—a dance hall.

Their plans were really pushed along by a friend who was the local stationmaster, Percy Hare. "He encouraged Harold to build a dance pavilion which would inevitably benefit the community by offering great social evenings," says George Day, Frances' husband.

Ken confirms the origins of the pavilion: "It was Harold Rankin Clark who constructed the building, on the urging of Percy Hare, who visualized such a site." Whether Percy actually contributed any financing to the project is debatable, but the idea certainly had merit, so Harold built Bayside Gardens, a very sophisticated and classy dance pavilion just across the street from the lodge, on the shore of the bay. Percy, incidentally, was the first person in the village to have a crystal radio set which he listened to with headphones.

The grand opening was in the year 1926. The building itself was a solidly constructed wooden pavilion with a covered porch and verandah out front. A fireplace was installed on the west end, and the interior was always well decorated with blue and white bunting and cut-outs of seagulls. A two-storey boathouse was located just a few feet to the east, where the various orchestras would live while they performed at the hall. An underground stream flowed beneath this boathouse.

"A number of popular bands played Bayside Gardens," Frances recalled. A young Moxie Whitney was a regular, as was Sid Fox and Cuth Knowlton from Kingston, and Eddie Stroud's orchestra from Toronto. Sid Fox was known for his dapper attire which included white gloves and spats. At that time there were many black bands that toured around Ontario, and they were also quite popular at Harold's pavilion. Jack Kennedy from Sarnia put Clark's on his itinerary when he was performing in this area.

A bonus for the tourists staying at the lodge was free admission to the dances, which took place every Tuesday and Friday from 9 p.m. to 1 a.m. Lloyd Downey writes from nearby Bath: "The Clarks were abstainers,

147

Collins Bay was the site of the popular dance hall, Bayside Gardens. This photo shows the corner of the building on the right, with benches overlooking the bay.
Courtesy of Frances Day.

and there was absolutely no alcohol allowed in the hall." In fact, as George points out, the hall quickly developed a reputation as a very elegant place to go. "The social graces of the time were very important; the clothes people wore were semi-formal, which meant evening dresses for the ladies, and usually grey flannel trousers and blue blazers for the men. Another popular dress for the men was a brown blazer ensemble."

The dance season began with the long weekend in May, and lasted until the second or third week in September. It was not an inexpensive night out for the times, with admission costing $1.00 to $1.50 per couple. People arrived in couples rather than attending stag, which was often the manner in which people went to dances in the area, particularly in later years to pavilions such as the Golden Slipper. Ken says the pavilion was an extremely classy place to dance and was well-managed, but during the Depression the admission fee was "a fairly steep price for the hard times people faced in those days." It operated Tuesday and Friday nights, and on special occasions as well. The Royal Military College held their annual graduation balls here for a few years. "It was a beautiful setting on the water," says Ken. "People would take boats out on the bay on a summer evening."

Even years later, the dance floor was "absolutely beautiful—incredibly smooth," recalls George Day. This was likely due to Harold's fastidious treatment of the surface. "I remember Dad used a weighted polisher which he pushed by hand around the floor to apply the wax," says Frances. "As a very young child I sometimes would sit on the polisher end as Dad pushed."

The pavilion operated until 1939, but even though the last dancer left the floor over 60 years ago, there are still many people who have fond memories of spending romantic summer evenings at Bayside Gardens.

"The pavilion was converted into two cottages with a dividing wall, and rented as part of the lodge for about ten years," says George. The building remained unused for the next 15 years until Harold brought to reality a dream he had been nurturing for his wife, Harriett.

"In 1965, my Dad promised Mom that he would build a small house for them on the water, on the site of the pavilion," says Frances. He started by tearing down the old building, and in 1970 the house began to take shape. As the original plans took on a life of their own, the house grew in size. Harold and Harriett moved into their dream house in the early '70s.

Driving along the Bath Road through Collins Bay one would never suspect that 60 years ago Bayside Gardens was one of the classiest dance halls in the region. On the other hand, Fran's ancestors in 1785 likely had no idea that 150 years later, their physical toil would eventually lead future family members into the hospitality business, a business which continues in restaurant form to this day.

Gananoque Canoe Club

If you enjoy live theatre then you'll probably agree with Shakespeare's famous observation that all the world is a stage. On the second floor of the Gananoque Canoe Club building the play today is indeed the thing, unlike a few years ago when young men might be heard quoting the phrase: "to dance or not to dance, that is my question." Fortunately for the people of Gananoque who appreciate their heritage, the Thousand Island Playhouse showed up in time to praise this wonderful building, not to bury it.

Shakespearean puns aside, The Gananoque Canoe Club (built in 1909) was the home of the famous rowing club which owned the structure, but as many people remember, the upstairs hall was the place where regular dances were held for decades. At the time it was advertised as "the largest dancing floor of any club in eastern Ontario." The local Rotary Club ran dances here from 1962 to 1982 at which time the building's function changed from a canoe club/dance hall to summer theatre.

W. G. (Glenn) Abrams shares excerpts from his essay about the orchestra his mother led in the Thousand Islands area. Both Glen and his older sister played in the band for periods of time:

Today the old Gananoque dance hall lives on as a centre for live theatre.

"Abrams' Orchestra

Her style was to 'play it as it's written,' with minimal embellishments. Thus, Bessie Abrams and her Orchestra became well known in the Gananoque/Thousand Islands/Leeds and Grenville area.

Mrs. Abrams started entertaining on piano in the 1930s for wedding showers, dance recitals, Christmas concerts, and with Harry Campbell's 'Troupe,' which entertained during the War. A highlight of being with the Troupe was providing entertainment for the forces at Fort Henry in Kingston.

From these beginnings, an orchestra evolved. The usual size was five pieces, with various combinations at different times of piano, violin, drums, sax, clarinet, trumpet, bass guitar and accordion. Musicians included Leo Slack, Roy Hampton, Norm

Hampton, Bill Lashea, Keith Clow, Betty Abrams, Glenn Abrams, Evans Graham, Jason Hawke, Sammy Seaman and Bill Tyson.

'Now Is The Hour' was established as a signature song early on, as the last dance ... immediately preceded by 'Show Me The Way To Go Home.'

Mr. McNeeley and Mr. Farquharson renovated the lofts in their barns to provide a different venue for dancing. Floors were sanded and polished, a small elevated stage was made, and canteen and washroom facilities were incorporated. To witness a square dance with the motion of eight squares on the floor at the same time is something to behold. There is no doubt that these barns were structurally sound!

Abrams' Orchestra played dances until the late 1950s, and will be remembered by many for its delivery of the popular old standards, Leo's fiddle

149

playing for square dancing, and the general ability to fulfil a request for almost any song, either by note or by ear."[5]

The Golden Slipper

Drivers on Highway #2, halfway between Kingston and Gananoque, may notice a set of stairs and a crumbling foundation. This was once the most popular dance hall in the Kingston/Gananoque region—The Golden Slipper.

Ellie Stuart recalls the enjoyable evenings she had here. "I spent many hours on the dance floor of The Slipper," she writes. "The favourite band for our gang was Don Johnson's, who played all of the big swing tunes of Goodman, Dorsey, Miller, Ellington and Shaw. The hall did not have a liquor license and so it was expected that we bring in our own 'libations.' I remember feelings of sad nostalgia when The Slipper burned to the ground..."

That was on Sunday January 21, 1962. But let's turn the clock back almost 40 years to the opening of what would be one of the most celebrated dance pavilions in the area. The Red Moon initially occupied this parcel of land, opening on Wednesday, July 21, 1926. Dances were scheduled three days per week, with afternoon tea available from 1 to 3 pm daily. Popular Kingston bandleader Sid Fox and His Serenaders began performing at The Red Moon. Harry Anderson and His Original Victoria Ragpickers were another popular attraction. Records were played on the Orthophonic.

Although transportation was provided by Walker's Bus, the Red Moon just could not attract enough people to be viable. In 1927, the business was purchased by Peter Lee who renovated the hall and opened the place for business under the new name, Grand Gardens, with a new large verandah, fresh interior paint, individual table lighting, a coat check room, a women's rest room and a highly polished dance floor. Peter brought in a good variety of entertainment featuring many local bands as well as some imports. Female singers, tap dancers and even musical comedy were all put on stage. Some of the orchestras included Leo Beauvais and His Melody Kings,

Everett Steven's Blue Jackets, Bob Warmington and His Troubadours, The Ambassadors and let's don't forget Eddie Lane the Human Cyclone who dazzled the crowds with his whirlwind and jazz dancing.

Peter Lee ran dances right up to New Year's Eve and into 1928. When the new season opened in May, customers marvelled at new decorations and lighting schemes along with a ventilation system that was guaranteed to keep the building cool in summer. The closing dance for the 1931 season in September featured Eddie Stroud's Snappy Five Piece Orchestra. Ownership of the Grand Gardens changed again, and two weeks later Jim Wood changed the name to the one most people recognize—The Golden Slipper. He advertised dancing every night, good food and no mosquitoes. The price was one dollar per couple, an admission fee that lasted until 1945 when it doubled to two dollars. The year 1932 saw many orchestras perform at The Slipper, such as the St. Lawrence Orchestra, the New Blue Jackets and even the Golden Slipper Syncopators. When the bands weren't playing, recorded music was spun on a brand new device—the Victrola Electrical Transcription Phonograph. The Dixie Aces played for the Christmas dance that year and came back a week later for the New Year's Eve bash.

Through the 1930s, many other orchestras were hired for the Golden Slipper—Jack Crawford, Jack Grant, Bentley Ford, George Saltstone, Charlie Hopkirk and Jack Denmark and His Jazz Orchestra, just to name a few. The World War II Victory dance on May 12, 1945, had music supplied by Dick Edney and His Orchestra. By the late '40s Hyman and Harry Rosen were at the helm of the Golden Slipper.

After 23 years of being the most popular roadhouse/pavilion in eastern Ontario, fire destroyed the Golden Slipper Dance Pavilion on Thursday July 28, 1949. A new Golden Slipper was rebuilt immediately on the same site and to the joy of dancers in the region, the doors opened in 1950 with Dick Edney providing much of the music. The Slipper began catering to private functions in addition to the public dances. A motel was added and the complex became known as The Golden Slipper Motel. The owners continued to book local acts such as Brian

The Slipper featured wall and ceiling murals depicting dancing scenes from around the world. These were painted by Ole Johansen. *Courtesy of H. Rosen.*

Brick, Doug Ziggy Creighton, Parr Lane and Cuth Knowlton. It was Cuth's orchestra who played one of the last dances at The Golden Slipper on January 5, 1962. Sixteen days later the dance hall and restaurant were completely destroyed by a fire which broke out in the early hours of the morning, cause undetermined.[6]

The Golden Slipper will hold a special spot in the hearts of everyone who recall the music and dancing they enjoyed at this hall. Frederick Joyce remembers it well and writes: "It had a sunken dance floor with tables around the outside; it was a lovely place." Rose Darling Moore writes with her thoughts: "About ten years ago I was at a Big Band Dance. This gentleman asked me to dance and he was sure that we had danced together before. We went over the places where we would have been at the same time. I was in Gananoque with the Army and he was in Kingston with the Navy. We knew then that it was The Golden Slipper."

Brockville: CNRA Dance Hall

One of Brockville's most popular dance halls was without a doubt, the CNRA hall. Jim Yeldon writes

that there were sometimes two dances a week here and the place was packed. "The tradition was to go to the outdoor rink on Saturday night and skate until 9 p.m., then go to the dance where some of the local bands would play—Sandy Runciman, Eddy Flannigan and Bruce Kerr. They had the place jumping."

A great tribute to this hall is from Ken Garrett who now lives in Inverary:

"The CNRA hall, which was the top-of-the-line dance hall in Brockville, was located in the middle of King Street. The full name of the club was the Canadian National Recreation Association, organized by a group of railway employees who were interested in saving their jobs by promoting the 'ship by rail' association. The hall was huge, located on the third floor over Leveret's Store—this building was torn down in the 1980s to make way for the Royal Bank. The dance floor was about 150 by 50 feet and was well braced; it accommodated about 100 couples comfortably. The hardwood floor was beautifully polished—I never saw another one that could compare. My brother Ian and I took tickets for the dances and were paid 50 cents and got some free dances. Our job was to keep unruly people out who may have been drinking. It was there I danced for the first time in my early teens and met my first date.

"I recall learning to jitterbug to 'In The Mood.' I must have lost a couple of pounds, dancing to this great song, played by Earle's Orchestra. There were so many girls who went unescorted to the dances, it usually took you a half hour to decide which girl to ask. The dance took place every Saturday night and all the local guys and gals danced

151

their feet off 'til midnight. Dances ran from the later 1930s to about 1950; I stopped going after I was married in 1946.

"Earle's Orchestra was the best. Mr. Earle played the trombone and trumpet and Bill Stratton really knew how to play the tenor sax. Also I recall Eddie Flannigan who was a fantastic piano player. Altogether there were seven members—I wish I could recall the drummer, he was the best.

"I think the CNRA Club should go down in history as the greatest club there ever was."

Charleston Lake Pavilion

Jim Heffernen, well into his nineties, wrote about the pavilion he built: "The first pavilion I remember was about ten miles west of Brockville, named Latham's. I went once or twice. The orchestra then was Ben Hokey from Hawaii. He also conducted outdoor dances in the district during the summer.

"My brother and I built a pavilion on property we owned on Charleston Lake in 1926. We cut the logs and had them sawed in Athens. Our pavilion was about 60 by 30 feet. Brockville is 22 miles from Charleston and the roads were gravel, so transportation was poor. But we had good music and good crowds. One of the orchestras we had was from Perth, called Victor Young. The dances were held on Friday nights. On February 13, 1931, a heavy snowstorm was too much for the roof and it collapsed. We used the two ends to build cottages, and these buildings are still standing."

Iroquois Pavilion

When the St. Lawrence Seaway was built, Iroquois was one of the villages that had much of its land flooded to make way for the ships that would soon ply the route in and out of the Great Lakes. Many of the buildings were moved while some were dismantled and used in the construction of new dwellings. Whatever happened to the Iroquois Pavilion is not exactly clear, but one fact is certain: its original site was flooded years ago.

J. Donald Bell sheds more light on this hall

in his letter:

"The Iroquois Pavilion was located on the banks of the St. Lawrence River in the old Village of Iroquois. I say 'old' because the village was uprooted to make way for the Seaway. Some of it was moved about one mile north of the river to what is known as Iroquois, which bears no resemblance to the original picturesque town. The pavilion was a large wooden structure which at night was brightly lit with coloured lights—it was fascinating and the sound of great dance music coming from it made it irresistible. On Saturday nights the voices of 200 or more happy people could be heard as you approached. Admission was maybe 25 cents and a five-minute dance was ten cents. Soft drinks were sold and no booze was allowed or available during those days of prohibition. And everyone seemed happier than they do now. Many great bands played there. One particularly good one which I remember was the Royal Ambassadors from Chicago. Bert Niosi's band from Toronto was a great attraction. Occasionally some passenger ships would dock close to the pavilion and bring Americans from as far away as the Thousand Islands. It was fun to ask these 'foreign' girls to dance and whirl around the floor with them."

Other interesting reflections on the pavilion come from John Gordier:

"It was owned by the Lannons from Winchester, and dances were held three times a week, Tuesday, Friday and Saturday. The house bands were usually hired for the season and came from Toronto. The upper half of the Iroquois Pavilion's walls were fitted with screens, and hinged wooden panels covered the openings when the building was not in use. The floor was hardwood and the band played from a raised dais at the opposite end from the entrance. The usual reflecting globe hung in the middle of the hall. Attendance was good until 1934 when it seemed to drop off. Before the next season came around, the pavilion had been sold, and the new owner converted it to a Cabaret. Tables occupied half the dance floor and the customer bought dance tickets. There was no longer a resident orchestra, but the void was taken care of by local bands and those travelling the circuit. One in particular caught my fancy, a competent all-girl orchestra. In another year or so the pavilion had closed and I had moved on, taking with me a host of musical memories. I treasure my collection of records and sheet music from those days."

Ron Stroud played sax in Eddie Stroud's band for over 25 years. The group performed at practically every major pavilion in Ontario, and had the distinction of being Gerry Dunn's first house band in Bala. Ron also has some thoughts about the Iroquois Pavilion: "For three seasons we headed East to play at several pavilions that made up Lannon's one-night stands. Our starting place would be from Mr. Lannon's home where we would leave in his bus after lunch to go to Gananoque, play the job and go back to his home after the job. We would try to sleep during the four-hour drive, and then once we reached Mr. Lannon's home, sleep until noon. Then the routine went on for about two weeks to other pavilions."

For a final thought on the Iroquois Pavilion, let's turn back to Donald Bell for his last words on the long-gone dance hall: "The site of the old pavilion is now many feet underwater. Maybe when ships now pass over it some feet begin to tap and happy sounds can be heard coming from the deep ...."

Cornwall: Pearson Central Ballroom

Cornwall had a few popular dance halls where local orchestras performed. Local historian Gary Villeneuve writes: "This was a large brick structure, one floor, located on Sydney Street between Water and First. I always knew this place as 'Pearson's Furniture,' which was its final function. It was certainly in business during World War II, possibly earlier, but was levelled in 1979, along with an entire city block, to make way for the Cornwall Square shopping mall."

From Elinor Kyte Senior, in her history of Cornwall: "Some of the drawing cards at the local dance halls were Burton Heward's Rhythm Knights and Charles James' Orchestra. Heward's first band included Dan Robertson, Mac Norris, Levi Leroux, Jack Gibson, Hamilton Kirkey, Charles Stewart, with Burton on drums. Later on, other members joined including Hal Lee, Harvey Boileau, Charles Heward,

Dick Loucks, Len DeCarle, Lionel Bouley, Eric Hudd, Gerry Burgess and vocalists Shirley McAteer and Ed Lalonde. Members in Charles James' Orchestra were Paul Comeau, Larry and Joseph Desrosier, Fern Moquin, Oliver Duhaime and Rheal Groulx."[7]

Cornwall: The Oasis

Gary continues with background on The Oasis: "This famous hall was located about four miles north of downtown Cornwall, on the border between the City of Cornwall and Cornwall Township, about 200 feet north of the intersection of Cornwall Centre Road and St. Andrews Road, the latter now being Highway 138. It was a classic-looking dance hall, wooden construction, with a castellated false front. I remember the place as a terminus for the Pitt Street bus line. Buses would turn around in front of the Oasis to head back downtown. It was still in operation at the time of its destruction by fire in 1966."

Cornwall: Collins' Dance Hall

Gary Villeneuve goes on to describe another spot for dancing in Cornwall: "Collins' Dance Hall was located on the upper floor of a long-gone building at the corner of Montreal Road and Marlborough Street. This hall may very well have catered more to the very large French-speaking population of East Cornwall."

The Cornwall Armouries

"I might also mention the Cornwall Armouries," Gary continues. "It was the scene of many gatherings and dances, even as late as my high school years in the 1960s. At least, this building is still standing. It is in superb shape and remains unaltered. Erected in 1939, it is also one of the last WWII armouries to have been built, and is considered to be among the very finest armouries buildings ever built in this province. Unlike the usual red-brick armouries, it is of yellow brick with a fabulous yellow-stone castle-front, a beauty to behold."

A couple of other dance spots in Cornwall

153

Green Valley Pavilion, built in 1933, operated until the mid-50s. *Courtesy of Jacqueline Bouchard.*

were the Labour Temple on York Street and the more fashionable Cornwallis Hotel.

Green Valley Pavilion

Jacqueline (Lajoie) Bouchard writes about the dance pavilion her family operated in Green Valley, located on Highway #34 between Lancaster and Alexandria:

"My Mom and late Dad, Leo Lajoie, were widely known throughout the years they operated the Green Valley Pavilion. I give them lots of credit for starting up such a business in the Depression years (1933 construction was started). Over the years it became the most popular rendezvous in Eastern Ontario for dances, wedding receptions and other social activities. Among the big bands that made several appearances were Don Messer and his Highlanders from P.E.I.

"My Dad had a quiet friendly personality which won him many friends. He was also a leader in the community and operated a general store and post office for many years. My Mom with her bubbling personality and love of people was in charge of all the food, and along with her several helpers did an excellent job. She is now 85 years old and enjoying life to its fullest. (Hard work doesn't kill!)"

One of the acts to perform at the hall in the early 1950s was the Rocky Mountain Rangers. In 1956 the pavilion was converted into a church. The Lajoie family home, built about 1945, sits beside the former pavilion.

154

Other Memories

Dorothy Power used to go dancing at the pavilion at Grippen Lake in the Lyndhurst area. "It was owned by the Sweet family. They always had good orchestras, one of which was Warmingtons from Kingston. The late Cyril Slack of Brockville was a pianist with them while he was attending Queen's University. He became a lawyer and lived in Mission City, B.C. There was also a hall called Pinehurst, near Blue Church Prescott. Another one in operation for many years was at Long Beach, about five miles west of Brockville. They had many good orchestras who played. There is a motel there now."

Jim Yeldon also remembers this last place. "The Hub at Long Beach was on the old #29 Highway. There was Dance Land which was down by the river past the Ontario Hospital. Then we also had the Armories; one night Jimmy Auld hired Gene Krupa for a party—it was sure packed that night! We often took the ferry across to Morristown to dance. I still love to dance—we just had Canada's Spitfire Band here and they are great."

Vera (Blanchard) Black writes about some of her favourite places. "I grew up in the village of Greenbush, 12 miles north of Brockville and began attending dances quite young with my older brother who would take me. One of the most popular halls was the Orange Hall in New Dublin. The music was provided by Frank Murray's four-piece orchestra—violin, piano, saxophone and drums .... I once attended a dance in the Merrickville Armories in the early 1930s when Guy Lombardo played."

Don Sherman is a retired musician (piano) in Brockville who remembers many of the halls that are long gone. "Early pavilions in Brockville in the 1920s were McCoy's and Deslisle's in St. Lawrence Park. Leo Beauvais' Melody Kings played there as a matter of interest. There were so many pavilions that once existed and were very popular in their day. Proceeding towards Brockville there was Crystal Beach (later Long Beach) where bands from Brockville played, such as Leo Beauvais and Carl McLennan. Out-of-town bands including Niosi, Stroud, the Royal Ambassadors and the Maryland Collegians often played there. It was demolished in the late 1940s.

"Further down by Prescott was the Colonial Inn. H. Thompson played there, often using itinerant Toronto musicians, such as Maynard Ferguson when he was hitchhiking from Toronto to Montreal. Going east to Iroquois was a very large pavilion where the Royal Ambassadors from Cleveland played. When the Seaway flooded out Iroquois, many other pavilions were taken out as well, such as Long Sault Rapids and Mille Roches.

"I played many of the pavilions with Smiths Falls musicians as well as Sandy Runciman from Brockville. I look back on these great nights with guys now long gone. It gives me satisfaction to have played with guys that went on to famous orchestras, including Niosi, The Dorseys and Spivak."

Chapter Eleven

FROM WHITBY THROUGH THE TRENT RIVER SYSTEM

"The Jube", one of Ontario's few remaining dance pavilions, as it once was.

Whitby: Club Bayview

Travelling along Highway 401 near Whitby, you'll see a tall green steel fence, erected to deaden the roar of traffic as well as protect residents from highway grime. Just a stone's throw to the north of this drab wall lies the remnants of a small and very old apple orchard which was once the location of Whitby's popular dance hall, Club Bayview.

Club Bayview was the creation of Whitby resident, Harold Rowley, who brought his dream back to Canada after World War II, feeling that the community would enjoy a clean, respectable club featuring dancing and entertainment. Using his Veteran's Benefits from the War, he purchased six and a half acres at the end of his street (Byron) and constructed his new club right in the middle of the apple

orchard. On October 7, 1946, the *Oshawa Daily Times Gazette* reported on Harold's dance hall. "Well underway in the southern reaches of Whitby is one man's post-war project. The walls and basement of H.D. Rowley's dance pavilion are completed and the trusses for the roof are ready to be raised. Mr. Rowley has located his amusement place in one of the most attractive spots in town, near the new highway."

The name Club Bayview was coined from the view of Lake Ontario which was visible from the balcony windows in the pavilion. When it opened on December 21, 1946, the place was filled with people who were anxious to see Harold's new project. Harold's house band was an Oshawa group called the Rythmaires, which featured Oshawa musicians such as Bill Askew, Otis Foote and singer Laurie Harmer, sister of well-known vocalist, Shirley Harmer. From

156

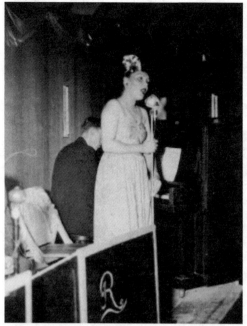

During the late 1940s Club Bayview featured many local orchestras as well as touring bands.

This photo *(above)*, circa late 1940s, is believed to be Cy McLean and his orchestra.

Both photos courtesy of the late Harold Rowley.

opening day Club Bayview was a very busy hall. Along with running three or four dances per week, banquets were also staged for various community and church groups. Running the business quickly became a family affair with Harold's wife, Pearl, managing the kitchen, along with daughter Maebelle (Sevcik) and son Bud helping out on a regular basis. "We would also have special event dances to coincide with the time of the year, such as Easter, Valentine's Day, New Year's Eve—something like the movie, Holiday Inn," said Harold. With the building located in the middle of an apple orchard, Harold staged a Blossom Ball every spring, which was a very romantic occasion for the customers who wandered around the apple trees during the evening.

Back in 1946, when Club Bayview was under construction, the *Times Gazette* reported: "Care is being taken to make the place as safe as well as attractive. The building is of cement block construction with a fireproof shingle roof, which will make it practically fireproof." Ironically, Club Bayview was destroyed by fire over the Easter weekend in 1964. Three weeks after our visit in 1994, Harold Rowley passed away.

The Jubilee Pavilion shortly after construction in 1927.
Courtesy of Ron Bouckley.

Oshawa: The Jubilee Pavilion

When the Dominion of Canada celebrated its 60th birthday in 1927, the City of Oshawa was determined to make the most of the affair. To honour this memorable occasion the new dance pavilion in Oshawa's Lakeview Park was officially opened on July 1, and named the Jubilee Pavilion. As one of the few dance pavilions remaining in the Province of Ontario, the Jubilee Pavilion has had a remarkable and rich history of presenting great music, and hosting many other events. "The Jube," as most people

157

Art Hallman *(photo right and standing above)* **performing with his band at the Jube in the early 1880s.** *Courtesy of Joe Kondyjowski*

affectionately call it, quickly gained a reputation as a hall that featured both the best dance bands and rock groups in Ontario. Over the years people have travelled from far away to enjoy music which has ranged from Big Band, to rock 'n' roll and even country & western, showcasing some of the finest talent and biggest acts of the various musical eras. A series of independent operators—the most well known and beloved being Owen McCrohan—directed the city-owned Jubilee Pavilion over the years; today the hall is managed by the Oshawa Central Lions Club.

The brown brick pavilion sitting in Lakeview Park in 1997 has been so radically altered from the original Jube that it's hard to believe most of the old hall is still intact behind the new facade. It was originally a wood frame building set on a cement foundation, with room below for coal furnaces. Most people will remember the large gleaming maple dance floor which is still there even today. Walkways 15 feet in width flanked this floor — the railings have since been removed.

Big Bands were usually hired for the whole summer, performing six nights per week, and would often stay in cottages very nearby. Initially jitney dancing was 10 cents a dance, and most people arrived stag in groups. With the RCAF flying school located just northeast of the city (now the airport), there was never a shortage of young men looking for dance partners at the Jube during World War II. Some of the popular bands to perform at the Jube included Ozzie Williams, Stan Williams and His Blue Marines, Boyd Valleau, Jack Denton and Pat Riccio. In fact, Pat Riccio, who was the winner of best dance band in Ontario contest in 1960, made his debut as bandleader at the Jube in 1957. From the 1960s on, the late Art Hallman was a fixture on the Jube's stage for regular Saturday night dances. "The Jubilee Pavilion is a one-of-its-kind place in all of Canada," he told a local newspaper in 1987.[1] Art

158

The new Red Barn was built in 1974.

played his final gig at the Jube in 1991.

Throughout the 1960s, '70s and '80s most every well–known rock group set up their equipment on the Jube's stage. Local Oshawa bands, Toronto groups and many Canadian touring rock 'n' rollers all performed for at least one night. A number of them returned on a regular basis, including perennial favourites Little Caesar and the Consuls.

Owen McCrohan guided the Jube through nearly half a century of music, from the swing era into the rock years. His office walls were literally covered in autographed 8″ by 10″ glossy pictures of the musicians who played here; bands always enjoyed playing the Jube, regarding it as one of the premier dance halls in southern Ontario. They also looked forward to visiting "Onie McCronie," hoping to glean some words of wisdom from a man who knew just about everybody and everything there was to know in the music business. Owen also had a personal connection with rock music—two family members joined Steppenwolf, a band with a string of hits in the late '60s and early '70s. Owen McCrohan was at the helm of the Jubilee Pavilion until he passed away in 1980.

The large mirrored globe still sparkles over the maple dance floor for regular dances.

Oshawa: The Red Barn

One of the people who quickly came to appreciate Owen McCrohan's vast experience in the business through working with him, was fellow Oshawan, Joe Kondyjowski. Joe has an enviable track record in the pavilion business himself. Garnering his initial knowledge through Owen's tutelage, he has owned or managed four major halls in Ontario, including the Red Barn in Oshawa. Following a tradition began by Owen McCrohan of asking every band for an autographed photo, Joe also has amassed a large collection of photographs of bands and orchestras that have played his halls. When Owen McCrohan passed away, the estate left Joe the photos he had collected over the years. These pictures portray one of the most complete visual compilations of music, from Big Band to rock.

DANCE Tonight

RUDY VELTRI
and his New
TRONADOS
playing the
NASHVILLE SOUND
featuring the lovely
MARIE HARRISON

RED BARN
"Oshawa's Friendliest Dance"

Today Joe continues to run his Red Barn Auditorium in Oshawa. "The present Red Barn was constructed in 1974," explains Joe." It replaced the old one that burned down on the 1973 May 24th weekend. "The old wooden pavilion was about 40 years old, built by Harold Reddick and was primarily a Country and Western venue." Joe says at one time the Red Barn was a mecca for country and western acts. "People came from all over to see acts like Johnny Cash, Ernest Tubbs and other big-name performers."

Oshawa: The Avalon

The Westmount Pavilion was constructed in 1932 on King Street West, across from the present Oshawa Centre. Steve Macko describes the hall. "It was an older wooden structure with a maple dance floor and a stage that extended into the audience for a few feet. The Avalon's crowd sometimes could be rough, with bikers from the Golden Hawk Riders motorcycle club along with their friends frequenting the dances on Sunday night at the Avalon. The kids who didn't want to meet trouble in a dance hall headed down to the Jubilee Pavilion for the rock dances on Friday nights."

Ron Bouckley, an Oshawa collector of local memorabilia and an historian as well, remembers the

159

Romping Ronnie Hawkins *(left)* **with his drummer, Levon Helm at the Avalon, early 1960s**
Courtesy of Ed Mazurkiewich.

Avalon from an earlier time. "I often attended Sunday night jazz concerts here and enjoyed the performances," he says.

Ed Mazurkiewich, who also played with Steve in the Lincolnaires at the Avalon on a regular basis, fills in some of the history: "In 1938 the hall's name was changed to the Avalon...When the dances closed in 1962, it became Harvey Dance Academy, then Honest Cal's furniture and appliance store in '63. By 1968 it was the Slot Car and Hobby Shop until April 20, 1969, when the building burned down." The Lincolnaires found their niche at the Avalon and enjoyed a number of years as the regular band. Ed talks about the usual after-dance tradition. "Both the bands and the customers would always gather at either the Hilltop or Wayside restaurants— the Hilltop was famous for their 12-inch hot dogs and strawberry shakes. People would come just to hang out after the Sunday night dances during the late 1950s or so. But then things changed when the local A&W opened—that's where people started going after dances."

Today, Ed leads a reunited and re-formed Lincolnaires, who specialize in music from 1956-64—their favourite years—and play around town at oldie dances. The walls in Ed's basement rehearsal room are filled with large displays of photos and memorabilia from their heyday which they bring

with them to their dances. The band even has an exact replica of the giant clock that used to hang on the back wall of the Avalon's stage.

Caesarea (Port Perry): Reg's Marina

Nestled on the east side of Lake Scugog lies a quiet collection of cottages and permanent homes which comprise the community of Caesarea. It's been over 20 years since the last public dance at Caesarea's pavilion. The Frayer family started the dance and marina business from scratch in 1930. Percy Frayer recalls the early days of his father Fred's venture, founded on the land his grandparents owned: "It began as a dance hall and a concession stand with the snack bar operating daily. A few years later my father began the marina portion of the business where he repaired and rented boats." Saturday night dances were a very big attraction at Caesarea and often brought in 600 to 700 people who danced to a variety of bands and orchestras hired by Fred.

Reg Renouf told me about his years of ownership: "I purchased the business 1958. Our family had a cottage in Caesarea and I was quite familiar with the small resort. When I learned the pavilion was being put up for sale, I felt that the business would be an ideal enterprise to operate during the summer months." Reg's Marina was born. (Reg's family had been in the business of operating pavilions, having leased Elm Park in Woodbridge from

1934 to the early 1940s.) Reg transformed the concession stand portion of the business into a restaurant where patrons could order a breakfast or lunch.

Some of the entertainers at Caesarea included Jack Fowler whose Big Band sound was a real crowd pleaser. Russ Creighton from Toronto also played here regularly with his brand of older style country flavoured music. Charlie Cochrane from Oshawa and King Ganam were also popular. Dancers travelled from Oshawa, Port Perry, Peterborough and other nearby towns on a Saturday night to dance at Caesarea. Says Reg: "I also booked a number of rock bands over the years, including Ronnie Hawkins, who had just come to Canada and was making his musical mark, and perennial favourites, Little Caesar and the Consuls."

As the 1960s moved along, the crowds became a little rougher at Caesarea, particularly on a Friday night when motorcycle gangs would arrive to party. As a result, Reg made strong alliances with the OPP, who were responsible for policing the area.

An aerial view of Reg Renouf's marina business circa 1960. Servicing boats, running the restaurant and staging dances all summer long kept Reg and his family busy. *Courtesy of Reg Renouf.*

Both Reg and his friend Morgan Sears remember some occasions when there would be cruisers at all entrances to Caesarea, two boats on the water in front, "and even a plane in the air above." Unfortunately, kids began to stay away from the pavilion. The change in clientele was one of the major factors behind Reg's decision to sell the business in 1968. The last time the building changed hands was around 1990 when a motorcycle group turned the building into a private dwelling. They throw two or three parties for their friends over the year, say locals, but mostly keep a low profile the rest of the time. The many "Private" and "Keep Out" signs are enough to warn the curious to keep their distance.

Bowmanville Beach Pavilions

Not far from the site of the former pav sits Mrs. Fowler's cottage, built in 1915 by her grandfather. As with most other established cottage areas in the province, family ties in many of these summer abodes stretch back for decades, providing a link from generation to generation. In many cases the

township owns the land and leases it back to the cottagers and homeowners. Mrs. Fowler fondly recalls the days when the pavilion was the centre of activity at the beach, with its dance floor, convenience store and ice hut.

But in order to really grasp an understanding of the significance of the beach to Bowmanville and the surrounding area, it helps to speak with someone who recalls the good years, and who has also witnessed the many changes which time has brought. To find such a person I needed to look no further than the popular town barber, Gary Cole.

Fortunately for my purposes, Gary has a direct connection with one of Bowmanville's two dance pavilions. The Bowmanville Creek actually divides the waterfront into the East and West beach areas. At one time there was a dance pavilion on both sides of this body of water where it empties into the lake. Gary recalls the dance hall on the east side. "The eastern beach pavilion was built by Fred Depew just after the First War," he says. "The structure was initially an open-air dance floor which was later covered as funds permitted. Some of the popular dances were the jitney dances where customers paid five cents to get up on the floor. Typical summer food such as hot dogs, was sold from a concession stand. There was also a post office located on the premises to service the cottages on the beach. This facility operated during the summer months only and was torn down during the 1970s."

But it was the pavilion on the other side of the river that ties Gary to the waterfront. "On the west beach another pavilion was constructed about the same time as the east pavilion—the late 19-teens. The building was actually used as a cottage during the First War and changed hands quite often, but the original owner was Joe Dilling who operated the hall until 1946."

162

A subsequent owner was Gary's uncle, Charlie Severs. He purchased it in 1945 and ran it until the mid-1950s. Dutch Butler took over later and kept it until its demise around 1960. It collapsed in the early 1990s. "The building itself was long and narrow, measuring 50 to 60 feet long and 20 feet in width," he continues. "Four additions were complet-

A group outing at west pavilion along Bowmanville's beach during the 1920s or '30s. *Courtesy of Gary Cole.*

ed over the years as money became available, enlarging the facility. A hardwood dance floor was built, providing dancers a great place to move their feet to both bands and in later years, a jukebox. Wooden shutters were pulled up when the pavilion was open, and screens protected the customers from bugs."

The east pavilion, owned by Depew, was also operating at the same time the Severs ran their business. In fact, the Severs offered a free boat ride across the channel to anyone wishing to leave the east side and visit their pavilion on the west. Irene said there was always friendly rivalry between the two dance halls, and yes, the twain did meet. There were a couple of owners after the Severs, but the pavilion and store eventually ceased operating in the early 1960s.

As recent as April 1995, Clarington (which includes Bowmanville) Mayor Diane Hamre was quoted in local papers as being very interested in restoring Bowmanville's beachfront to its pristine state of many years ago. Modern waterfront townhouses on the river are contrasted with many of the remaining cottages which sit in a sad state of disrepair. With limited government funding available for even the most essential services today, it is difficult to estimate how much time will pass before this wonderful lakefront property will finally see re-development.

Cobourg Pavilion

In Cobourg's Victoria Park, the site to the west of the

bandshell where people once came to dance and make romance is now a mini-putt. The last dance at the Cobourg Pavilion was held Saturday, April 24, 1976. On of the best descriptions of the Cobourg Pavilion and how much it meant to people is conveyed by Marion Sherwin who writes about her personal memories of this dance hall:

"The music floated across the park and spread along the beach. The moon, shining on the lake, added its golden touch but I was not happy. I was crying. How could I leave this scene? Cobourg Pavilion was everything to me—the music, dancing, friends and good times. It was 1938. I had finished high school and was leaving the next morning for New York. Cobourg Pavilion! Two or three nights a week my brother, my friends and I met there to enjoy dancing to the music of the Blue Marines. The pavilion was a large frame building; cool lake breezes wafted through the screen windows and the wooden floor shone like satin. It was a popular spot for young people and they happily danced the summer away.

"The year 1939 found me back in Canada dancing at the Cobourg 'Pav.' However, things were changing. In the fall War was declared. We were shocked that almost immediately some of the boys joined up and gradually many familiar faces were missing. When the manager of the pavilion enlisted, Stan Williams, the leader of the Blue Marines, took over the responsibility for the entertainment. Stan was also an accomplished pianist. When the band took intermission, Stan played piano solos, slow pieces and waltzes. The lights were lowered. A spot light shone on a revolving globe in the ceiling. It sent delightful shimmering coloured rays all over the dancers and the dance floor. The couples pressed closer, dancing cheek-to-cheek, stealing kisses now and then. They were in another world. It was seventh heaven.

"It was the Big Band Era and on occasion we thrilled to the music of Mart Kenney and Art Hallman who came to our pavilion. 'Blue Moon,' 'Amapola,' 'Moonlight Cocktail' and 'Blueberry Hill' were favourites. We were going through hard times, but dancing was not expensive. The fellows bought tickets—ten cents a dance. Gas was rationed, but

when we had a full tank we sought adventure further afield at Chemong, Lakefield, Campbellford and Little Lake.

"One night my girl friends and I noticed a different uniform across the floor. We identified it as American with ribbons showing that this soldier had taken part in the Italian Campaign. All the girls were hoping he would ask them to dance. Then we saw him heading our way. I didn't think I stood a chance, but would you believe it, he came straight to me and asked me to dance. He fed me quite an interesting line and then he began asking a lot of questions about my family and me. The next day he turned up at our farm. He was in fact a cousin from Washington, D.C.

"Stan Williams and the Blue Marines went on playing at Cobourg Pavilion for many years. The young people kept coming, dancing to pieces like 'Star Dust,' 'Paper Doll,' 'String of Pearls' 'In The Mood' and 'Beer Barrel Polka.'

Happy, Happy days!"

One musician who travelled the dance hall circuit extensively and was no stranger to the Cobourg Pavilion was Tommy Cinnamon. He devoted his career to the passion he loved—music. This talented musician passed away May 27, 1995, aged 85. He was still actively performing well into his 80s.

Tommy's musical journey began when he joined a dance band formed by members of the Cox family of Oshawa. In the 1930s, Tommy was playing bass with Win Phillips, and travelled to Montreal. He became involved with vaudeville and even shared the stage one evening with a very young Sammy Davis Jr. During World War II, Tommy served overseas where he was able to keep working in the field he loved, entertaining hospitalized troops. After the War, he settled into a steady gig with the Moxie Whitney Band, travelling to Banff for 17 summers and playing the Royal York Hotel for 23 years. After leaving Moxie's band in 1971, Tommy continued performing with the Oshawa Symphony, teaching and playing various gigs at area hotels. He also loved to participate in impromptu jam sessions whenever the opportunity arose. Along with the bass, Tommy was proficient on piano, drums and fiddle. Tommy performed

163

in nearly every dance pavilion in southern Ontario during the 1920s and '30s. From Mossington Park at Jacksons Point in 1923 and 24, to Riley's in Trenton, to Rye's in Peterborough, to Quick's Pleasure Palace at Presqu'ile Point, Tommy set his bass on almost every stage where dances were held.

He will always be remembered as one of the original troopers who lived to make music.

Brighton: Spring Valley Dance Pavilion

"The Spring Valley Dance Pavilion may sound like an innocent enough dance hall, but don't let the name fool you," says Basil McMaster. "It could just as easily have been labelled 'The Bucket of Blood,' or, as some of us called it, 'Hog Wrestle'," according to this long-term resident of Brighton

This roadside dance hall is not written up in local history books. No, the Spring Valley Dance Pavilion was everything that the pavilion at the Presqu'ile Hotel—Quick's Pleasure Palace—was not. To begin with, access was easy. You simply walked a

few steps north of town (less than a mile) and *voila*, Hog Wrestle awaited you. Basil says that the emporium operated between the mid-'20s and the mid-'30s, finally going down in a blaze of glory when fire destroyed the hall.

The Kenney family ran Spring Valley, offering dancing every Saturday night. Entertainment was usually in the form of a fiddle player and caller, often accompanied by a pianist. Fiddlers played for their honour and reputation and so did the callers, and both usually donated their time.

Basil also draws the comparison in many ways between the fancier, more conservative facilities at the Point, where a dress code was always in effect, to the rougher atmosphere at Spring Valley. While dancers were gracefully moving their feet to square, round and fox trot dancing at Quick's Pleasure Palace, Hog Wrestlers followed the calls to square dances only, just north of the little town of Brighton.

Brighton: Little Lake Pavilion

Just past the exit to Brighton on eastbound Highway 401 is a small body of water off to the right. This large milky blue puddle is called Little Lake.

Although not visible from the freeway, there's a pavilion sitting on the south shore of the lake in a park-like setting, appropriately called Little Lake Pavilion. In 1995, John and Barbara Kremer operated the business primarily as a restaurant and catering venture. There were a few seasonal trailer sites (22 hook-ups), but as these were vacated, newcomers were not sought. Little Lake is 110 feet above Lake Ontario, and from the top of the hill to the south of the pavilion, you can see both lakes.

John says that dances have not been held during the 20 years he and Barbara owned the pavilion, but that was not always so: "The original pavilion dates back to the 1800s when it was the only structure on the lake—now 150 cottages have been built around this small body of water. The old pavilion had wooden doors which would be propped open

Little Lake Pavilion today is a restaurant and banquet site with a few trailer sites. Dances are no longer held here.

when the hall was being used. People came by horse and buggy to stay overnight." There have been at least two fires, resulting in extensive re-construction. The Kremers put on significant additions over the years including a patio where during the summer many people eat on outdoor tables.

A wide circle of people attended dances at Little Lake, but you needed transportation because the hall was three or four miles from town. Spring Valley, on the other hand, was just north of the town limits.

Presqu'ile Hotel: Quick's Pleasure Palace

When the contents of the Presqu'ile Hotel were auctioned off on May 19, 1972, Basil McMaster was there with others who remembered the hotel in its grand days when U.S. visitors would take their holidays at the Point, and when the dance pavilion operated every night of the week. "It was sad seeing all of those items being sold off for a few dollars—there were just too many memories," says Basil. "I attended the sale

for a short while, but I couldn't stay."

Presqu'ile Point is home to one of Ontario's most popular provincial campgrounds. But long before tents were pitched and trailers were hauled, an entirely different type of vacationer found pleasure at the Point. The Presqu'ile Hotel opened July 1, 1905. Eight years later, an ambitious 26-year-old local entrepreneur by the name of Grant Quick built a pavilion opposite the hotel and advertised free dancing Wednesday and Friday evenings with a Belleville orchestra supplying the music. And the name he gave his dance hall might raise some eyebrows—even today:

"Quick's Pleasure Palace—where you get first class service and can always enliven yourself."

The *Brighton Ensign* in 1913 confirmed that Quick was on to a good thing. "Dancers were there in big numbers...words failed the majority to express the praise they wished for the charming music...this coupled with the excellent condition of the floor made the lads and lassies whirl in ecstasy ...." The following year the Hotel Presqu'ile was sold to the Presqu'ile Hotel Company, managed by Grant Quick, who also held well over half the shares of the

Today the government dock and the old stairway are the only visible reminders of the glory days of the hotel and dance pavilion. A modern home now sits on the grounds of the pavilion.

165

business.

In 1937 and 1938, Basil gained first-hand knowledge of the hotel and the pavilion as an employee: "The first year I worked as a bellhop and then the following year my duties were varied, but mostly devoted to the dance hall." Basil has his own unique recollection about maintaining the dance floor. "One of the musicians would be trussed up in a wool blanket while two others would drag him over the surface. This helped to shine the floor as well as remove the road dust that would collect through the open windows." Basil remembers Quick's strict dress code. "Men traditionally wore white flannels and blue blazers." Local cottagers would pay Grant $10 for dance privileges anytime during the summer. Presqu'ile Pleasure Palace ran on Standard Time, in order to add an extra hour in the evenings.

Trenton musician Ted Snider led one of the many bands who performed for the season at the Pleasure Palace. As Ted remembers: "We were booked for both the 1946 and 1947 seasons and received $16.80 per man per week plus room and board. We bunked down in the barracks at the back of the pavilion." According to Ted, Sunday concerts and evening sing-songs at Presqu'ile were very popular. Soon after Ted's stint at the pavilion, live radio broadcasts were transmitted from the hall. Some of the bands who performed at Presqu'ile Pleasure Palace during its remarkable history were: Art Jewitt, Gordon Winters, The Windsor Four (later the Windsor Seven), The Blue Jackets, Frank Barnard, Eddie Musgrove, Al Saunders Rainbow Review, Skip Vaughn (who later operated the Bobcaygeon's Edgewater Pavilion), Tom Gimley, Herb Bell and His Merrymakers, Joni Greer, Bud Marsh and The Mell-O-Tones, and Wayne Ring's Four-Piece Band & Trumpets. Pianist Peggy Mitchell was hired as piano soloist one year; she painstakingly located large whitewashed stones to create a four-foot-high landmark 'Presqu'ile' sign which, when completed, was visible from both the water and the air.

Bette Donaghy Moore shared some of her memories of the pavilion with me. "My mother and father spent their honeymoon at the hotel, so our family does have deep roots at Presqu'ile," she says. "Grant Quick would carefully scrutinize the crowd at each dance—he would know exactly who had paid and who had not and would walk around with a wad of bills in his hand." In the 1940s, the crowd would sometimes approach 800, attracted by the large number of posters put up in the area advertising the dances.

Ben Thompson writes: "My wife, Pat, and I together with our teenage friends, spent hours every

Ted Snider led the house band in the mid-1940s. At 20 years of age, he was the old man of the group. He had made a solemn promise to the mothers of the Italian lads that he would look after their boys: ensure their clothes were clean, that they attended mass regularly and that they washed and showered regularly. This photo, taken on stage at the pavilion in 1947 shows: Joe Melo, piano; Bob Wilkinson, drums; John Garriere, Cliff Wilson and Ted Snider, trumpets; and in front: Al Zippoly, Al Colantanio, Frank Contini and John Bartucca, reeds.
Courtesy of Ted Snider.

day at the hotel government dock and in the pavilion. In the summer of 1942, I played a slide trombone in the orchestra. The pavilion was almost a second home for all the teenagers." Only two reminders of this hotel and pavilion remain today—the cement staircase leading up to a large vacant lot where the hotel sat, and the government dock, rebuilt in 1939.

Sandbanks: Lakeshore Lodge

Even though hotels and lodges are not the focus of the book, there is one very special location in Prince Edward County that cannot be overlooked.

If you have ever camped at Sandbanks Provincial Park you may have taken the time to explore the remains of Lakeshore Lodge. This vacation resort stood beside Lake Ontario for 102 years, from 1870 to 1972. The main lodge burned down in 1983 after which the remainder of the buildings were taken down for safety sake, but there are still many visible reminders of the fun and the elegance this hotel provided for guests during its century of operation. And what is most interesting for this book, is that the terrazzo floor, with the letters "LSL" is still solidly entrenched in the ground, as if waiting for the next couple to make their way to the dance floor.

A number of owners were associated with the lodge during its years of operation. One of the first ones was Daniel McDonald. Each new owner made various changes, improvements, upgrades and additions to the facility. The lodge itself was constructed in four stages between 1870 and 1892, at which time it could serve meals to 100 guests.

Dances at Lakeshore Lodge were originally held in a building near the site of the terrazzo floor. This old structure also housed an ice cream parlour, billiard room and bowling alley. A new combination dance hall and games room was built in the early 1960s and it was at this time that the high quality floor was laid. Dancing took place most nights, usually to a live band.

One area band who enjoyed playing Lakeshore Lodge was The Aces. In 1994, The Aces' leader, Jack Grant, told the *Belleville Intelligencer* newspaper's 'Remember When' section, "Lakeshore

was our favourite spot, I think. We drew tremendous crowds there." Jack hooked up with The Aces in 1930 and it wasn't long before the band was playing five nights per week. The group would travel in pianist Jack Denmark's big 1926 Cadillac, playing gigs in Kingston's Roy York Cafe, Queen's and the Golden Slipper as well as Lakeshore. By 1935 Jack and others formed a new band out of Havelock, called Jack Grant and His Aces.

During its century of operation it is estimated that over one million people visited Lakeshore Lodge. The property was sold in 1972 to the Ministry of Natural Resources and became part of Sandbanks.

And on a moonlit night in July or August, if you quietly make your way to the ruins of Lakeshore Lodge, you just may see the silhouette of a couple who have been mysteriously drawn from their tent, swaying on the smooth weather-beaten floor, gently moving their feet over the initials "LSL."

Oak Lake: Oaksmere Pavilion

It's a tiny lake, located just south of Stirling, but during the days when the pavilion was up and running it was one of the hottest spots north of Belleville.

Choosing a location between Bird's Beach and Sarle's Beach, Mrs. Barager opened Oak Lake's first dance hall in the 1920s and called it the Oaksmere Pavilion, originally just a converted barn. After its demise in 1936 her son, Arthur, built a larger hall on the very same spot. Arthur's interests did not include running a dance business, so he leased the property to three partners — Harold Carruthers, Sid Samuels and Theodore Maraskas, who together ran the Trianon Ballroom in Belleville. They ran dances here from 1937 to 1942.

Most Saturday nights featured local talent, usually from Belleville. In fact, the newly re-formed Commodores Orchestra played their first gig here in 1941. By this time the pavilion was known as the Oak Lake Casino. On special nights some very big acts were brought up to the hall, including such names as Earl Hines and Dick Rogers.

Farley and Bertha Lindenfield danced at

167

Special ATTRACTION
OAK LAKE CASINO
Presents
DICK ROGERS
VOCALIST COMPOSER
and his Famous Orchestra
Direct from Million Dollar Pier, Atlantic City
MONDAY, JULY 21
15 ARTISTS
Featuring Bobby ENGELS Vocalist

Advance Sale Tickets 75c per person
on Sale at Reward Shoe Store and Oak Lake Casino
REGULAR ADMISSION: $1.00 per person

It has been many years since the Oak Lake Casino operated, but when it did there were some big names who graced the stage, including Dick Rogers *(he married Mary Pickford)* and Earl Hines in 1941. Belleville's Commodores were one of the local bands to play here as well.

EARL HINES
Exclusive XXX *Management*
WILLIAM MORRIS AGENCY
ROCKEFELLER CENTER
1270 SIXTH AVENUE
NEW YORK
LONDON · CHICAGO · HOLLYWOOD

Oak Lake in the 1930s when they were about 15. In an interview with the *Belleville Intelligencer* in 1992, Farley recalled his experiences. "Most people came out to a dance in groups, five or six to a car," he said. "A lot came out to the beach during the day and stayed for the dance at night. Sometimes people would quietly sneak out for a drink once in a while, but who wouldn't!" But generally speaking, money was too scarce for any luxuries like booze and gas. Occasionally the OPP visited the hall, but the operators made certain they had a couple of bouncer-types who insured that any troublemakers were firmly escorted out of the pavilion.

Farley said that everyone danced at Oak Lake. "You didn't come there to sit and chew the fat. Aside from the long benches and the rail around the dance floor, there were no tables or chairs."[2] Dim lights with coloured shades lit the room. The windows were square holes in the walls with wooden shutters that were lifted during dances—no screens, by the way.

Items like tires and gas were rationed during the War resulting in business falling off as people simply couldn't travel out of town to dances. And with alcohol rationed as well, the opportunities for a snort outside during the dance were few and far between. The partners did not renew their lease after 1942.

The winter of 1943 was particularly unfortunate for the Oak Lake Casino. During a heavy snowfall the roof collapsed under the weight of the white stuff and the pavilion was not re-built. Today, Puttman's Camping can be found in the same general area of the old hall.

Gerry Robinson recalls dancing at many of the pavilions in this part of the province, including Oak Lake. He writes: "I remember dancing at a few of those outside halls filled with flying objects like mosquitoes and bats occasionally, and eel flies and other interesting creatures. There were no coffee shops, usually just a bar at one corner where they sold cold drinks and as the night got warmer and the ice

An aerial shot of the old Cedardale Dance Pavilion and campground. Part of the wooden floor was used in the park's new recreation hall. *Courtesy of Dirk Safioles.*

melted, the drinks also got warmer. It was also that era when jitney dancing was in vogue—three tickets for a quarter. In my age group we learned to dance and there was body contact. Also a bit of drinking in cars but that was limited due to a money shortage. They often had a list of dances so one could sort of wait for the one you were most proficient at, and jump in if you could find the willing girl."

Trenton Area: Cedardale Dance Pavilion

The old park and dance pavilion called Cedardale, just southwest of Trenton, have since been replaced by "A beautiful retirement lifestyle park" named "The Meadows of Cedardale," as the business card states. But the three partners of this park are reminded on a regular basis by some of the senior residents of the mobile home community about the history behind this parcel of land.

There have been many owners of Cedardale over the years, including Jack Dingle. Another owner was Mr. Booth, who still has a mobile home in the park. Dirk Safioles is one of the current partners and talks about the park.

"Years ago, Cedardale was more of a day use park, where people would come out to the beach and swim during the day, and take in the dance at the old

pavilion in the evening. There was some camping as well," he says. Dirk feels the original pavilion was constructed in the 1920s, about the time the Murray Canal was built. This waterway initially provided access to the area for pleasure boats which brought people to the region.

"During the 1960s the old hall was dismantled, but the original dance floor was used in the new recreation hall for the park. It functions as a centre for meetings, bingo, suppers and of course, dances."

Tweed Park Pavilion

The Tweed Pavilion is surrounded by a grove of mature maples in Tweed Park, on the shore of peaceful Stoco Lake. It's been there since 1929, the year it was built and officially opened in a ceremony attended by dignitaries from far and wide. You can see a couple of the original fixtures from the building on display in the town's Heritage Centre—curator and dedicated Tweed historian, Evan Morton, proudly points out the old wooden box where dancers would deposit their tickets for jitney dancing in the 1930s, along with two dance tickets that Doug Connor found while restoring the box on July 11, 1992. Over in the corner sits an ornate cast iron toilet complete with a solid oak seat, "wrestled by Evan" from the pavilion's old plumbing pipes.

Evan gave me a guided tour of the building. "It is a grand old pavilion, but it is in need of repairs to maintain the structure," he says. A plaque on the outside west wall indicates that some renovations were carried out on the pavilion under the 1967 Centennial of Confederation Park Improvement program. "A cement block foundation was installed and steel beams were put in place to reinforce the floor," he says. Once inside the hall you are immediately taken back in time

169

Built in 1929, the Tweed Pavilion *(above)* **remains along the shore of Stoco Lake.**

The old wooden jitney ticket box *(left)* **is on display at the Tweed Heritage Centre.**
Both photos courtesy of Evan Morton, Tweed Heritage Centre.

to a period when this pavilion was considered to be one of the major dance halls in this part of the province. Open shutters bring in the beauty of the water, the original benches where young men and women sat and relaxed between dances line the wall, and the old wooden railings still have the gates which allowed dancers to enter the floor.

When the weekend dances were held the pavilion would be packed. "People would look forward to the Friday night dances all summer long. They came from Madoc, Kaladar, all over the general area," says Judy Desjardins, whose family operated a refreshment stand in the park. "We would beg to work at the canteen on a Friday night so we could go over to the dance for fifteen minute intervals." A local band who performed on a regular basis was the Sands of Time, who played music by the Righteous Brothers and other big acts of the era. Judy says, "At that time, the roadway wound down around the pavilion, and many a night a young man would leave the grounds squealing his tires, barely making the turn." Today, community events are held in the building including aerobics and kids' programs during the summer, craft sales and so on. Dianne Brick grew up in nearby Madoc and knows the Tweed

Pavilion very well. She writes: "In the summer of 1994 I was in the building for a family reunion. Like most of the old dance halls, you could almost hear the walls talking."

Once back at the Heritage Centre, Evan offers another interesting fact about his town: "Tweed is the birthplace of Mart Kenney—he was born here on March 7, 1910, and spent the first year of his life here before moving to Vancouver." Curiously, although Mart played many towns and cities in Ontario, his orchestra never did hit the Tweed Pavilion.

Erinsville: Beaver Lake Pavilion (Palmetto)

"Memories of Erinsville
Palmetto stands beside the lake, her dancing space
so fine,
The old and young go there for fun, when the stars
begin to shine.
A sea of autos parked around, from home and foreign
land,
Attest the magic of the spot, where you get the welcome
hand ..." [3]

Fire consumed the Beaver Lake Pavilion in 1989 — a family operation for 61 years. *Courtesy of Barb O'Neill*

"Memories of Erinsville"—an excerpt from a poem attributed to an individual by the name of Uncle Josh—no last name. He was so moved by his memorable vacation experiences at Beaver Lake that he put his thoughts to rhyme. In the first verse Uncle Josh refers to "Palmetto." It was the name on the lighted sign that for many years rested on top of the roof of the pavilion at Beaver Lake. H. Carroll Paul, of nearby Tamworth, spent many a happy summer evening dancing at the Beaver Lake hall, owned by the O'Neill family for 61 years. Charles O'Neill built it in 1928 and his brother James took over the operation in 1940, adding cottages on the lakefront property. It became a very popular destination for both Canadian and American tourists. Mr. Paul wrote to say that "James farmed his land, ran the dance hall, rented summer cottages, did the mail route and was the tax collector—he had everything but the potato bugs!"

In 1963, Joe and James Jr., the two sons of James O'Neill, acquired the family business. When James Jr. retired in 1987, Joe and his wife Barb managed the business themselves, continuing the tradition of weekly dances for the cottagers on the lake, as well as the general public who travelled from Kingston, Napanee, Belleville and Tweed to the weekly dances. The hall became a real community gathering place, which as the O'Neill family explains, is reflected in the name Palmetto. "People rented the

pavilion for anniversaries, family reunions, wedding receptions and many other special gatherings," says Barb. Barb and Joe's own 25th anniversary was celebrated with friends and family in the cosily decorated hall. H. Carroll Paul recalls dancing to bands such as Toronto's George Wade and His Corn Huskers, The Aces and Don Johnstone and His Serenaders. Later bands included the Land O' Lake Cruisers, Harmony Kings, Shiloe, Dakota and the Red Rose Express, all hailing from the general area. The late Ed Hopkins, proprietor of the local general store had the distinction of dancing at the opening night of the Beaver Lake Pavilion, and was also present at the last dance on July 15, 1989. In the early hours of July 16, a flash fire destroyed the interior of the hall, and the pavilion had to be torn down. No doubt Uncle Josh would be saddened at the loss of his beloved pavilion, but the strong feelings of friendship and human spirit still remain at Beaver Lake.

Trenton: Twelve O'Clock Point

This area was located on the north side of the entrance to the Murray Canal. Around the turn of the century it was a popular summer resort, complete with lodge, amusement park and steam-driven merry-go-round. Camping also was popular. In the early days people would gather for sing-songs, corn roasts and bonfires. The lodge did have a dance hall, which attracted a number of people. The building on the site is apparently the original lodge, once owned by the Groff family, although there is little resemblance in architecture, since there have been additions and new siding installed over the years. Jack DeLong says that after the War the park was bought

171

by Mrs. Henrietta Dewey of New York State. The resort was refurbished, but the original pavilion was in bad shape and consequently had to be torn down.

Trenton: Riley's

Riley's was one of the better known dance pavilions in Trenton, located on the south side of Highway #2, a couple of miles east of the city. Between the 1920s and 1940s many travelling bands stopped here, including Moxie Whitney who got his first big break in 1937 when his band, then known as the Pacific Swingsters played here. Moxie would later develop a long-term association with the Royal York Hotel in Toronto as the house orchestra. Bayside High School now sits across from Riley's old site.

Belleville: Club Commodore and
The Trianon Ballroom

Stan Wiggins' Commodores Orchestra in Belleville has the distinction of being one of the only groups to perform continuously for seven decades (members have changed during this period), and are a musical institution in this city. The Commodores are also one of the few orchestras in the province who owned and operated their own dance hall—Belleville's famous Club Commodore dance pavilion. Formed in 1928, the very first job the Commodores played was on

May 24 of that year, at the Bay of Quinte Country Club to mark Queen Victoria's birthday.

Originally comprised of six members, the band's dress approach to its work was formal. When one of the original members left, the Commodores decided to expand the group; this is when Stan and others joined, bringing the membership up to 10 pieces—three trumpets, four saxes, piano, bass and drums. The first engagement for the newly formed orchestra was at Oak Lake Casino in August 1941.

The Trianon Ballroom in Belleville was also a hot spot for many years. "There were line-ups every Saturday night," says Stan. "In the cold months the dance hall was so steamed up by the end of the night that moisture literally ran down the walls and windows." The Commodores were regular entertainers at the Trianon during the first half of the 1940s.

In 1942, The Commodores Orchestra opened their own dance pavilion. "We negotiated a lease from the city of Belleville on one of the fair buildings at Exhibition Park, with the intention of running our own dances," explains Stan. From the beginning, the band's Park Pavilion was a co-operative effort. A good deal of the profits earned were re-invested to upgrade the facility. On one particular dance night they had 989 paid admissions throughout the evening, due to the large number of air training bases in the area. During the War, The Commodores played for many benefit concerts and shows such as the Kinsmen Milk for Britain Fund and IODE drives, all to assist the war effort.

Five years later the name of the pavilion was officially changed to Club Commodore with Mayor Frank S.

The Club Commodore was located in Belleville about 100 yards west of the Ben Bleeker Auditorium. The original members of the Commodores Orchestra, in this photo from May 22, 1942, are: (front seated l to r) Tony Giosefitto, Larry Brown, Art Kemp, Jimmy Large, Bud Haines, Phil Huddleston; (standing l to r) Jimmy Elliott, Frank Howard Sr., Stan Wiggins. (Drummer Reg Scriven is absent.) Courtesy of Stan Wiggins.

A watercolour sketch of Club Commodore by artist Linda Barber was presented to the Commodores on Sept. 4, 1994, when the orchestra was honoured for its musical contribution to the City of Belleville. *Courtesy of Stan Wiggins.*

dances were reduced to Thursday and Saturday nights only, and the group rented out the hall for other functions during the rest of the week. In 1963, the band closed down the pavilion and the buildings were dismantled. The Commodores Orchestra was still busier than ever, though, travelling to perform for functions at various locations from Toronto's Royal York Hotel to Queen's University in Kingston.

Stan describes the musical path his group has followed: "The original band in 1928 styled itself after the Guy Lombardo Orchestra. As the band added more members in 1941 we changed the style to that heard in the Big Band era. We still follow the styling of Miller, Dorsey, Goodman and Ellington, with some contemporary music added."

In recent years The Commodores Orchestra have made recordings of Big Band music, demonstrating the versatility of the musicians and the excellent arrangements of the songs. One of the proudest moments for Stan and his orchestra was on September 4, 1994, when the Quinte Exhibition and Raceway officially recognized The Commodores Orchestra and Club Commodore. "For the Pleasure of Dancers Everywhere" the plaque reads, and lists the names of the band as well. Artist Linda Barber also presented the group with a watercolour painting of their pavilion. It is fortunate that Stan had the foresight to hold on to much of the memorabilia associated with the group's history. A look through the articles, advertisements, posters, tickets and other

Follwell cutting the ribbon on May 23 to mark the occasion. The building now had heat and full plumbing so it could operate year-round. "We also built a kitchen and a chef was hired to prepare the food," says Stan. Local businesses and organizations held their parties and events at Club Commodore. The Commodores would often provide the entertainment for these private events, as well as for their own dances, which ran three days per week during the summer months. Well-known orchestras were also booked into the Club, giving people a regular variety of visiting bands. But by the very early 1950s,

GALA DANCE

In aid of Belleville Kinsmen Milk for Britain and Fag Fund

"DANCING"

PARK PAVILION
BELLEVILLE

THURS., JULY 30

10-PIECE
COMMODORES ORCHESTRA
with Guest Artists

All Services for this Worthy Cause Donated

Tickets - .50 each

173

memorabilia establishes the realization that this orchestra is a musical cornerstone in the city of Belleville—a musical tradition that many people hope will survive for years to come.

Other Trenton and Belleville Area Halls

There are likely few people with the knowledge of dance halls and pavilions in the Trenton/Belleville area than Jack DeLong. A retired public school principal and historian residing in Trenton, Jack can also look back to those memorable days when he played in a band.

That band was the Trenton Valley Ramblers, an orchestra that played a combination of modern and oldtime music, "to please all tastes," as Jack says. At the time, remote radio broadcasts from many of the pavilions were popular. Jack's first paying gig brought in seven dollars. For the whole band.

"In those days there were virtually no fire regulations for any of these pavilions," says Jack who remembers one occasion when his band was playing, "smoke arose from somewhere and the piano player jumped right out of the building! The fire was minor but it took over an hour for the rest of the band to persuade the musician to return to the hall and resume playing!"

Jack provides some background about pavilions in general. "In the early 1900s the buildings were very simple in construction. The basic pavilion would have a rectangular dance floor, roofed over with open sides which could be closed in inclement weather with wooden flaps. These were designed for summer use only. The seating would usually be a bench around the inside and in some cases pop and ice cream would be sold at the opposite end of where the stage was situated."

He notes a few exceptions to this design. "In some instances an open-air dance floor was first built, usually at a summer resort for use by picnic patrons. This seems to have been the case at local places such as Massassaga Hotel, Lakeshore Lodge and Club Cedars north of Belleville. "In the case of Idlewylde at Roblins Mills (Ameliasburg), Albert File built a pavilion right on the side of his house in 1920! It was

later winterized and used as a Parish Hall for St. Alban's Church. It was demolished in the '70s. The Quinte Inn on Rednersville Road was originally a small square cottage/house. The interior walls were removed, the windows became doors, and a verandah was built on three sides with tables and chairs. Glassed-in windows were installed, which were open in summer. This place was later winterized for year-round use. Howard Weese built this in the 1930s; it was later converted into apartments in the '50s."

The following list of pavilions are ones about which Jack has been able to supply some limited information. In most cases there is no sign that the buildings ever existed, and photographs are rare—in many cases none likely exist:

• Hillcrest: Located on the south shore of Consecon Lake. It was popular in the 1920s and was used sporadically during the '30s for special events. School fairs used it as an exhibit hall before it was torn down in the '40s.

• Wellington: There was a pavilion on the lake-shore, just west of Sand Beach which had limited use in the '20s and '30s with local bands.

• Palace of the Moon: With a name like this the hall should still be standing, but, unfortunately, it too disappeared. It was built in the '30s at the outlet from East Lake to Lake Ontario and had a fair run of popularity, surviving well into the '40s. Both Trenton and Belleville band played here, and a few specials were tried with name bands from Toronto. This hall was so named because of its unique construction. The building was located behind a large landform of sand which had been naturally created as a windbreak. In order for the people to see the water over this mound of dunes, the Palace of the Moon was built up on stilts.

• Massassaga Hotel: Located on the picturesque point of land southeast of Belleville, this popular hotel operated in the late 1800s and early 1900s. Most people came by boat which brought them over from Belleville. An advertisement in the early 1900s spoke of a dancing platform. According to records, this became a pavilion around World War I and was very popular until the advent of the automobile, which killed the boat service. A lawsuit closed road

174

The Edgewater Park Pavilion, pictured here in 1951, was owned by Charlie Wickens. Many Peterborough musicians such as Alex Ingram found regular employment at this popular Campbellford dance hall. *Courtesy of Alex Ingram.*

dance halls—a heady experience for our high school romantic encounters." I drove by this site in late 1994. The hall appears to have been demolished and a large empty lot remains beside the flowing waters of the Moira River.

access in the 1920s, effectively preventing people from attending dances. All buildings were torn down. The land is now a Conservation Park.

• Crowe Lake Pavilion: Located just north of Marmora on Highway #7. Local bands and limited popularity.

• Iroquois Pavilion: This hall was built on the east side of the Trent River north of Frankford by Claude Copeland, a Trenton musician who came into some money. It was not a great success.

• Glen Ross: James Read and his wife owned and operated this pavilion. Their son, Woody Read, had a local career as a piano player and entertainer.

• Belleville Harbour: Apparently in the late '20s and early '30s a pavilion operated here at the water's edge. Canoes and rowboats were rented at the water level, and the dance floor was up top.

• Club Cedars: Starting as an open-air dance floor along the Moira River at Cannifton, it began in the '30s and was transformed into a covered pavilion and winterized by the '40s. Club Cedars was used year-round with local bands for many years. Dianne Brick writes with her thoughts about this hall: "One of the most well-known dance halls in this area was Club Cedars, complete with big band, candlelit tables, and starlight ceiling on the dance floor ... truly a romantic spot and one of the first classy BYOB

Campbellford: Edgewater Park and "The Pavilion"

It was a warm June afternoon when I drove down a hill behind a service station on Bridge Street in Cambell-ford in search of information about the dance hall that at one time was located in the area. Nestled beside a meandering stream with the charming name of Trout Creek, I discovered a small mechanic's workshop. When I asked the owner if he knew anything about the old dance pavilion, he paused, smiled and told me that it was his family who ran the operation for many years.

Bob Wickens today makes his living just a few feet from the lot where his dad, Charlie, operated the Edgewater Park Pavilion. In his late '80s, Charlie was in a nursing home when I spoke with Bob, but the mechanic has vivid memories of living through the years of music which drew dancers from small towns and villages surrounding Campbellford. "In 1948, my father purchased the hall from Wesley Sweet; it was a wooden building with the largest dance floor in the area, with the ceiling designed so that it was hung from inside with no posts interfering with the dancers," describes Bob. "It resembled a large barn."

Fran Douglas of the Campbellford Heritage Society provides more background on the construction of Edgewater Park. In her letter, she writes, "It was built by Harvey Donald for Wes Sweet in 1944."

"Regular dances were scheduled on Fridays and Saturdays," recalls Bob, "although the Friday

175

The original owners of Riverside, Gert and Jack Wineberg are shown outside the pavilion. *Courtesy of Fran Domenic.*

night affairs were cancelled after a few years. Sunday midnight dances were also very popular. We also held many banquets and the hall could be reserved for special occasions and operated year-round." The Wickens family lived in quarters attached to the building.

Not all people in Ontario were Big Band music fans. Once you moved out of the larger centres and into some of the smaller towns and hamlets around the province, it was not unusual to find country music being the preferred music form, and Campbellford was no exception. "The Golden Valley Boys out of Oshawa were a regular band with George Potter and Floyd Lloyd," Bob remembered. Entertainers from Peterborough also made their way to the Edgewater. When Charlie Wickens first purchased the pavilion, live music from the dance hall was broadcast over a local radio station.

One of those musicians was Alex Ingram who regularly gigged at the Edgewater: "Although the Wickens' hall did not sell booze, young men often arrived after bending the elbow." Curiously, when men drink, their thoughts sometimes turn to vandalism, and Charlie Wickens' establishment regularly felt the effects of young men's aggression when supplemented by booze. "I recall that after Charlie lost a number of porcelain toilets in the men's room to hefty kicks from men who had too much to drink, he finally built cement thrones, with a toilet seat attached on top. His problem was solved," says Alex.

The Edgewater was closed in 1968 and sold, but the new owner did not operate it as a dance hall. Bob said that by 1960 the crowds were beginning to change. People wanted to drink and dance, and the Edgewater never did acquire a licence. The building burned in 1970 and the remains were demolished. Charlie later purchased land across the river from the old pavilion, which Bob later bought from his dad. After running a Shell station up the small hill from his present location, he now operates his business on this site.

The other dance hall, known simply to local folks as "The Pavilion," was located on the corner of Doxer Avenue North and Market Street, according to Fran Douglas. "It was run by Gerald Hay, and then later used as a body shop by Harold Pearce," writes Fran. "Then Floyd Adams operated it as a service station, followed by Hector Macmillan who used it as a garage. Finally, Keith Brunx started a car dealership which was then purchased by Stewarts Motors of Norwood as a Chrysler dealership. They still own the property but it is vacant."

Hastings: Riverside Pavilion

Hastings' Riverside Pavilion – one owner lost it in a poker game, and another owner was hassled through bylaws and tax increases to the point he was forced to stop running dances.

This dance hall has passed through a number

of hands since the hall opened in 1939 on the north side of the Trent River, just west of Hastings. Originally called Riverside Park and Cabins, the pavilion has been a popular spot for many years, the first dance being held in August, 1939. George Potter and His Danceland Band were one of the early groups to play for the Tuesday night square and modern dances, with the Sevenaires Orchestra from Peterborough becoming a regular fixture on Fridays.

Two large field-stone fireplaces give the pavilion a cosy feel especially in the cooler months. The fireplaces were so coveted on dance night that couples would telephone ahead requesting a table beside them. In the earlier days people would often bring an armload of wood to the dance and tend the fireplace over the evening, in exchange for a free ticket into the dance. The red steel roof you see on the building today was installed in recent years, as was the exterior siding of rough cedar lumber that covers the hall's original clapboard.

Riverside drew regular crowds from all the small towns as well as from Peterborough and Cobourg. The hall was originally located far enough away from town so that any music and traffic noise didn't pose a problem. In fact, people in cottages across the river quite enjoyed the music floating over the water during the summer. In 1958, Hank and Jean Taschereau, along with Hank's brother Richard and his wife, Mary, purchased the business from Mr. Thompson. Says Hank, "Jean and I were originally from London and had enjoyed dancing at Wonderland and down at the Stork Club in Port Stanley." Hank and Jean decided to move to the town and live in the apartment adjoining the pavilion, while Richard and Mary would stay in Toronto, commuting to Hastings on the weekends to help operate the dances. The families ran dances from 1958 to 1971, when they sold the business.

One of Jean and Hank's children is Lynda Taschereau who writes with her own recollections of growing up with the dance hall. "There were dances on Friday, Saturday and, on long weekends, the Sunday midnight dances. During the time of our ownership the bands were usually 'house bands' and we had a few through the years—Jack Skitch and the Sevenaires,

the Jaguars, Paul DeNoble, Joey Henderson, and the Pastels who were from Cobourg. We went through several musical eras at Riverside. I believe we were one of the first pavilions to move from Big Band to rock 'n' roll with the Sonics around 1960-61. I can remember my aunt teaching me to do the Twist in an empty dance hall with bright sunshine coming in through the windows. I'm sure there are many many people with fond memories of magical nights on the banks of the Trent River in Hastings."

In 1977, Les Brittan assumed ownership of Riverside and his problems were just around the corner. As a talented auctioneer, Les thought that the Riverside Pavilion would be the perfect investment for his business, giving him a permanent hall for weekly sales as well as dances. If the Taschereaus introduced rock music in its early, more gentler form during the innocent years of the 1960s, by 1977 the preferred rock music for party-goers was loud and heavy.

And just as music had changed, so had the little town of Hastings. Riverside Pavilion, which once sat by itself in the middle of acres of fields and trees, was now surrounded by sprawling suburban ranch-style homes with manicured lawns stretching down to the river's edge. And here we have the beginning of real conflict: the right of a business owner to carry on entertainment activities that began in 1939 versus the right of people to live private lives in a country setting they assumed would be quiet and peaceful. Neighbours started complaining about the drinking, trespassing, noise and the hours of these late-night affairs, dubbed the "Hastings Howl."

By the mid-1980s the Riverside Pavilion was being attacked on many fronts. A small but vocal group of residents wrote letters of complaint to politicians, the Fire Marshall and police. They even circulated a petition. Local newspapers reported that Hastings village council set the wheels in motion to initiate bylaws that would regulate crowds at the midnight dances. But as Les says, "Midnight dances were held at Riverside for years, long before I took over the business. And many of the people complaining today seem to forget that they themselves used to come here as young people to have a good time."

177

Richard (left), now deceased, and Hank Taschereau's love of fishing brought the brothers and their wives to Hastings where they eventually purchased the dance hall and ran the business for thirteen years. This photo was taken beside the pavilion about 1960. *Courtesy of Hank and Jean Taschereau.*

midnight dances promptly at 3 a.m. and even stopped booking the "heavy metal" bands in favour of more mainstream rock groups. But as he told a local newspaper, "telling me to stop making noise at a dance hall is like telling a blacksmith to stop all that hammering!" As the vendetta against Les mounted, writers to the editors of papers expressed bizarre and irrational fears. Many came to his defence, however, sending notes of support to the same publications. The ante was upped a notch when OPP stepped in one year and blocked every possible route into the town of Hastings itself and conducted intensive R.I.D.E. checks. A few charges were laid and attendance at the dance was down drastically. By 1992 the dances were finished at Riverside.

In a letter to a local paper Les announced the Hastings Howl had uttered its last yelp. Then Les put the hall up for sale. In a personal letter to Les and Linda, a former business associate wrote with his condolences over the demise of the pavilion. "I've always enjoyed booking your dances, making your commercials and watching the full house have a great time! You put up an admirable fight but sometimes it's just not worth it. Good luck with the auctions!"

The local police chief felt that the incidents were not as serious as some people stated and asked that common sense prevail. To appease the complainants, Les installed more outside lighting, hired additional staff to monitor the crowd both inside the hall and in the lot, erected an eight-foot fence to give neighbours privacy, double-insulated the east wall behind the stage to cut down on noise and kept the east windows and doors closed. He concluded the

When the highway was straightened to cross the river, removing the curve, Coral Gables Casino in Trent River (then known as Trent Bridge) ceased operations. Here is the old Trent Bridge, circa late 1920s. *Courtesy of Agnes Nazar.*

Chapter Twelve

MUSKOKA: DUNN'S PAVILION/THE KEE TO BALA

Gerry Dunn's new pavilion, which opened in July 1942, was constructed 75% over the water of Lake Muskoka. This 1995 popular watercolour of The Kee by artist Pam Turner-Wong hangs in many Muskoka cottages. *Used with permission of the artist.*

"If you build it, they will come." Long before the fictional movie "Field of Dreams," Gerry Patrick Dunn felt the same real-life urge to push ahead in 1941 with an idea so grandiose it left some people scratching their heads in amazement. Gerry erected the most ambitious dance pavilion ever built in Ontario cottage country. It was to become the province's most successful summer dance venue: Dunn's Pavilion— "Where All Muskoka Dances."

When it was completed and opened its doors for business in the summer of 1942, people began to realize that Gerry's gift to Bala was a treasure. It attracted dancers from near and far, all of whom dressed in their finest attire to dance in an atmosphere that was first-class all the way. The new pavilion was an immediate hit with everyone, featuring dancing six nights a week throughout the summer,

with at least one major Big Band attraction coming in every week for an engagement. Gerry instinctively knew the secret to creating a good business, long before he built his new hall. It was his personal charm and attentiveness to every detail that ensured Dunn's Pavilion would enjoy a long run in Bala. A gracious host, Gerry made every person feel special as he greeted them personally at the door.

Little did he know at the time the pavilion was built on Lake Muskoka that, for six decades, the tradition he began would continue every summer. There have been a succession of owners since Gerry, but Dunn's Pavilion, which for over 30 years has been called The Kee to Bala, continues to draw thousands of people who attend dances with one intention—to have a good time, just like their parents and their grandparents did in their own way in previous years.

Before Gerry Dunn purchased his drug store/dance platform in 1929, the business was operated by the Langdon family, pictured here in front of their store in 1925. Standing, left to right: ___ Langdon, Reginald Thompson, Chuck Lyon, ___ Langdon, Norm Amer, Douglas Thompson, Clark Thompson. Seated: Fanny Thompson, Madelaine Thompson, Grace Thompson, __ Embleton, unknown, unknown.
Courtesy of Kay Thompson.

The tradition Gerry Dunn started with his pavilion in 1942 for his generation, repeats itself year after year as new generations of young people discover the musical shrine Gerry conceived.

Gerry Dunn passed away in December, 1999, in his 98th year; I feel very fortunate to have been able to meet with Gerry in the summer of 1994 at his Acton Island summer home, located on his beloved Lake Muskoka.

"I was a pharmacist, graduating from the University of Toronto in 1927," says Gerry, who was born in Bracebridge. "Although I could have gone on to medical school at McGill on a hockey scholarship, the chance came up to purchase Langdon's Ice Cream Parlour in Bala in 1929. After I bought the store—I paid $11,000 for it—I could see there was great potential for the area to open up and could see that the store and the open-air dance pavilion in the rear might be a pretty good business opportunity. So I lived in Detroit in the winter, working at a pharmacy during the day and playing hockey at night." This arrangement lasted a few years and helped Gerry pay

off the initial investment he made in the business.

"Most people have always assumed that the dance pavilion was my main income, but the store did just as well," says Gerry. There was a long lunch counter/soda fountain, pharmacy items and a large variety of clothing, fishing equipment and hardware stock. Dunn's Drug Store was the only pharmacy between Gravenhurst and Parry Sound.

Remembering the Original Pavilion

George Allison recalls in his letter some of the early days on the original dance platform: "Dunn's was the old dark green pavilion-type clapboard and lattice place with the drug store and souvenir area in front and Gerry Dunn always present in white shirt, tie and smart slacks, greeting and welcoming folks. We teens rowed the skiff or canoe to the dock by Dunn's Pavilion after lunch to meet, have ice cream sodas, dance to the resident jukebox and try to make dates for the evening or for swims the next afternoon. In the evenings people came from quite a distance, by road and by water, especially if a known Big Band was playing. Some of the launches you now see at Antique Boat Shows came loaded with the more affluent young adults, and tied up at the pavilion dock. The travelling Big Bands were the highlight of the summer dances. There was no liquor sold so it was BYOB in a plain paper bag or satchel."

Leone (Palmer) Fisher also writes about the fun to be found at Dunn's long before the famous pavilion was constructed: "About 1937 to '45 my sister Frances and I had a glorious time in summers. We would walk or canoe, into Dunn's. They also had costume evenings and we won first prize one evening for dressing as hula dancers. Years later we went there with our husbands to hear the big name bands for old times sake."

Marshall Louch was as well-known around the pavilion as Gerry himself. Sadly, Marshall passed away in his 97th year, just a month after Gerry. For over 60 years the two men had been close friends. According to Marshall, customers would sometimes confuse the two of them, people were known to have called him "Gerry" on more than one occasion.

Born in London, Ontario, Marshall became involved in the performing end of the music industry, and played banjo with Guy Lombardo in 1919. "During the Depression I was booked in with the Stanley St. John Band to the 21 Club in Port Carling, which was just opening in the mid-'30s," recalls Marshall. He ended up managing the club for five years. Through a mutual business interest in slot machines, Marshall became acquainted with Gerry Dunn who was expanding his operation in Bala at that time. Gerry eventually contacted Marshall to see if he might be interested in joining him at the pavilion. Dunn's resident photographer, Don McIndoe, remembers Marshall: "He helped to maintain a high standard in the way the crowd dressed and how they behaved."

Slot machines are not a recent source of amusement for the gambling public in Ontario. During the 1930s, these Vegas-style one-arm bandits were as common as gum-ball machines in some parts of the province—such as Bala. An entrepreneur had a circuit of locations where he had placed these slot machines, according to Marshall. Rumour had it that he distributed enough incentives to key people so that when a check was to be made by the police, he was given the word which he then passed on to his operators, including the 21 Club and Dunn's. The slot machines were then quickly squirrelled away to safe hiding places, such as the grease pit in Dunn's Garage.

Bruce Brocklebank remembers the slots. He writes: "Gerry had a dozen machines always on the go. I remember him carrying a slot machine into his little office and take the back off and out would pour an ocean of nickels; he even had 25-cent machines."

As the 1930s drew to an end, the crowds became so large at the old pavilion that Gerry decided to tear down the hall and build what would become his famous pavilion. He had visions of bringing the best bands in the business to Muskoka, but knew that he would need a hall that could hold enough people to pay for the big acts. "I designed the pavilion myself—no architect was involved," says Gerry. "It took some time on my part, coming up with different designs that I'd draw on the brown paper we used in the store to wrap things." Finally, with the help of local boat livery owner Mac Cunningham, the two men came up with a unique design for a hall with a 75-foot span that would be built out over the water. With a crew of 14 men, the pavilion began to take shape in late 1941. By utilising a gin pole fashioned from a tall pine tree cut along the Moon River, they raised the upper rafters into place with Gerry poisitioned at the top, nailing them down.

An early picture of the new hall shows material hanging down from the ceiling. "These were natural cedar boughs dipped in calcium chloride for fire protection and then hung from the rafters for looks," says Gerry. The silver-coloured boughs served two functions—they camouflaged the wooden rafters plus they helped improve the overall sound of the hall. Gerry says, "Bands always said they could play as loud as they liked and still sound good—there was

181

Originally streamers were hung from the exposed roof to camouflage the wooden supports. Later, cedar boughs dipped in a fire retardant replaced the streamers and the famous fountain was installed in the middle of the floor.
Courtesy of Jack Lomas.

no vibration."

When the fountain with coloured lights was later installed in the centre of the dance floor, it became the focal point of the hall. The artificial potted palms and flowers throughout the hall all blended together to enhance the atmosphere. Even the stage was a conversation piece. It was raised about 18 inches from the floor, so dancers could be very close to the musicians. The ambience created by the stage blended in well with the Muskoka environment; the backdrop of the bandstand was the facade of a small cottage with flower boxes underneath the windows, and palm trees and lamps adorned the platform. There were a number of private boxes in the hall, each of which could accommodate about 20 people. These partitions were popular when a group of individuals wanted to celebrate a special occasion.

The summer of '42 was a memorable one for Eric Lynd and his friends who would regularly gather at Dunn's Gas Station and Soda Fountain; names not known. *Courtesy of Eric Lynd.*

That first summer of 1942 in the new pavilion is memorable in many respects. James Gilmore remembers the thrill of the new dance hall. He writes: "Fifty years ago I was courting my bride-to-be in Barrie. Construction on the "new" Dunn's Pavilion had been started in the fall of 1941 and, when I arrived in Bala, there it was in all its splendour. Many a night we attended the dances, some of them the Big Bands, but more often to dance to the music of Howard Cable and his band and to hear his wonderful singer Norma Locke, who became Mart Kenney's

wife."

"We had a staff of about 35 working in the store and the pavilion," says Gerry. "Almost everyone lived on the property for the summer." Cathy Barber, Marshall Louch's daughter, worked in Gerry's drug store at the pavilion for many years. She says that the staff and residents in the area were very much like a family. "Service was so personal in the store. Patrons were welcomed back year after year. We kept track of our customers because we really cared about them."

As seen in this circa 1940s photo, Gerry was a hands-on owner who put in long days serving patrons at his filling station, selling merchandise in his store and greeting customers at the evening dance. *Courtesy of Jack Lomas.*

Patricia Arney also remembers the summer of 1960 when she worked for Gerry and recalls experiences ranging from "living in an attic with 12 other girls sharing a gas station washroom and working four-hour shifts seven days a week, to almost running off with a drummer from Larry Elgart's band. My husband and I also have done business and been friends with all the subsequent pavilion owners."

In his autobiography, Mart Kenney reflects on his first visit to Dunn's. "On August 2, 1942, we drove north to Dunn's Pavilion at Bala ... out over the water at the back of his drug store Gerry Dunn had built a pavilion with a good dance floor and seating for close to a thousand people .... We played a midnight frolic from 12:01 a.m. to 3 a.m. Sunday night before the Monday Civic Holiday and the dance was such a success that we went back year after year on

To celebrate the 50th Anniversary of Dunn's Pavilion, Mart Kenney returned to Muskoka's treasured dance hall (now called The Kee to Bala) on August 20, 1992. As guest of honour, Gerry Dunn was chauffeured to the pavilion by his former employee, Eric Lynd, in Eric's 1950 Dodge Wayfarer sportabout roadster convertible. Gerry and Mart had a grand reunion and hundreds of couples relived memories of the Big Band years on the dance floor.

Courtesy of Eric Lynd.

the closest Sunday to July 1, and the Sundays preceding Civic Holiday and Labour Day. It became a "must" event. Gerry Dunn was held in great esteem by the hundreds who knew him, including old softie Gordon Sinclair, who was a fellow summer resident of Bala." [1]

Mart Kenney and his orchestra did remote broadcasts wherever they performed, including Dunn's Pavilion. From an old tape of the event, radio fans heard the familiar introduction of the June 29, 1952, show as follows: "From beautiful Bala, Muskoka, CBC Dominion presents the Mart Kenney

show...yes, tonight from Dunn's Pavilion at Bala in the heart of the great Muskoka vacationland, the music of Canada's first man of show business, Mart Kenney, some happy holiday talk between Maestro and friends, and some singing by the quartet, Four of a Kind—Wally Koster, Norma Locke, and Mart's guest tonight Chicho Viaje." [2] It was a special night in 1994 when Mart Kenney returned to Dunn's for a memorable evening of nostalgia, with Gerry Dunn the guest of honour. A similar reunion was held again in 1998 when Mart made yet another unforgettable appearance with Eddie Graf and his orchestra.

Since such a night at Dunn's Pavilion was very special, it was only natural that people would want a souvenir or memento to remind them of the experience. Gerry hired resident "roving photographers" Don McIndoe and his wife, Winnifred, to circulate around the hall during the first portion of the evening, taking candid snaps of couples at the fountain, or groups of people at their tables. Today

Beginning in 1948, Don McIndoe and his wife, Winnifred, looked after the photo duties at Dunn's Pavilion. Although their photography business was based in Hamilton, their summer work was with pavilions from Galt through to the Muskokas. Couples could receive photos in a souvenir folder before the evening's dance finished.

Courtesy of Don McIndoe.

183

End of summer photos were a must for the staff at Dunn's Pavilion. Don and Winnifred McIndoe always gathered the gang together for a souvenir group shot in front of the stage, as seen in this late 1950s photo.

Courtesy of Don McIndoe.

and often gave away these shots to patrons and people in the bands.

Don talks about some of the entertainers he saw at Dunn's: "When a band like Les Brown played, musicians would arrive from everywhere to watch and appreciate the fine talent in this band—never a bad note. Musicians also loved to watch Count Basie for the quality of professionalism he had on stage. Entertainers like Louis Armstrong and Duke Ellington were also great showmen. And the crowd would immediately respond to the Glen Miller orchestra when they played tunes like 'Moonlight Serenade' and 'String of Pearls.' "

Louis Armstrong's appearance at Dunn's in 1962 is still regarded as the most memorable night in the pavilion's history. It was one of those rare occasions when all the elements necessary for the creation of a magical night of music somehow came together, as if Gerry knew his days at the hall were coming to an end, and he wanted to give his customers one very special evening they would never forget. The sky glimmered with a million stars, the evening air was warm and gentle, the water of Lake Muskoka was calm, reflecting the stars as well as the welcoming lights of the pavilion and surrounding cottages.

many people still have a cardboard folder with "Souvenir of Dunn's Pavilion" printed on the front, and the five-by-seven black and white picture tucked safely inside.

"Our first year at Dunn's was 1948," says Don. "Winnifred would take pictures of couples throughout the evening while I worked feverishly in the darkroom developing prints. The photos were ready in a souvenir folder before the dance finished." Don also photographed the entertainers who played the hall. He has many informal and original photos of some of the biggest names in the music business,

Over 2,100 people heeded the urge to make their pilgrimage to Dunn's to see the greatest jazzmen of their time perform. Another estimated 1,000 people lolled on the grass outside, or quietly drifted around the bay in every imaginable type of vessel, from canoes to gleaming varnished wooden watercraft, enjoying Louis Armstrong's music as it wafted from the pavilion's open windows into the soft night air. Gerry Dunn remembered that night: "Louis Armstrong drew the largest crowd ever; we sold over $5,000 in mix and ice alone. Admission was five dollars, the most we'd ever charged to that point."

Probably the most touching letter received for this book comes from Mrs. D. Castaldi, who wrote about her unforgettable experience the night that Louis Armstrong played at Dunn's Pavilion: "My aunt and uncle had a cottage just down the lake from Bala Bay. As youngsters, my cousins and I used to go into Dunn's and wander through the store with our little bit of spending money deciding from all the exciting things we found there, what we would buy. Then the day came when we became big enough to go with our families to the dance upstairs. What a great room it was with its sunken dance floor and tables all around. We sure felt like big girls. One evening when we were there for the dance to listen to Louis Armstrong and his band, my father asked me to dance. I'm sure I was probably the youngest person there. Boy, did I think I was grown up and special. And what happened next has stayed with me my entire life. Louis was singing, and when an instrumental break came, he stepped down from the bandstand and asked me: 'May I have this dance with you?' You could imagine the thrill that this was for me, and for my parents too. This memory has been one of my fondest all my life, and I never hear Louis' music that I don't remember this special moment."

Introducing The Kee

When Gerry decided to sell the pavilion in 1963, it came as a surprise to many people who assumed that both Gerry and his dance hall would go on indefinitely. Gerry Dunn at no time in his career sat back and simply assumed business would come his way. He worked at his enterprise extremely hard; he was a hands-on proprietor, a people person, a warm and likeable individual who gave the people what they wanted at the time. Gerry didn't have much time to put up his feet.

The subsequent owner, unfortunately, lost the pavilion to the bank a few years later. When Ray Cockburn entered the Bala picture in 1968, the pavilion Gerry Dunn had built in 1942, and carefully nurtured into one of the most successful dance halls of its type in Canada, had declined into a sorry state of financial woes and physical disrepair.

Purchasing the pavilion in Bala was not particularly risky for Ray after ten years under his belt as owner of the immensely popular Pavalon (The Pav) on Lake Couchiching in Orillia. The bank had approached Ray Cockburn to see if he was interested in acquiring a second venue. "I agreed, and purchased the hall for a reasonable amount," says Ray. "The existing store in front of the building had been condemned and had to be demolished." Ray then built the extension on the front of the Bala pavilion. He also re-named the hall. The label "Kee" came about as a solution to remove the uncertainty in customers' minds regarding the hall's name. "A short label, easily remembered, was what I wanted, and when someone suggested that the pavilion was the 'key' to Bala and the surrounding Muskoka area, I jumped at the idea and changed the spelling to KEE,"

Gerry often socialized with the entertainers who played his hall. Seated around the table with Gerry (centre) are: (l to r) Patrick (Gerry's son), Les Elgart, Eddie Stroud and Larry Elgart, circa 1950s. *Courtesy of Don McIndoe.*

185

says Ray. The new name has held since 1968.

The largest crowd at The Kee was the night The Stitch 'n Tyme and Lighthouse played, drawing 2300, 200 more than attended the Louis Armstrong dance in 1961. Another night saw 2250 cram into the hall. There was standing room only. It was Ray's idea to book two rock bands per night into The Kee. "With two bands on stage, live music was continuous, leaving little time for kids to become distracted," Ray explains. In 1971, Ray was approached by the Parry family who indicated they were interested in

purchasing the pavilion.

Bev Parry and her family had many successful years at the Kee, taking the pavilion through the 1970s and into the next decade. With music being an art form that never sits still, the Parrys had to move with the various phases of rock 'n' roll. As the cost of doing business rose, so did the price they had to charge at the door. It became obvious that for the Kee to remain viable and compete with bars and other forms of entertainment available to people, a liquor license had to be obtained, so they set the wheels in motion. The Kee has now had a license for over 25 years. During this time a larger stage was built on the east side of the dance floor, and the old cottage front was converted into a bar. A very young Adam Parry (Bev's son) was learning the dance pavilion business during this time. He swept floors, sold admission tickets, cooked food and learned how to hire entertainment. He and his wife Andrea later went on to purchase Greenhurst Pavilion on Sturgeon Lake.

In the late 1980s Joe Kondyjowski assumed ownership. As a person who loves to preserve the original integrity of older buildings, taking over the Kee presented a number of challenges. The pavilion Gerry Dunn had built was well out over the water, and much of the structure sat on cribbing and pylons that had been installed in 1942. As Joe says, "We had much work to do!" And work he did. Fortunately for Joe, with his experience and sound management, the pavilion brought in great rock 'n' roll acts and consequently large crowds, generating sufficient revenue to support the huge expense incurred in bringing this marvellous old building up to the standards necessary to keep it operating.

"I owned The Kee for six years and in that time I did more work on it than any previous owner after Gerry Dunn," says Joe. "I had a new Viceroy home built on the property. We poured asphalt for a parking area, installed a new roof and built a new deck." Joe also brought back the Big Bands three times per season during his stay, the first owner to do so in many years. "We had to put in new cement cribs, and very slowly, in stages we jacked up the building because it had begun to sink. The pilings underneath were all replaced. A new kitchen was put into the building and we painted the outside." Joe was the first operator of The Kee to start booking big name rock acts, beginning with Burton Cummings. The most special moment for Joe arrived when he invited Gerry Dunn to stop by the pavilion. Says Joe, "Gerry said he was very pleased and commented 'the place had not looked this good since I sold it in 1963' That was the ultimate compliment for me."

In the late 1980s, Joe sold the business to Norman Arbour, who ran the pavilion for just one year. Sanober Patel then purchased The Kee and assumed responsibilities as owner. Joe returned to

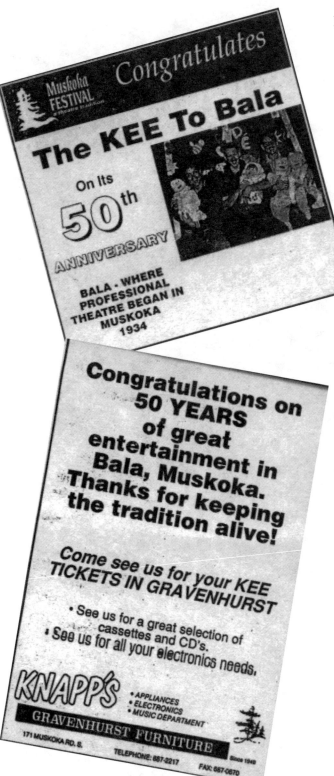

Bala and spent a summer helping her with various aspects of managing the pavilion, imparting some of the advice and techniques which had been passed on to him by veteran pavilion owners such as Mrs. Lines at Greenhurst and Owen McCrohan at Oshawa's Jubilee Pavilion.

During the summer of 1994, Sanober Patel was approached by concert promoter and entrepreneur Stephen Wyllie, who asked her if she would be interested in selling the business. [3] The transition began in 1995, with Steve assuming full ownership of the property in 1996. Every new operator of The Kee to Bala has brought his or her plans, hopes and dreams for the pavilion. They realize that it is not simply another concert hall or dance hall; there is so much history behind Dunn's Pavilion that ownership also brings with it a responsibility to the residents, cottagers and visitors to Muskoka who regard the pavilion as one of the most familiar and significant landmarks in the region.

Steve has a deep awareness of the importance that The Kee holds for so many people and he immediately set the wheels in motion to honour the rich past of his pavilion. Re-painting the pavilion to its original Muskoka white was Steve's first job on his long list of jobs. In the past few years the dance floor has been refinished to its original patina, the interior has been freshened up with new paint, the old fountain has been located for future restoration and for the first time in 25 years the original stage has been used for the orchestra when Big Band dances are scheduled. Steve even had a large sign painted to hang behind the band: "Dunn's Pavilion, Established 1942."[4]

For many years a small but interesting building has sat beside The Kee, and has often been referred to simply as "The Garage." Built well over six decades ago, it was used by Gerry Dunn as a gas and service station. In 1997, the entire structure was

187

Count Basie

Les Brown

Stan Kenton

Warren Covington

During the 1940s, '50s and into the early '60s, the biggest names in the music business performed at Dunn's Pavilion, and Don McIndoe was there with his wife, Winnifred, to capture them all on film. Here are but a few: Count Basie, Warren Covington, Stan Kenton and Les Brown. These were just a few of the greats who travelled up to Bala every summer. *Courtesy of Don McIndoe.*

188

resurrected under the name Dunn's Station, an ice cream parlour and coffee shop.

They originally came to Dunn's to see the Big Bands, and today they're still coming to The Kee. Most of the hundreds of thousands of people who have entered this building can likely recall their own special thought or memory about their experience here. And it's not just the building itself that makes the memories—it's the people. Dunn's Pavilion/The Kee to Bala has been a conduit, bringing people together for one purpose, and that has been to meet, dance, enjoy music and have an evening of fun.

In July 2000, a special memorial service was held at The Kee to honour Gerry Dunn. Hundreds of people showed up to reminisce about Gerry and recall the great days of Dunn's Pavilion.

In 2002, The Kee changed hands again. Along with the regular season-long concerts, the new owner has added Big Band dances throughout the summer, opened up the outdoor deck of the hall for lunch and dinner (the Kee Patio) and transformed the hall into a night club setting every Friday. Once again innnovation and hard work combine to demonstrate that The Kee to Bala will continue to be a musical landmark in Muskoka.

Chapter Thirteen

PAVILIONS OF THE NEAR NORTH

Eddie Sarlo's group, The Northernaires Orchestra (pictured here in 1952), held down house band duties at the famous Top Hat Pavilion on the shore of Lake Nipissing in North Bay. When Eddie's band had a night off, members would often travel down to Bala and take in the name bands booked by Gerry Dunn. *Courtesy of Eddie Sarlo.*

As former Timmins resident George D. Babcock writes, "I must say that there is no place like the 'North' for friendship and congeniality!" There are thousands of Ontarians who would agree with George. Even though the winter weather can often freeze you to the marrow, the people's hearts are as warm as you would find anywhere. And what better places to find warm hearts than in some of northern Ontario's dance halls!

North Bay: Top Hat Pavilion

Eddie Sarlo recalls the Top Hat pavilion in this city very well—he played in orchestras here, and at many of the halls around the North Bay area. Eddie writes: "I remember the very good times of the 1930s, '40s and '50s during the popular era of dance pavilions, in

particular our own famous Top Hat Pavilion on the shore of Lake Nipissing here in North Bay. As a teenager and on, I played in the dance bands that performed at Top Hat as well as dance halls in the area. I played lead alto sax and clarinet in the Big Bands of Andy Cangiano's Orchestra, then in the Lucenti Dance Band, later with the Northernaires dance orchestra and then with the Norm Mauro Big Band. In those early years, we played for jitney dances—five cents per dance set; it was hectic playing our tunes of the day with shortened arrangements. But generally, it was Park Plan with one admission for the evening.

"During that era name bands of Canada and the United States played here at Top Hat, which drew full houses. People from all around the area and tourists attended with great delight. Our house band

190

played the weekends mostly. Some of the Canadian bands to appear at Top Hat more than once were: Bert Niosi, Mart Kenney, Art Hallman, Bobby Gimby, Norm Harris, Trump Davidson etc. American and internationally famous entertainers included: Louis Armstrong, Les Brown, Jimmy Dorsey, Charlie Spivak, Johnny Long, Guy Lombardo, Warren Covington and others. Several of us musicians would travel to Dunn's Pavilion in Bala through the years to dance to the name bands there. Top Hat burned down in the early 1960s, and in its place is the Dragon's Chinese Restaurant."

Timmins to South Porcupine

Once again, it is George Babcock who writes about some of the pavilions he remembers, particularly the one in Timmins which has special meaning for him: "I recall the Miami Beach Pav in North Bay, the Edgewater Pavilion at Porcupine and last but not least, the Olde Pavilion in Timmins. I must admit that these famous old dance spots are long gone, but the memories linger on. The Timmins pavilion was located at the bottom of Wilson Avenue across the old Matagami River bridge. It was a large building with railed dance floor, rotating light and bandshell. The floor was solid hardwood and it actually vibrated to the music beat and dancers' feet. The acoustics were perfect. My memories go back to the 1930s when I took my wife to the 1936 Valentine's Dance; we were married May 12, 1937, and danced there that night! The Saturday night dances were a must. Most of the big fancy functions and dances were held there for years, and these were formal too—service club affairs, weddings, anniversaries, you name it! The bands were second to none. The Perrini Brothers, Andy Cangiano, Gene Rocco (composer, clarinet and tenor sax), Ole Brandes (trumpet), Cliff McKay (Happy Gang back-up), Henry Kelneck (ex-RCAF band, trumpet) all held fort there until the building burned—I can't remember the exact date.

"There were many memories made at the Olde Pav. Truth pledged, hearts broken—and some mended too! The dancers were the best! You play it, they could dance it. One of the famous ones was Leo

Delvillano, a real Fred Astaire. The girls—ah, the girls—they were super too. Waltz, fox trot, tango, sambo, swing, boogie, if you didn't know how to dance it, one would be sure to break you in. And it was easy on that floor with that grand music. I was back up to Timmins/Porcupine area a couple of years ago—there's no pav there now. Damn few old-timers like me either!"

Charles Budd writes with a few thoughts of his own: "I've been in Timmins since 1930. I have had the pleasure of knowing Mr. Wilson, who owned the Riverside Pavilion. Also, I worked at the Edgewater Pav from 1934 to 1938 as square dance caller and Floor Manager. Mr. Red Cummings was the owner and operator of this pavilion. Other dance halls in Timmins were the Oddfellows Hall, the Polish Hall and the Finn Hall. There were others that had some big-time bands such as Don Messer's boys, the Henry Kelneck Band and Lou Rotondo and his gang."

Ulysses Levinson operated his own dance pavilion for a few years. "I ran the Arcadia Dance Hall," he writes. "The band was called the Club Royal Band. We held regular dances, and on weekends we had square dances with Lou Rotondo on violin, Mary Gervais on piano and Andy McGinn who was the square dance caller."

Cochrane: Oxville Hall

George Ray's family owned and operated a popular dance hall just north of Cochrane near Clute in the 1930s, called Oxville Hall. "It was built it in the mid-1930s and we ran it until the beginning of the War," he writes. "It was a frame structure, with the roof covered in tarpaper. Oxville Hall was very popular during the summers, and the highlight of the season was the annual corn roast towards the end of August. Our music was 90% country and western, with some round dancing thrown in. The building was torn down in 1940 and the materials were used elsewhere. Our family then moved to Toronto." The pavilion is still vivid in George's mind, clear enough

191

for him to compose a poem in May 1991 entitled *'Oxville Hall.'* Here are a few verses:

There was a place in the north country
That was known by one and all
Where people danced the night away
At a place called Oxville Hall.

Admission charged was a quarter each
And very cheap as I recall
For that included cake and coffee
At a place called Oxville Hall.

The building is no longer there
There is no sign of it at all
Only good time memories linger still
Of a place called Oxville Hall."

Interior of Fort William's (now Thunder Bay) Chippewa Park Pavilion, circa 1940. Its rustic interior was enhanced with large beams, many of which were still covered in bark. *Courtesy of Irene Winslow.*

Thunder Bay (Fort William and Port Arthur)

Long before the city of Thunder Bay was established, the twin cities of Fort William and Port Arthur stood side by side on the north shore of Lake Superior. Each town had summer dance pavilions, the two most popular being Chippewa Park in Fort William, and Current River Park in Port Arthur.

The pavilion in Chippewa Park is still standing, though the last dance finished many years ago. Marie McInnis grew up in the Lakehead and sends a few words along: "Around 1957 all of us would go to the Chippewa Park Pavilion and dance in a very romantic setting by the shores of Lake Superior. I remember dancing to band music and coloured lights hanging from the ceiling. It is a log building so it was really a camp setting not far from the water; we could stroll on the sandy beach. Oh, it was a very romantic time."

Marnoni Johnson was also brought up in Fort William and went to dances with her brothers at this park set "about eight miles from the centre of town," she says. "Ted Goodsell and his orchestra played for dances Tuesday and Thursday evenings. On Friday night there was a square dance with Art Sparks' band. The steamships *Hamonic* and *Noronic*

came into Fort William where the passengers would be taken to Chippewa Park for lunch and a tea dance. The ship's band went to Chippewa as well to play for the dance. Street cars ran from town out to the park, with the last car leaving at one a.m."

During the summer, Marnoni often stayed at the park in a cottage. "These cottages were built on leased land," she explains. "Some of these buildings were called canvas cottages, clad in a heavy canvas type of material, which would keep out the elements, but get very wet in the rain." Marnoni's family eventually sided their canvas structure with wood in 1955 and to this day she still has her cottage. A local theatre group used the Chippewa Pavilion to stage summer performances for a short while, but have since obtained their own facilities, according to Marnoni. [1]

Volunteer Researcher with the Thunder Bay Museum, Joan Hebden, adds more information about Chippewa Park Pavilion. "It was built in the 1920s with an outdoor bandstand, located nearby offshore on a small peninsula. As far as I know the building still exists though it has been some time since dances were held there regularly."

Irene Winslow worked at Chippewa Park and sent along a photograph which she took 60 years

ago of the pavilion's interior. "I worked as a life guard, and later in the tourist camp area during the summers of 1940 and '41," she writes. "I was 19 or 20 at the time and have fond memories of the park with its natural log buildings and of this dance floor. On occasion we would all help out whoever was in charge of polishing the dance floor, enjoying pushing the many big brushes around."

Mildred Arnold often went dancing at Chippewa and also at the Elks Hall with her husband Wilf, and their friends Bill and June Klomp. One of their favourite orchestras was Ted Goodsell's band, and Mildred sends along a list of the members and their instruments: Leader and pianist, Ted Goodsell; soloist and sax, Roy Knox; drums, Red Burr; trumpet, Arne Malo; sax and trombone, Maurice Jackson;

soloist upon occasion, June Chambers. The band was seen regularly from 1936 to 1946.

It took a few attempts to finally erect an operating pavilion in Port Arthur's Current River Park, as Joan Hebden describes: "This pavilion was developed late in the 19th century. The Dancing Platform was set up in 1904 and bandstand the following year. A full Pavilion was built in 1908. Unfortunately, that same year a disastrous flood burst through a dam on the Current River, plunging a CPR freight train into the river, killing three, and taking out the pavilion along with the park restaurant. A petition for a new pavilion soon circulated and in 1910 the 'Merry Night Pavilion' opened. A replacement, variously called the 'Palais de Dance' and the 'Casino Dancing Pavilion' opened in 1922 but burned down in 1938 and was not, to my knowledge, replaced."

Joe Turner's orchestra was the headliner at Current River and performed Monday and Wednesday evenings throughout the summer, says Marnoni Johnson. Rudy Hansen often sang with Joe's band. Other members included: vocals, Gladys Smith (Sands); sax, Duncan McIntosh; bass, George Rudd; sax and clarinet, Angus Appelte and Roy Saari; drums, Ed Butler; trumpet, Leo Saari. Joe was leader and pianist. Joe's band also played the pavilion at Boulevard Lake—the Casino—where there was regular friendly rivalry with fellow musician and bandleader Roy Corran.

The Elks Hall was also a favourite of Irene Winslow's. She adds, "Mart Kenney and His Western Gentlemen visited our area several times during the War years (definitely my favourite with their 'The West, A Nest and You, Dear'), but usually played in

Port Arthur's Current River Park Pavilion, 1929.

National Archives of Canada
PA-043682

the local arena, drawing large crowds."

Charles Thomas remembers both the pavilions and the bootleggers in the area. "I attended all the Thunder Bay pavilions in my youth," he writes. "Roy Corran's orchestra played at Chippewa Park and the Current River Pavilion. Most of the bands in my time were country and western as that was the choice of music then. One of the most notable pavilions was the one at Kakabeka Falls. This hall was situated overlooking the falls, and in those days a large amount of alcohol was consumed at the dances. But if my memory is correct, no one ever fell over the falls. Years ago bootleggers flourished in and around Fort William and Port Arthur, so a lot of peple—especially teenagers—would go there first before heading to the dances! I met my wife Olga at the Current River Pavilion in October 1953, and we were married in May 1954. We have been together ever since, so writing this has brought back pleasant memories."

Chapter Fourteen

THE LAST WALTZ

The musicians silhouetted in this photograph were members of an orchestra led by a Mr. Campbell in 1937, likely taken in Peterborough *Courtesy of Andy Rutter.*

It is interesting to see that new music reminiscent of the swing era, along with the original swing standards by Goodman, Shaw, Miller, Dorsey and so many other artists, are being enjoyed by people everywhere. The exceptional Canadian magazine devoted to this music—*Big Band World*, published by Diamond Entertainment—continues to grow in popularity and circulation. Ballroom dance lessons are in more demand than ever before.

Does this mean there will be a resurgence of dance halls and pavilions? Probably not in the same form that once existed in Ontario. The ones which have survived—The Palais Royale, The Kee To Bala, The Dard, the Jubilee Pavilion and others—will, it is hoped, continue to be healthy as they cater to their customers' changing musical tastes. Today, many of the new venues featuring music are urban-based.

Toronto has dozens of clubs providing something for everybody, but although these places are gathering spots for people to meet and enjoy music, they are not really similar to the traditional dance halls or dance pavilions.

Many people look at pictures of some of the Lake Huron and other beachfront pavilions and wonder if there would ever be a chance of seeing this type of unique and romantic entertainment house again. This is not unlike looking back at an old steam locomotive with great nostalgia and wondering if those iron horses will ever be seen plying the rails across Canada again. The short answer is no. These have had their time, served their purpose, but to try and resurrect a dance pavilion for a three-month-per-year operational life would be impossible.

Do you know that the National Anthem

used to be the last song of the night at dances? It was usually God Save the King (or Queen); people actually stood at attention on the dance floor as the house lights were turned up, signifying the end of the dance, and people made an orderly exit from the building. That tradition seemed to disappear in the late '50s or early '60s, and one of the rare occasions one hears the anthem played regularly today is at sporting events.

It is hoped that the people today who are able to dance and go to concerts in the few remaining pavilions in the province appreciate the impact these halls had on so many lives. The good times that people are having today will be their special memories tomorrow, just as thousands of people before them have enjoyed the same experience. Whatever era you remember, or whatever music you enjoyed, the songs you grew up with—Big Band, country, or rock 'n' roll—the emotions you felt and the experiences you had were likely similar.

The decline of dance pavilions in Ontario has been slow but steady, particularly over the last 25 years. As will have been noted in this book, some of the buildings have burned down, others demolished, and a few of the remaining halls have fortunately been saved and are being used for various purposes.

Today it is difficult to imagine a summer dance pavilion operating six nights a week and drawing large crowds every evening, but that was the norm in the 1930s and '40s. In terms of competition, there was very little else for people to do for entertainment. But today, typical homes as well as many cottages have televisions, VCR's, stereo equipment and more than likely computers with Internet connections. A person is quite capable of amusing themselves for lengthy periods without having to leave the home. But not so long ago when people wanted to meet one another, what better place to socialize than at a dance?

By 1950 other forms of entertainment began to compete for spare-time attention. With leisure time and entertainment dollars usually limited, choices are made as to where one goes for amusement and where cash will be spent. Gradually, dance pavilions began to feel the pinch of this competition.

As North America's love affair with the automobile increased, particularly after World War II, the population became more mobile and the drive-in movie theatre business grew at a tremendous rate. People also began to travel more extensively than ever before, rather than staying close to home and taking in local entertainment. Probably the most severe impact on dance pavilions was the invention of television. Once the "box" made its way into people's homes it completely changed a way of life. And as the province loosened up some of the entertainment laws, sporting events became more popular than ever.

As Big Band music gradually gave way to Rock, the transformation took many halls as casualties. This was not always the fault of the hall or the location, but sometimes due to the unwillingness of the owner to move with the times, especially if the owner was either reluctant or thinking about selling or retiring. Those who, seeing the change, decided to book in rock bands did very well since they catered to the huge bulge of the population born after the war. But ultimately, it was the lowering of the drinking age that really dealt a final blow to the pavilions in the early 1970s. Bars, which formerly catered to an older crowd, now became meeting places for the late teens and the early 20s crowd. Rock bands replaced lounge acts, small dance floors were built to accommodate those restless dancing feet and people loved it. They could buy a drink, see a band and dance. Pavilions could only offer the music and the dancing. Drinking sometimes took place in the pavilion parking lots, but that also began to cause trouble in some towns.

By the late 1960s and early '70s, a new phenomenon began to take place. That was the rock concert, largely an offshoot of Woodstock and Monterey Pop. Outdoor rock concerts, where people could take in as many as 15 bands over the period of a weekend, were staged all over Ontario. A pavilion could offer perhaps two bands at most in an evening, but could not compete with a weekend of camping and music. By the late 1970s business for most of the remaining pavilions had seriously declined. Dancing was just one of many things to do for fun—not the only activity any more. The physical condition of many of

196

these old wooden buildings was poor, necessitating significant upgrades just to preserve them. Some owners simply decided to tear down their building.

As I mentioned, Big Band music is enjoying a resurgence in popularity as a younger audience discovers the excitement in this music form. Canadian rock groups from the 1960s and '70s continue to reunite and play gigs. The summer of 2000 saw The Guess Who reunite for a cross-country tour, bringing their great music to sold-out concerts. In Oshawa alone, two local rock groups—The Lincolnaires and Pink Cadillac—are busy every month. The music does indeed live on—it's only many of the halls and pavilions which are relegated to memories in people's minds and pictures in this book. Still, it is sad for many people to see a part of life which was so popular in this province gradually disappear. They are gone now, but remain as part of social history.

It is hoped that through this book readers were able to relive a happy time from recalling musical experiences—a hall, a pavilion, a band, a fond memory contributed by someone whose experience may have been similar to yours.

Peter Young

Appendix

SCRAPBOOK OF MEMORIES

Stanley St. John and his University of Toronto Dance Band performed many society gigs, starting in the 1920s. *Courtesy of Ross Brethour.*

Bigwin Inn's octagonal grand dance hall on Muskoka's Lake of Bays provided shelter below for the Inn's boats, which were berthed underneath, circa 1940s. Some of the original buildings still sit in a state of deterioration, while the site awaits redevelopment plans. *Courtesy of Alex Ingram.*

A talented musician and bandleader, Bobby Gimby gained national fame with the theme song he composed for Canada's Centennial (1967) – "C-A-N-A-D-A". *Courtesy of Ron Bouckley.*

Billy Bissett at the piano (he was later known as Billy Bishop) and his band inside the Silver Slipper at Toronto, circa 1930s. *Courtesy of Jack Lomas.*

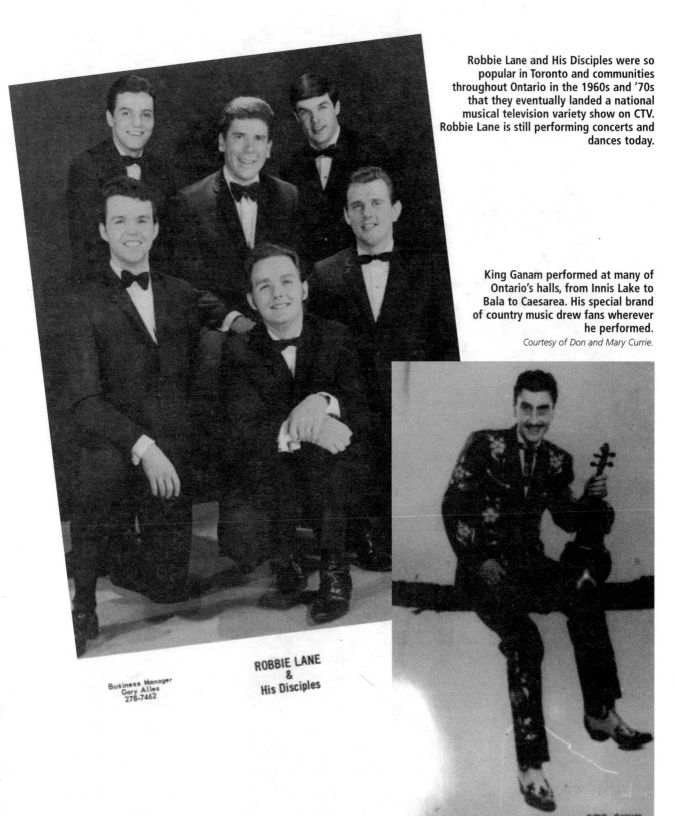

Robbie Lane and His Disciples were so popular in Toronto and communities throughout Ontario in the 1960s and '70s that they eventually landed a national musical television variety show on CTV. Robbie Lane is still performing concerts and dances today.

King Ganam performed at many of Ontario's halls, from Innis Lake to Bala to Caesarea. His special brand of country music drew fans wherever he performed.

Courtesy of Don and Mary Currie.

Business Manager
Gary Alles
278-7462

ROBBIE LANE
&
His Disciples

KING GANAM

199

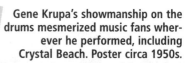

Gene Krupa's showmanship on the drums mesmerized music fans wherever he performed, including Crystal Beach. Poster circa 1950s. *Courtesy of Cathy Herbert.*

Bill Haley and His Comets are synonymous with early rock 'n' roll and are known worldwide for their first hit song "Rock Around The Clock." Haley (shown upper right) and his group continued to do rock revival shows well into the 1970s.

200

The Seacliffe Park Dance Pavilion in Leamington featured an outdoor stage for fair-weather dancing. If rain began, the orchestra turned around to play and dancers went indoors to the covered dance floor where they continued dancing, circa 1940s. *Courtesy of Johnny Downs.*

Sources & Notes

The research for Let's Dance has come from a variety of sources. Since there are no books dedicated solely to this topic on an Ontario basis, I decided to turn to the general public for assistance, initially through letters to editors of many newspapers. *The Sunday Star* provided the first responses and they were overwhelming. People wrote about their favourite halls with a passion, and provided me with leads and other sources to investigate. I tracked down many people who had worked in the business, either as hall owners or their surviving family, staff members or musicians. I am grateful to so many of these individuals who took time to speak with me about their experiences, either in person, on the telephone or through written correspondence. Many of the photos and other visuals you see in this book are courtesy of generous people who searched their personal collections and shared their memories with me. Over the years, newspapers have often featured a "Looking Back" piece on some aspect of local history; this was another source of information about various dance pavilions. Along the same vein, a number of

THE TORONTO STAR Sunday, August 21, 1994

Do you remember dance pavilions?

Perhaps you swayed across the dance floor at Dunn's Pavilion in Bala (now called "The Kee") to the bands of Duke Ellington, Tommy Dorsey and Louis Armstrong. Or maybe you grew up in the '60s and rocked and rolled to Little Caesar and the Consuls, Crowbar, Ronnie Hawkins, Lighthouse and many of the other superb bands from southern Ontario who played regularly at The Pav in Orillia, Sauble Beach Pavilion, the Jubilee in Oshawa, Greenhurst Pavilion near Bobcaygeon or Peggy's Pavilion in Stroud.

Summer nights. Summer romance. Great music. Good times.

But, sadly, with the exception of a couple of notable pavilions such as The Kee and Greenhurst, few of these wooden summer dance halls still exist.

I am writing a book on the summer dance pavilions in Ontario and I would like to include personal anecdotes. Do you have even one memory to share about a special time at a summer pavilion? Which hall was your favourite? Were you a staff member? Did your orchestra or band play at some of these great Ontario pavilions? Do you have any photographs? Do you have a book? All pictures will be returned.

I would be willing to visit your location to copy a picture or to conduct an interview, or if you prefer, please send your memories to:

PETER YOUNG
Pavilions

local history books have also devoted a paragraph or two to a local dance hall. I have used a few quotations from other books as well, when I felt a specific line related directly to the topic of dance venues, dancing and music in general. During my years in the music business I also accumulated a range of personal material, some of which is used in this book.

201

Chapter 1: Introduction to the Era of Pavlions and Dancehalls

A. Sources

Conversation with Pauline Dutton (Grafton) Oct. 19, 1994.

Letter from Bruce Gosnell (Thornhill) Sept. 27, 1994.

B. Notes

1. Ronnie Hawkins and Peter Goddard, *Ronnie Hawkins: Last of the Good Old Boys* (Toronto: Stoddart Publishing Co. Limited, 1998) page number unknown.

2. Levon Helm with Stephen Davis, *This Wheel's On Fire* (New York: William Morris & Co., 1993) 43-44.

3. Mart Kenney, *Mart Kenney and His Western Gentlemen* (Saskatoon: Western Producer Prairie Books, 1981) 26.

4. The Savoy opened December 14, 1926, and closed in 1958. Two-storey ballroom spanning the block of 140th Street to 141st Street on Lennox Avenue in uptown Harlem. The Cotton Club had its first review in 1923, with one of the house orchestras led by Duke Ellington, followed by Cab Calloway. Located at 42nd Street and Lennox Avenue.

5. From an Artie Shaw Documentary by Brigitte Berman, *Time is All You've Got*, 1984.

6. Professor Pasquele Vanuta, according to the late Dr. Morris Wearing of London, Ontario. "The London Marconi Club was prosperous enough to import a professional conductor for its concert band. His name was Professor Pasquele Vanuta, who came to London in 1913." Written by Dr. Wearing in his article "Dance Bands and Dance Halls: Another London Heritage." Received July 12, 1995.

7. Levon Helm, *This Wheel's On Fire*, 40.

8. Ronnie Hawkins, *Ronnie Hawkins: Last of the Good Old Boys*, 48.

9. Scott Young, *Neil and Me* (Toronto: McClelland & Stewart, 1984) 48.

10. Attributed to Luria Catsell in Ralph J. Gleason, *The Jefferson Airplane and the San Francisco Sound* (New York: Ballantine Books, 1969) 2.

11. Ralph J. Gleason, *The Jefferson Airplane*, 22.

Chapter 2: Toronto and Surrounding Area

A. Sources

1. Interviews
   Jack Ainslie (Peterborough) June 13, 1995.
   Bet Armstrong (Weston) Oct. 20, 1995.
   Don & Mary Currie (Innis Lake III, near Caledon East) June 6, 1995.
   Margaret Duggan (Erin) Oct. 20, 1994.
   Ernie Ince (Bridgenorth) March 30, 1995.
   Richard Kosztowniak (at Palais Royale, Toronto) June 8, 1995.
   Ron McLean (Bolton) May 12, 1995.
   Joe McNulty (Balmy Beach Club) Nov. 4, 1997.

2. Letters
   Hon. John Arnup (North York) Aug. 23, 1994.
   Roberta (Niosi) Baldwin (Mississauga) April 10, 1995.
   Bruce Brocklebank (Scarborough) Aug. 24, 1994.
   Adele Bromby (Toronto) Sept. 2, 1994.
   George Gordon (Scarborough) Aug. 21, 1994.
   Louaine Parten (Scarborough) Aug. 16, 1995.

3. Telephone Conversations
   Elma Billingsley (Erin) Aug. 26, 1994.
   Anne Kline (Picton) May 12, 1995.
   George Strachan (Toronto) April 12, 1996.

B. Notes

1. Mart Kenney, *Mart Kenney and his Western Gentlemen*, 118.

2. Attributed to an authentic family story, related by Joan (Livings) Young who accompanied Bill

Livings, her cousin, who took the photo on January 23, 1942.

3. Mart Kenney, *Mart Kenney and his Western Gentlemen*, page number unknown.

4. Ibid.

5. Ross Brethour, *"The West, A Nest And You, Dear": A Bio-discography of Mart Kenney and his Western Gentlemen* (Nomadic Records, 1988) 106.

6. Mart Kenney, *Mart Kenney and his Western Gentlemen*, page number unknown.

Chapter 3: Around the Bay by Burlington to the Shores of Lake Erie

A. Sources

1. Conversation

Pauline Dutton (Grafton) Oct.19, 1994.

2. Interviews

Betty Coates (Simcoe) Aug. 2, 1995.
Ruby Conway (Port Colborne) Aug. 3, 1995.
Cathy Herbert (Ridgeway) Aug. 3, 1995.
Gordon Ivey (Port Dover) Aug. 1, 1995.
Fred Knechtal (Port Dover) Aug. 2, 1995.
Leola McCloy (Port Dover) Aug. 1, 1995.
Bert Oldershaw (Burlington) Nov. 17, 1994.
Darrin Schott (Glen Meyer) Aug. 2, 1995.

3. Letters

Margo Kerber (London) Sept. 1994
Mary Wintle (Niagara Falls) Aug. 23, 1994.
Tom Zareski (Welland) Aug. 14, 1995.
4. Telephone Conversations
Helen Lorriman (Port Dover) Aug. 1, 1995.
Elaine O'Neill (Burlington) July 24, 1995.

B. Notes

1. Dorothy Turcotte, *Port Dalhousie, Shoes, Ships and Sealing Wax* (Erin, Ontario: Boston Mills Press, 1986) page number unknown.

2. Taken from *The Life and Times of Crystal Beach*,

a video documentary by the Crystal Beach Video Group, 1994.

3. Levon Helm, *This Wheel's On Fire*, 110.

Chapter 4: Across Southwestern Ontario from Woodstock to Amhertsburg

A. Sources

1. Interviews

Gerry Costello (St. Thomas) Sept. 28, 1995.
Chuck Jones (Wonderland, London) Nov. 15, 1994.
Maurice Smyth (Chatham) Sept. 27, 1995.

2. Letters

Norma Aiken (London) April 4, 1995.
Burns Bedard (Burlington) Jan. 11, 1995.
Nick Corrie (London) July 9, 1995.
J. Frarey (Nepean) April 15, 1995.
Tom Hammond (London) April 5, 1995.
T. Murray Lynch (Moncton, N.B.) 1995.
Alf Murray (London) April 9, 1995.
Cecil Pearson (London) April 1, 1995.
Dorothy Ratcliffe (Exeter) April 18, 1995.
Barbara Richards (London) March 25, 1995.
Cheryl Sanregret (Edmonton, Alberta) Sept. 29, 1994.
V.P. Smith (London) March 30, 1995.
Harry Vandersluys (London) March 30, 1995.
Daniel Wilson (London) March 30, 1995.

B. Notes

1. Excerpts from a photocopy of a letter written by Louis Armstrong to Harry Vandersluys, June 9, 1941. Made available by Harry Vandersluys.

2. The late Dr. Morris P. Wearing generously provided much information through his letters and his research, received over a period of time from March 26, 1995, to December 26, 1995.

3. Excerpts from Alan Mann's colum "History Trail," in the *Wallaceburg News*, Nov. 20, 1985.

4. Quotes from *The Brass Factory Bulletin*, a

newsletter printed in Wallaceburg by the Brass Factory Band, dedicated to the memory of the Bob Jacks Orchestra, April 1995.

Chapter 5: Pavilions on Beaches from Owen Sound to the Shores of Lake Huron

A. Sources

1. Interviews

Leah Breckenridge (Goderich) Sept. 25, 1995.
Johnny Downs (Port Stanley) April 22, 1995.
Margaret Garon (Clinton) Sept. 25, 1995.
Douglas Kennedy (Sarnia) Sept. 26, 1995.
Genevieve Kennedy (Corunna) Sept. 26, 1995.
Pat McGrath (Port Elgin) Sept. 15, 1994.
Dick Rose (Sarnia) Sept. 27, 1995.
Esther Scott (Southampton) Sept. 15, 1994.
George Scott (Inverhuron) Sept. 16, 1994.
Jim Steele (London) Nov. 15, 1994.

2. Letters

Bill Baldock (Sarnia) Aug. 15, 1995.
Ken Bowes (Port Elgin) Aug. 22, 1994.
William Boyd (Sarnia) Aug. 29, 1994.
George Cairns (Willowdale) Aug. 28, 1994.
Anne Ellis (Scarborough) Aug. 24, 1994.
Geri Kirkpatrick (Owen Sound) Aug. 21, 1994.
William "Mac" MacKenzie (Oliphant) Oct. 24, 1994.
Robert McKee (Goderich) Aug. 21, 1994.
Jeanette Ovens (Lucan) March 26, 1995.
Ethel (Jowett) Poth (Goderich) Aug. 28, 1994.
Vicki Storm (Kingston) May 10, 1995.

B. Notes

1. Amabel Township Historical Society, *Green Meadow and Golden Sands: A History of Amabel Township, 1851-1982* (Wiarton: Echo Graphics, 1984) page number unknown.

2. Helen Hammond, "To A Dance Hall." Published in *The Port Elgin News*, Aug. 26, 1970.

Chapter 6: From Brantford North to the Georgian Bay Area

A. Sources

1. Interviews

Jack Beauchamp (Midland) May 5, 1995.
Tom Crowe (Orr Lake Golf Club) Oct. 7, 1994.
Johnny Downs (Port Stanley) April 22, 1995.
Guy Johnstone (Midland) May 5, 1995.
Jack McGrattan (Kingston) July 18, 1995.
Warren Ovens (Kitchener) Nov. 16, 1994.
Michelle Seip (The Dardanella, Wasaga Beach) June 6, 1995.

2. Letters

Erwin Daniels (Brantford) Sept. 11, 1995.
Gloria Ferringo (Guelph) Aug. 15, 1995.
Doreen Fraser (Cambridge) Aug. 31, 1995.
Vi (Marsh) Hoare (Etobicoke) Sept. 22, 1994.
Dorothy Jones (Kitchener) Sept. 21, 1995.
Margo Kerber (London) Sept. 4, 1994.
Chester Kirk (Erin) Aug. 15, 1995.
June Nicholson (Brantford) Aug. 5, 1995.
Margaret Renton (Acton) Aug. 25, 1994.
Frank A. Smith (Thornhill) Aug. 19, 1994.
Dorothy Young-Yeandle (Drumbo) Aug. 20, 1995.

B. Notes

1. Jean Somerville, *The Bands Played On: The Story of the Frank Family and Their Music* (Acton, Ontario: Published by Jean Somerville, 1995) 7.

2. Information from Alan Waters (Toronto) on The Dard (1939/40), in a telephone conversation, June 11, 1995.

3. Information from Gayle Collins (Anten Mills) on the Pine Crest Dance Centre, in a telephone conversation, May 2, 1995.

Chapter 7: Around Lake Simcoe

A. Sources

1. Interviews

Ray Cockburn (Barrie) Aug. 16, 1994.
Orville Fleetham (Barrie) Oct. 4, 1995.
Bob Matiuska (Orillia) Aug. 16, 1994.
Carl McDaid (Orillia) Aug. 16, 1994.
Barb Parsons (Toronto) Nov. 3, 1994.
Jack Phillips (Barrie) Oct. 4, 1995.

2. Letters

Vera Battalia (of Orillia) Oct. 30, 1994.
Ruth Beeforth (Keswick) Oct. 3, 1994.
Jack Bissett (Scarborough) Sept. 10, 1994.
Dan Bonner (Orillia) Oct. 31, 1994.
Doug Brown (Sutton) Aug. 21, 1994.
Vale Clark (Sutton) Oct. 3, 1994.
Terry Ann (Lee) Elliot (Orillia) Nov. 6, 1995.
Vita Epstein (North York) Aug. 20, 1994.
Audrey Fettes (Scarborough) Aug. 24, 1994.
Dorothy Forsythe (Belfountain) Dec. 29, 1994.
Jean Jardin (Carleton Place) July 1, 1995.
Andrea Kostek (Mississauga) Aug. 30, 1994.
Pat Langman (Newcastle) Oct. 29, 1994.
Else McConachie (Richmond Hill) Aug. 23, 1994.
Bill O'Neil (Brampton) Aug. 29, 1994.
Marlene Phillips (Jacksons Point) Aug. 28, 1994.
Anne Reeves (West Hill) Nov. 28, 1994.
Verna Scott-Creber (Pefferlaw) Feb. 1, 1995.

B. Notes

1. From a telephone conversation with Bill Burridge of Toronto, Sept. 6, 1994.

2. From a telephone conversation with Norman Hills of London, March 29, 1995.

3. "Beginning History of Alcona Beach Club," a personal written recollection by Muriel (David) McDermott, March 21, 1990.

4. From a telephone conversation with Betty Shillinger, Aug. 15, 1995.

5. In conversation with a staff member at Bonnie Boats Ltd., Jacksons Point, July 13, 1995.

6. In conversation with a librarian at the Sutton Library, July 13, 1995.

Chapter 8: Through the Haliburton Highlands Into the Kawarthas

A. Sources

1. Interviews

Helen Lines (Lindsay) June 1, 1994.
Steve Macko (Oshawa) May 17, 1994.
Jim Marshall (Fenelon Falls) Sept. 7, 1994.
Bud & Muriel Medley (Minden) Aug. 13, 1994.
Adam Parry (Thurstonia) May 7, 1994.
Annie Robertson (Coboconk) Oct. 25, 1994.
Ken & Ida Young (Crystal Lake, near Kinmount) Sept. 4, 1994.

2. Letters

Peggy (Reynolds) Challice (Bailieboro) Dec. 1, 1994.
Gord Daniels (Kinmount) Aug. 28, 1994.
Margaret Dobbie (Bobcaygeon) March 30, 1995.
Joan Farrell (Ayr) Oct. 3, 1994.
Freda Hopkins (Pointe-Claire, Quebec) Dec. 8, 1994.
Marg Lucas (Puslinch) Aug. 23, 1994.
Joan Olesuk (Oshawa) Sept. 30, 1994.
Hope (McPhee) O'Rourke (Southampton) Oct. 1, 1994.
Janette Parker (Lindsay) Aug. 29, 1994.
Stanley Redman (Midland) Sept. 2, 1994.
Florence Reynolds (Oakville) Oct. 12, 1994.
Edna Templeton (Bala) Aug. 27, 1994.

3. Telephone Conversations

Eugene Sheedy (Peterborough) Oct. 3, 1994.
Skip Vaughan (Brampton) July 3, 1995.

B. Notes

1. Mart Kenney, *Mart Kenney and his Western Gentlemen*, 104.

205

Chapter 9: Peterborough and Environs

A. Sources

1. Interviews

Jack Ainslie (Peterborough) June 12, 1995.
Marjorie Armstrong (interviewed by Debra Young at the Rotary Laughlen Centre, Toronto) Oct. 25, 1994.
Marlow Banks (Peterborough) Sept. 22, 1994.
Ruby Conway (Port Colborne) Aug. 3, 1995.
Fran Domenic (Lindsay) Oct. 12, 1994.
Geoff Hewittson (Peterborough) June 12, 1994.
Katharine Hooke (Juniper Island Pavilion, Stony Lake) July 20, 1995.
Bea Ianson (Mt. Julian) Aug. 17, 1995.
Bobby Kinsman (Bridgenorth) March 30, 1995.
Betty Knox (Crowe's Landing) July 20, 1995.
Steve Macko (Oshawa) May 17, 1994.
Don & Winnifred McIndoe (Bracebridge) Sept. 1, 1994.
Sean Pennylegion (Woodview General Store) Oct. 28, 1994.
Stanley Redman (Midland) April 14, 1995.
Reg Renouf & Morgan Sears (Caesarea) July 17, 1994.
Andy Rutter (Young's Point) Oct. 5, 1994.
Herb Rye (Peterborough) Nov. 5, 1994.
Helen Willcox (Bridgenorth) Sept. 7, 1994.

2. Letters

Sylvia Ducharme (Peterborough) Oct. 4, 1994.
Stanley Redman (Midland) Sept. 2, 1994.

3. Telephone Conversations

Percy Frayer (Taunton) July 14, 1994.
Joyce Turner (Bridgenorth) Sept. 7, 1994.

B. Notes

1. Helen Willcox, *The Chemong Park Story* (Archival and History Committee of Smith Township, 1986) page number unknown.

Chapter 10: Through the Ottawa Valley to the Seaway

A. Sources

1. Interviews

Vera Boyd (Osgoode) Nov. 4, 1995.
George & Frances Day (Collins Bay) July 26, 1995.
Ed Hall (Ottawa) Nov. 7, 1995.
Val (Revell) McEwen (Kingston) July 26, 1995.
Jack McGrattan (Kingston) July 18, 1995.
Dave Peplinski (Combermere) March 16, 1996.
Bernadette Plebon (Barry's Bay) March 16, 1996.
Ken Reid (Collins Bay) July 26, 1995.
Florence Scott (Westport) July 27, 1995.
Herb Simmons (Menoke Beach, near Orillia) July 13, 1995.
Gary Villeneuve (Cornwall) July 19, 1995.
Stan Wiggins (Belleville) Nov. 25, 1994.

2. Letters

J. Donald Bell (Toronto) Sept. 2, 1994.
Vera (Blanchard) Black (Kingston) Aug. 12, 1995.
Jacqueline (Lajoie) Bouchard (Woodstock) Aug. 8, 1995.
John Boyd (Lansdowne) May 3, 1995.
Helen (Chaput) Clouthier (Pembroke) May 16, 1995.
Lloyd Downey (Bath) May 13, 1995.
Gordon Durant (Smiths Falls) Aug. 6, 1995.
John Ferguson (Manotick) Dec. 9, 1995.
John Gordier (Ottawa) May 20, 1995.
Teresa Halpenny (Pembroke) Aug. 28, 1995.
Jim Hefferen (Brockville) Oct. 5, 1995.
Olive (Clement) Hogan (Bath) May 11, 1995.
Frederick Joyce (Kingston) May 18, 1995.
Cuth Knowlton Jr. (Seeley's Bay) Aug. 15, 1995.
Barbara Logsdail (Kingston) May 9, 1995.
Teri Lyn Martin (Eganville) Aug. 8, 1995.
Ann McCahill (Kingston) June 9, 1995.

Marion Mills (Ottawa) May 21, 1995.

Rose Darling Moore (Ottawa) Aug. 10, 1995.

Dorothy Power (Brockville) Aug. 6, 1995.

James Reid (Kingston) May 16, 1995.

Don Sherman (Brockville) Aug. 14, 1995.

Iona Skuce (Ottawa) May 14, 1995.

Ron Stroud (Stroud) Nov. 1, 1994.

Ellie Stuart (Kingston) July 26, 1995.

Jim Yeldon (Brockville) Aug. 9, 1995.

B. Notes

1. From the Ottawa Status Report #2, Ottawa Archives, date unknown.

2. *Ottawa Citizen*, July 4, 1995.

3. Diane Aldred, *The Aylmer Road: An Illustrated History* (Aylmer Heritage Association, 1994).

4. Information on Mac Beattie from Mac Beattie, *This Ottawa Valley of Mine* (Beattie Music Inc., 1982) page number unknown.

5. From an essay by W.G. (Glenn) Abrams of Brockville, November 1995.

6. From a paper by Gordon Smithson, "Dance and Romance: The Golden Slipper Dance Hall" in *A Collection of Talks of Historical Interest* (Kingston: Pittsburgh Historical Society, 1986).

7. Elinor Kyte Senior, *From Royal Township to Industrial City: Cornwall 1784-1984* (Belleville: Mika Publishing, 1983) 521.

Chapter 11: From Whitby Through the Trent River System

A. Sources

1. Interviews

Ron Bouckley (Oshawa) May 24, 1994.

Les Brittain (Hastings) June 14, 1994.

Gary Cole (Bowmanville) June 14, 1994.

Jack Delong (Trenton) Oct. 21, 1994.

Alex Ingram (Seagrave) July 10, 1995.

Joe Kondyjowski (Oshawa) April 13, 1995.

John Kremer (Little Lake Pavilion, Brighton) June 14, 1994.

Steve Macko (Oshawa) May 17, 1994.

Ed Mazurkiewich (Oshawa) March 9, 1995.

Basil McMaster (Brighton) Aug. 9, 1994.

Betty Donaghy Moore (Presqu'ile Point) Oct. 21, 1994.

Evan Morton (Tweed) June 2, 1995.

Barb O'Neill (Beaver Lake, near Tamworth) June 2, 1995.

Reg Renouf (Caesarea) with Morgan Sears, July 7, 1994.

Harold Rowley (Whitby) May 31, 1994.

Dirk Safioles (Carrying Place) Sept. 12, 1995.

Irene Severs (Oshawa) Aug. 8, 1994.

Hank Taschereau (Hastings) Oct. 19, 1994.

Ben Thompson (Brighton) Nov. 25, 1994.

Bob Wickens (Campbellford) June 14, 1994.

2. Letters

Diane Brick (Kanata) May 16, 1995.

Bruce Brocklebank (Scarborough) Aug. 24, 1994.

Fran Douglas (Campbellford) Sept. 15, 1994.

H. Carroll Paul (Tamworth) May 19, 1995.

Gerry Robinson (Pembroke) Aug. 6, 1994.

Marion Sherwin (Baltimore, ON) Sept. 12, 1994.

Lynda Taschereau (Mississauga) Oct. 7, 1994.

Ben Thompson (Brighton) Aug. 24, 1994.

Gladys Wythe (London) Aug. 23, 1994.

3. Telephone Conversations

Tommy Cinnamon (Whitby) Aug. 8, 1994.

Judy Desjardins (Tweed) Nov. 2, 1994.

Percy Frayer (Taunton) July 14, 1994.

B. Notes

1. *Oshawa This Week*, 1987.

2. *Belleville Intelligencer*, 1992.

3. Published in the "Poet's Corner" section of the *Tweed News*, 1989.

Chapter 12: Muskoka: Dunn's Pavilion/The Kee to Bala

A. Sources

1. Interviews

Cathy Barber (Bala) Aug. 16, 1994.
Ray Cockburn (Barrie) Aug. 16, 1994.
Gerry Dunn (formerly of Bala) July 5, 1994.
Joe Kondyjowski (Oshawa) April 13, 1995.
Marshall Louch (formerly of Bala) Aug. 16, 1994.
Don & Winnifred McIndoe (Bracebridge) Sept. 25, 1994.

2. Letters

George Allison (Hanover) Aug. 23, 1994.
Patricia Arney (Bala) Aug. 28, 1994.
Leone (Palmer) Fisher (Oshawa) Sept. 8, 1994.
Bruce Brocklebank (Scarborough) Aug. 24, 1994.
James Gilmore (Bala) Aug. 24, 1994.
Mrs. D. Castaldi (Mount Forest) Aug. 23, 1994.

B. Sources

1. Mart Kenney, *Mart Kenney and his Western Gentlemen*, 78.

2. From a CBC archival audio tape, June 1952.

3. From conversations with Stephen Wyllie over the summer of 1996.

Chapter 13: Pavilions of the Near North

A. Sources

1. Letters

Mildred Arnold (Thunder Bay) Jan. 23, 1996.
George D. Babcock (Alton) Aug. 22, 1994.
Charles Budd (Timmins) Aug. 4, 1995.
Joan Hebden (Thunder Bay) Jan. 16, 1996.
Ulysses Levinson (South Porcupine) Aug. 4, 1995.
Marie McInnis (Toronto) Aug. 28, 1994.
George Ray (Stroud) Aug. 8, 1995.
Eddie Sarlo (North Bay) Nov. 2, 1994.
Charles Thomas (Atikokan) Aug. 8, 1995.
Irene Winslow (Thunder Bay) Nov. 20, 1994.

B. Notes

1. Memories of dances and summers at Fort William taken from a telephone conversation with Marconi Johnson of Etobicoke (Toronto) on Nov. 29, 1994.

Index

209

214

215

Miller, Glenn, 9, 23, 61, 150, 173, 184, 195
Miller, Wilf, 106
Milligan, Denzel "Denny", 98
Milligan, ___ (Mrs.), 98
Mills Brothers, 15
Mills, Marion, 136
Minacola, Paul, 116, 117, 125
Minacola brothers, 121
Minden (ON), 109, 110
Minet's Point, 101, 102
Minet's Point Pavilion, 101
Miss Diana Motor Hotel, 124
Mission (BC), 26, 155
Mississauga (ON), 76
Mississippi River, 143
Mitchell, Ginny, 59
Mitchell, Joni, 29
Mitchell, Kim, 127
Mitchell, Peggy, 166
Mitchell, Peter, 62
Modernaires, The, 61, 77
Mohawk Lake, 81
Mohawk Park Pavilion (Brantford), 81, 82
Moira River, 175
Monroe, Vaughan, 64, 80, 87
Montreal (PQ), 163
Moonglowers, the, 98
Moore, Bette Donaghy, 166
Moore, Harold, 109
Moore, Jimmy, 57
Moore, Rose Darling, 151
Moquin, Fern, 153
Morello, Gus, 53
Morgan's Point (Lake Erie), 41, 42, 125
Morgan's Point Trailer Park, 41
Morgan Thomas and His Orchestra, 48
Morrisburg (ON), 137
Morristown (NY), 155
Morrow, Buddy, 11
Morsehead, Bruce, 116
Morton, Evan, 169, 170
Morton, Gav, 33
Mose Yokum Orchestra, 122
Mossington, Thomas, 105
Mossington Park Pavilion, 105, 164
Mowry, Ferde, 4, 30, 70, 71, 115, 118, 129
Moxie Whitney Band, 163
Mueller, Al, 2
Murray, Alf, 48
Murray, Frank, 155
Murray, Violet, 103
Murray Canal, 169, 171
Musgrove, Eddie, 166
Muskoka (District), 179, 181-183, 189, 198

Musicians' Union, 112, 136, 145
Musselman's Lake (ON), 30
Mutual Radio Network (see CBC)
Mutual Street Arena (Arena Gardens/The Terrace), 23
Myers, Peter, 101
Myers, Sandy, 127
Myles, Allanah, 88

Namaro, Jimmy, 33, 59, 75, 77
Napanee (ON), 141, 171, 175
Neff, Lloyd "Vic," 41
Nelson, Billy, 17, 18
Nelson, Ozzie, 34
New Blue Jackets, 150
New Orleans (LA), 7
New York (NY), 7, 47, 64
Newtons (family), 105
Niagara Falls (ON), 36, 37, 123
Niagara Region, 36, 39-41, 125
Nicholson, June, 81, 82
Nine Royal Collegians, 76
Niosi, Bert, 12, 19, 21, 22, 30, 33, 36, 76, 77, 119, 152, 155
Norfolk Mountaineers, 46
Norm Mauro Big Band, 190
Noronic (steamship), 192
Norrena, Alvin, 101
Norrena, Beverly, 101
Norris, Mac, 153
North Bay (ON), 190, 191
Northernaires (dance orchestra), 190
Norwich (ON), 51
Novotny, George, 129

Oak Lake, 167
Oak Lake Casino, 167, 168, 172
Oaksmere Pavilion (later Oak Lake Casino), 167
Oasis, The (Cornwall), 153
Octagon (Sauble Beach), 68, 69
Oddfellows Hall (Kingston), 144
Oddfellows Hall (Timmins), 191
Old Elora Armouries (Elora), 86
Old Mill, The (Toronto), 1
Olde Mill (Guelph), 85
Olde Pavilion (Timmins), 191
Oldershaw, Bert, 33
Olesuk, Joan, 115
Oliphant (ON), 67, 68
O'Neill, Barb, 171
O'Neill, Bill, 103
O'Neill, Charles, 171
O'Neill, Elaine, 32
O'Neill, James, 171
O'Neill, James Jr., 171
O'Neill, Joe, 171
Orange Hall (Hew Dublin), 155
Orbison, Roy, 11, 102

Orillia (ON), 97-100, 102, 107
Orillia Packet and Times, 99
Oro Beach (ON), 100
O'Rourke, Hope (McPhee), 112
Orr Lake Dance Hall, 95, 96
Orr Lake Orchestra, 96
Oscopella, Eddy, 108
Osgoode (ON), 136, 137
Orthophonic (record player), 150
Oshawa (ON), 3, 30, 75, 106, 116, 123, 159-161, 165, 176, 197
Oshawa Centre, 160
Oshawa Central Lions Club, 158
Oshawa Daily Times Gazette, 156, 157
Oshawa Symphony, 163
Otonabee River, 6, 119
Ottawa (ON), 4, 115, 133, 135-138, 142
Ottawa River, 137, 138
Ottawa Valley, 12, 138, 139, 140
Ottawa Valley Country Music Hall of Fame, 141
Ott, Wilber, 86
Otts, Frank, 17
Ovens, Jeanette, 77
Ovens, John, 77
Ovens, Stuart, 77
Ovens, Warren, 69, 86, 87
Owen Sound (ON), 28, 67, 69, 84
Oxville Hall (Cochrane), 191, 192

Pacific Swingsters (Moxie Whitney), 173
Page-Hersey Hall (Welland), 36
Page-Hersey Works (Stelco), 36
Palace, The (Chemong Park), 127
Palace of the Moon (Prince Edward County), 174
Palace Pier, The, (Toronto), 13-15
    Queensway Ballroom, 13
    Strathcona Roller Rink, 13
Palace Pier Condominium, 15
Palace Theatre (Hamilton), 34
Palais de Dance (Casino Dancing Pavilion) (Port Arthur), 195
Palais Royale Ballroom (Toronto), 19-22, 27, 76, 195
Palmer, Benny, 48, 52-54
Palmer, Carl, 52
Palmer, Frances, 180
Palmetto (see Beaver Lake Pavilion)
Palomar Ballroom (Los Angeles), 8

Paradise Gardens (Guelph), 85
Paramount (New York), 8
Parent, Bernie, 144
Parker, Charlie, 94, 95
Parker, Harold, 101
Parker, Harry, 11
Parker, Janette, 117
Parklyn Holdings, 16
Park Pavilion (Toronto), 25
Parkside Pavilion (Midland), 94, 95
Parnaby, Hap (Taylor), 99
Parrott, Larry, 98
Parry, Adam, 117, 186
Parry, Andrea (Smith) (Mrs. Adam), 117, 186
Parry, Bev, 186
Parry Sound (ON), 180
Parsons:
    Barb, 103, 104
    George, 103, 104
    Peggy, 103, 104
Parson's Dance Hall (Stroud), 103, 104
Parten, Louaine, 23
Pastels, The, 177
Pastor, Tony, 34, 50
Patience, Jim, 56
Patel, Sanober,
Patton, Russ, 55
Patton, Stan, 33, 77
Paul, H. Carroll, 171
Paul Minacola and His Orchestra, 115
Pauline Johnston High School (Brantford), 82
Paupers, The, 70
Pavalon, The (Couchiching Park Pavilion/Club Pav/The Pav) (Orillia), 97-100, 102, 185
Pavilion, The (Campbellford), 176
Payne, Herb, 120, 127
Pearce, Annie, 110, 111
Pearce, Gertrude, 110
Pearce, Harold, 176
Pearce, Nathan "Natie," 110, 111
Pearson, Cecil, 55
Pearson Central Ballroom (Cornwall), 153
Pederson, Stan, 109
Peggy's Pavilion (Stroud), 103, 104
Pembroke (ON), 137, 138, 140
Penetanguishene (ON), 93
Pennylegion, Sean, 130
Peplinskie, Cy, 139
Peplinskie, Dave, 139
Peplinskie, Don, 139
Peplinskie, Ed, 139

217

INDEX

219

About the Author

Peter Young is a freelance writer and runs his own communications company. For many years he played Hammond B-3 organ with a number of Toronto-based rock bands and travelled extensively throughout much of Southern Ontario, performing in many of the province's popular dance pavilions. His first book published in May 1997—*The Kee To Bala Is Dunn's Pavilion*—was received with great enthusiasm in Muskoka and beyond. Peter's second effort in 1998— *Lake Huron's Summer Dance Pavilions: Sand, Surf and Music*—chronicled the places and people who brought song to this golden coastline from the 1920s to the present. *Let's Dance* is the third book in this series and covers many more of Ontario's popular dance venues.

Weston's own "Who & The Blazes" pose in front of the town's fire department in July 1965. From left to right: Peter Young, Brian Beech, Pete Hayden, Keith Wallace and Martin Dollery.